THE DOOMSDAY SYNDROME

THE DOOMS-DAY SYN-DROME

John Maddox

McGraw-Hill Book Company

New York • St. Louis • San Francisco • Düsseldorf

Mexico • Panama • São Paulo

Library of Congress Cataloging in Publication Data

Maddox, John Royden, date
   The doomsday syndrome.

   Includes bibliographical references.
   1. Human ecology. I. Title.
GF47.M3 1972   301.31   72-3844
ISBN 0-07-039428-8

First McGraw-Hill Paperback Edition, 1973

07-039429-6

2 3 4 5 6 7 8 9 MU MU 7 9 8 7 6 5 4 3

Preface

This is not a scholarly work but a complaint. In the past decade, since the publication of Miss Rachel Carson's *Silent Spring*, the people of North America and, to a lesser extent, Western Europe have been assailed by prophecies of calamity. To some, population growth is the most immediate threat. Others make more of pollution of particular kinds, the risk that the world will run out of food or natural resources or even the possibility that economic growth and the prosperity it brings spell danger for the human race. And there is talk of potentially horrific uses for genetic engineering and even of the possibility that the temper of modern science may undermine the structure of modern society. But, although these prophecies are founded in science, they are at best pseudo-science. Their most common error is to suppose that the worst will always happen. And, to the extent that they are based on assumptions as to how people will behave, they ignore the ways in which social institutions and humane aspirations can conspire to solve the most daunting problems.

If this book is an attempt to show why these prophecies should not keep people awake at night, it is not however a tract in favour of population growth or of pollution. One of the distressing features of the present debate about the environment is the way in which it is supposed to be an argument between far-sighted people with the interests of humanity at heart and others who care not tuppence for the future. Those who are not ardently for the preservation of the environment are thought to be against it. This false dichotomy conceals a host of important issues—the part played by the reductions of infant mortality and other social benefits in moderating the growth of quickly growing populations, for example, and the way in which freedom from pollution must be reckoned, in advanced societies, increasingly as a kind

The Doomsday Syndrome

of consumer good which less fortunate communities may not yet be able to afford.

Scientists have not played an especially creditable part in the environmental movement. They have too often made more of the facts than the conventions of their craft permit. Too often, they have expressed moderate or unsure conclusions in language designed to scare, sometimes with the open declaration that exaggeration is necessary to "get things done," but with the result that other people have been alarmed and mystified, not enlightened. Frequently they have accompanied prophecies of doom with recommendations for political and social change which serve chiefly to strengthen the false popular belief that scientists know very little of the real world but which have powerfully enriched the folklore of the strange affiliation between liberal ideals and authoritarian methods. The word "ecology" has come to be used as if it were a slogan, not the name of a branch of science, but the concept has been mischievously misused.

It goes without saying that this book makes no claim to be a cut-and-dried recipe for the survival of the human race. If anything, it is a reminder that certainty about the future is no more possible now than it has ever been. The most serious insidious danger in the environmental movement is that it may sap the will of advanced communities to face the problems which no doubt lie ahead. Throughout history, hope for the future has been a powerful incentive for constructive change. What will happen if it is now needlessly blighted?

This book would not have seen the light of day without the help of my secretary, Mary Sheehan—and at least one small boy thinks it may be entirely her own work. And I am grateful for the forbearance of my family, the indulgence of my colleagues and the affection of my friends, few though they may be in this unpopular pursuit.

JOHN MADDOX

London
March, 1972

Contents

THE
DOOMSDAY
SYNDROME

Is Catastrophe Coming?

Prophets of doom have multiplied remarkably in the past few years. It used to be commonplace for men to parade city streets with sandwich boards proclaiming "The End of the World Is at Hand!" They have been replaced by a throng of sober people, scientists, philosophers and politicians, proclaiming that there are more subtle calamities just around the corner. The human race, they say, is in danger of strangling itself by overbreeding, of poisoning itself with pollution, of undermining its essential human character by tampering with heredity and of perverting the whole basis of society with too much prosperity.

The questions which these latter-day doomsday men have raised are subtle and interesting; the spirit in which they are asked is usually too jaundiced for intellectual comfort. Too often, reality is oversimplified or even ignored, so that there is a danger that much of this gloomy foreboding about the immediate future will accomplish the opposite of what its authors intend. Instead of alerting people to important problems, it may seriously undermine the capacity of the human race to look out for its survival. The doomsday syndrome may in itself be as much a hazard as any of the conundrums which society has created for itself.

Nobody should doubt the wish of the contemporary prophets of calamity to find ways out of trouble, and nobody will dispute that modern society is confronted with important tasks which must urgently be tackled. In advanced societies, machinery must be devised for the more equitable treatment of the poor and the disadvantaged. Urban life, although better than it used to be, can be improved. Even where medical care is excellent, ways need still to be discovered of preventing untimely death and unnecessary disease. And in less-developed societies, there are more primitive tasks to be undertaken. Nourishment is still

The Doomsday Syndrome

too fitful. Schooling remains for many a luxury. Housing is shelter for some and a source of envy for others. The whole world knows, after what happened in Bengal in 1971, that Calcutta, for example, presents problems of race, poverty, disease, and freedom that affront and sometimes paralyze the conscience of industrialized societies. The question which the doomsday prophets pose for those who share their compassion for society is whether the energies of the human race should be spent on problems like these which, however difficult, can be solved or whether they should be spent on the avoidance of more distant trouble.

The doomsday cause would be more telling if it were more securely grounded in facts, better informed by a sense of history and an awareness of economics and less cataclysmic in temper. In an age of empiricism, of course, it is always tempting, especially for busy people anxious to get things done, to concentrate on tangible issues and to postpone a consideration of less immediate questions. This, no doubt, is why the doomsday movement has so wonderfully captured the allegiance of the idealistic youth. But is there not an opposing danger that too much preoccupation with the threat of distant calamity may divert attention from good works that might be done? On what horizon should well-intentioned people fix their gaze?

The defect of the case for thinking that calamity is the more important menace is its imprecision. There are some who fear that the burning of fuel on the scale to which modern industry is accustomed will wreck the climate on the surface of the earth, but few meteorologists are able unambiguously to endorse such prophecies. Some fear that the use of pesticides will irrevocably damage the human race, but that is an overdramatic statement of the need carefully to regulate the way in which such chemicals are sprayed on crops. Some fear that modern biology, with its artificially fertilized eggs and its detailed understanding of genetic processes, will degrade humanity; by doing so, they fly in the face of the past five centuries of the history of medicine, a consistent record of human endeavor. In short, the weakness

Is Catastrophe Coming?

of the doomsday prophecies is that they are exaggerations. Many of them are irresponsible.

The flavor of the prophecies of disaster is well illustrated by the work of Dr. Paul R. Ehrlich, who startled a good many people with the publication in 1968 of his book *The Population Bomb*. "The battle to feed all of humanity is over," he says. "In the 1970s the world will undergo famines, hundreds of millions of people are going to starve to death in spite of any crash program embarked on now." Dr. Ehrlich goes on to describe in a somber way the rate at which the population of the world is increasing, the inconveniences which are likely to result therefrom and to describe some ways of striking a better balance between population growth and available resources, especially in developing parts of the world. He is against sterilants in drinking water but for compulsory sterilization by other means.

Nobody will deny that it is important to control, if not the size of a population, then its rate of growth. In advanced societies, population control is increasingly a part of good government. In developing countries, it is a prerequisite of economic progress. But famine is now an unreal scarecrow. There is a good chance that the problems of the 1970s and 1980s will not be famine and starvation but, ironically, the problems of how best to dispose of food surpluses in countries where famine has until recently been endemic. Population control is therefore desirable not as a means of avoiding calamity but because like other social benefits, health care for example, it can accelerate the improvement of the human condition.

Implicit in the fears of the consequences of population growth which are now rife is an oversimple method of prediction. If the population of the world is at present doubling every thirty-five years, does it not follow that the population will multiply by four in the next seventy years, so as to reach 14,000 million by the year 2040? In his book *The Population Bomb*, Dr. Ehrlich is scornful about those whom he calls "professional optimists . . . who like to greet every sign of dropping birth rate with wild pronouncements about the end of the population ex-

The Doomsday Syndrome

plosion." In his more soberly written *Population, Resources, Environment,* he chooses to base calculations of the future population of the earth on the most pessimistic calculation of the United Nations, which assumes that there will be no change in the fertility of women of childbearing age between now and the end of the century. But in reality, there are already signs that fertility is declining in developing communities in exactly the same way, but possibly more rapidly than fertility declined in Western Europe between fifty and a hundred years ago. One of the strangest features of the Ehrlich description of the population explosion is the bland assumption that developing countries may somehow be unable to follow the path of development along which advanced societies have traveled. Is it any wonder that the predominantly Western preoccupation with the population explosion seems like patronizing neocolonialism to people elsewhere?

In much the spirit in which environmentalists worry about food, unnecessarily as events have shown (see Chapter 3), so too they worry about natural resources. In the United States, at least, this is an honorable tradition going back to the end of the nineteenth century. Then, Governor Gifford Pinchot was wringing his hands over the prospect that timber in the United States would be used up in roughly thirty years; that anthracite would last for only fifty years; and that other raw materials such as iron ore and natural gas were rapidly being consumed. Sixty years later, the same complaints are to be heard in the United States. The environmentalists have coined the phrase "our plundered planet" to express the anxiety they feel about the probability that petroleum will be much less plentiful a century from now than it is at present and that the time will come when high-grade copper ores are worked out.

The truth is, however, that society is by no means uniquely dependent on the raw materials now in common use. If copper becomes scarce or merely expensive, aluminum will have to be used instead. If natural diamonds are expensive, then make them synthetically. In any case, although supplies of raw ma-

Is Catastrophe Coming?

terials like these are known to be limited, the point at which they seem likely to be exhausted recedes with the passage of time so as to be always just over the horizon. Indeed, in spite of what the environmentalists say, the present time appears to be one at which forecasts of scarcity are less valid than ever. Petroleum may be much harder to obtain a century from now, but the past few years have laid the foundations for winning energy from hydrogen and minerals such as uranium in such large quantities that future decades will be much better off than anybody could have expected in the 1950s. And, strange as it may seem, the real economic cost of extracting metals such as lead and copper from the ground is still decreasing as exploration and techniques of mining and metallurgy become more efficient. In economic terms, the earth's resources seem to be becoming more plentiful.

Famine is only one of several hypothetical catastrophes supposed to flow from population growth. Dr. Ehrlich is one of those who have argued that crowding caused by population growth is a cause of individual disorientation and psychological disturbance and of social tension and upheaval. One common argument for supposing that crowding as such is bad for people starts from experiments which have been carried out with laboratory animals, principally rats and mice. The best-known experiments, due to Dr. R. Colhoun, showed that rats kept in conditions of crowding to which they were unused developed all kinds of psychological disturbances—mother rats took to infanticide, males became unnaturally aggressive and death was accelerated. So is it not reasonable to suppose that people living in cities will be more disturbed than those who live in rural areas? With growing population densities, will not social aberrations such as civil violence or international conflict become more prevalent? These are common suspicions. Dr. Ehrlich and his wife Anne, in their book *Population, Resources, Environment,* say that there are "very high correlations among rates of population growth . . . and involvement in wars."

The trouble is that the analogy between rats and people is

The Doomsday Syndrome

at best a tenuous analogy—gregariousness of the kind that led to the development of cities some thousands of years ago distinguishes the human race from rodents. And the belief that violence and war are accompaniments of crowding rests on the most shaky and disputed statistical basis. Who, after all, would think that the Netherlands, the most crowded of all the nations in Western Europe, is more given to violence than, say, the United States?

Ecological catastrophe is also high on the list of public fears for the future. As Dr. Barry Commoner puts it in *The Closing Circle*, "in our unwitting march toward ecological suicide, we have run out of options." What he and the less moderate people who echo his opinions wish to imply is that the interrelation between human beings and the natural environment is so delicate, and the dependence of the human race on the environment is so complete, that many of the effects of human activity on the natural world may destroy the capacity of the earth to support life.

One recipe for disaster, for example, is that pollution of the surface layers of the oceans by insecticides or chemicals may destroy the microscopic plants which turn the energy of sunlight into chemical form, thus helping to support marine life of all kinds and to replenish the oxygen in the atmosphere. Another is that the accumulation of carbon dioxide produced by the burning of fossil fuels may so increase the temperature on the surface of the earth as to transform the present pattern of weather and perhaps even to melt the Antarctic ice. Fortunately, these chains of events are by no means inescapable. For one thing, the processes which are supposed to lead to disaster are only imperfectly understood. Second, their scale is still puny compared with that of the envelope of the earth in which living things exist—the ecosphere as it is called. The fear that pesticides might so affect oceanic plant life that the world's supply of oxygen would be reduced, first introduced in 1969, was recognized by 1970 to be based on hopelessly gloomy calculations.

In all this gloomy speculation about potential calamity, the

Is Catastrophe Coming?

puzzle is why so much is made of remote and improbable happenings when much less emotional energy is lavished on other threats to human life and happiness—poverty, injustice and avoidable death. All these, of course, are tasks for which society must deliberately commit resources, men and money. Is it possible that the attractiveness of preoccupation with distant calamity is that it usually suggests policies of inaction? After all, the best way to prevent the accumulation of carbon dioxide in the atmosphere is not to build power stations. The best way to insure against the remote risk that DDT may be damaging to people is not to use DDT. In this sense, the environmental movement tends towards passivity, true conservatism. It is understandable that policies of doing nothing should seem easier than policies which require vigorous and expensive action, but widespread acceptance of what the doomsday men are asking for could so undermine the pattern of modern economic life as to create social stagnation.

If the human race manages to avoid the destruction of the environment on which it depends, is there not a danger that it may destroy itself more directly? In the past few years, the character of biological research has been repeatedly held up as a potential threat to continuing survival. Genetic engineering is, it is true, a somber phrase, conjuring up visions of the perversion of people's genetic inheritance, sometimes against their will. But the concept is less awesome when it is recalled that horse breeders and plant breeders have been doing it for centuries. And why should communities which have set their faces against the eugenic devices already possible—forced choice of marriage partners, for example, or selective infanticide—throw their principles to the winds now that molecular biology has come along?

Even the quite real prospect of fertilizing human eggs in test tubes does not contain the seeds of an unwelcome upheaval in society which many people suppose. The truth is that the most obvious uses of these new techniques are therapeutic, not subversive. To be sure, biological research has raised novel ethi-

The Doomsday Syndrome

cal problems. How, for example, should doctors decide which of several equally needy patients should have access to an artificial kidney machine or should receive a kidney that becomes available for transplantation? But the fact that these problems are awkward as well as novel is neither an argument for putting an end to the new techniques nor a justification for the belief that biological research is full of hidden dangers to society. What justification can there be for the supposition that the same medical men who have developed antibiotics for the treatment of infectious disease and vaccines for its prevention will seize on the new developments to pursue malevolent objectives?

But what of the possibility that science and the applications of science may in much more subtle ways undermine the integrity of society? This is an old fear, of course, which in its crudest form amounts to unregenerate obscurantism. In the past few years, the theme has been revised and made more vivid. Dr. Rene Dubos, a distinguished bacteriologist, in his book *Reason Awake* says, for example: "Man has always lived in a precarious state, worried about his place in the order of things. In the past he was threatened chiefly by natural forces that he could not control, and he experienced fear because of ignorance of the cosmos and of his own nature. Now threats and fears derive in large measure from science and its technologies, paradoxically the most characteristic products of human reason." Elsewhere he says, "Most would agree that science and technology are responsible for some of our worst nightmares and have made our societies as complex as to be almost unmanageable."

The flaw in these protestations is that they label technology, and the science from which it sometimes springs, as a subversive force in society. It is true, of course, that most technical innovations will frequently have unexpected and even unpredictable consequences. This has always been the case. Who would have guessed that the motor car would create the suburbs of North America? The introduction of the wheel into primitive societies must similarly have been attended by unforeseen developments. It is the same now—the immediate benefits of innovation may

Is Catastrophe Coming?

be predictable, but the more distant consequences, beneficial or otherwise, are harder to predict. The moral, of course, is what it has always been—that the governments have a responsibility to ensure that in the process of technical innovation, society reaps mostly benefits. To pretend that such discrimination is impossible, and that all technology is therefore suspect as Dr. Dubos appears to suppose, is to suggest that society is powerless to regulate its own affairs. The belief that technology is an all-powerful juggernaut wringing the humanity out of society seems usually to be a cloak for a pessimistic belief in the importance of social institutions. The test is not to keep science and technology at bay but to control them and, in particular, to make sure that they do not become dehumanizing or even misleading influences.

One of the most common misconceptions about technology is that it consists entirely of gigantic programs, supported by taxpayers' money, for sending rockets to the moon, for destroying other people's rockets when and if they are fired in anger, or for building advanced aircraft that airlines have no wish to buy. In reality, however, most technologists work towards much less spectacular objectives—building safer (and cheaper) bridges, for example, or devising ways of drying coffee without loss of flavor. Those who complain of technology and all its works would be on stronger ground if they were worried instead about the best way of deciding how society should exploit science and technology. Who says what innovations are worthwhile? Some decisions have to be made by individuals in their role as purchasers of goods. Others are left to manufacturers. Still others, which have a political flavor in the most general sense, must be taken by governments acting on behalf of the communities which they represent. Governments have all too often been unwilling to shoulder their responsibilities. In all advanced societies, governments have waved on the introduction of jet aircraft without thinking sufficiently about the extra noise that they would cause. They have encouraged industrial development without thinking sufficiently of the unavoidable side effects of

The Doomsday Syndrome

industry, pollution chief among them. They have encouraged urbanization without paying enough attention to city planning.

If these were the complaints which the environmentalists were making, their cause would be entirely laudable. By slipping into the pretense that science and technology have between them established such a powerful hold on the development of society that the human race may be undermined, they have chosen a lazy way of escaping the need to work out ways of making decisions for the beneficial exploitation of technology. But there is no reason now to think that technology will be less valuable in the future than it has been in the past in liberating men and women from drudgery and improving the quality of life not merely with material goods but with leisure. The environmentalists are therefore in danger of persuading society to turn its back on an indispensable agent for survival. Paradoxically, the environmental message, at least in its crudest form, is self-defeating.

Where did the environmental movement spring from? At the end of the Second World War, scientists were among the first to sense that the development of nuclear weapons would change the character of international relations and at the same time pose a real threat to the human race. This is too easily forgotten by those who now complain that the profession of science has been neglectful of its social responsibilities. But in 1945, Dr. J. Robert Oppenheimer, the scientific director of the program at Los Alamos for the development of the first atomic bombs, put the point eloquently if melodramatically when he said: "In some crude sense which no vulgarity, no overstatement can quite extinguish, the physicists have known sin, and this is a knowledge which they cannot lose."

Many of Oppenheimer's colleagues and particularly the group centered on the Chicago laboratory of the Manhattan Project—that in which the first self-sustaining nuclear reaction had been established—sought to influence the way in which nuclear energy would be used in the postwar world. To begin

Is Catastrophe Coming?

with, they founded the Federation of Atomic Scientists, now the Federation of American Scientists. The leading lights were distinguished people—men like Dr. Leo Szilard. They founded the *Bulletin of the Atomic Scientists* and began to urge that the United States government should deliberately design legislation for the control of nuclear energy in such a way that the military authorities in the United States would not have sole charge of the manufacture of nuclear weapons and that the United States would do everything it could to prevent the spread of nuclear weapons overseas.

In retrospect, it is curious how comparatively slowly people recognized the potential destructiveness of nuclear weapons. The fact that a single explosion at Hiroshima killed close on 140,000 people was an awesome piece of information, but at the end of a period during which a hundred times as many had been killed by conventional bombing, military action and the more old-fashioned bestiality of the concentration camps, the immediate importance of Hiroshima and Nagasaki was that they signaled the end of the war.

An influential group of scientists was on its toes right from the start. In the heady days immediately after the Second World War, Professor Eugene Rabinovitch, one of the founders of the Federation of Atomic Scientists, expressed the solemnity with which his colleagues regarded the arrival of atomic energy by saying: "Mankind has been given the power to use the immense energies locked up in the atomic nucleus for whatever purpose it may see fit—destroying itself in atomic war or building a more prosperous and secure world." Throughout the 1950s and 1960s, the potential ambivalence of nuclear energy was the theme that dominated most discussions of the social and economic value of nuclear energy. Nuclear fission was at once a way of bringing the world to an end and an almost magical way of solving what threatened to become a chronic shortage of conventional fuel.

The first tangible success for the scientists' lobby in the United States was the McMahon Act, which did place responsi-

The Doomsday Syndrome

bility for developing nuclear weapons firmly in the hands of a nonmilitary agency—the United States Atomic Energy Commission. This piece of legislation made it much easier for a strictly civilian nuclear industry to grow up alongside an industry for the development and manufacture of nuclear explosives. The now much-maligned Atomic Energy Commission is hardly recognizable as the most important political prize of the atomic scientists in the United States. Those who fought for the McMahon Act, and who applauded the way in which it restricted the freedom of the United States government to release information about the technical development of nuclear explosives to other governments, would not now be happy to acknowledge that the same legislation was a powerful spur to the independent manufacture of nuclear weapons in Britain in the late 1940s and in France a decade later.

It is ironical that one of the most influential postwar books on nuclear weapons, Lord Blackett's *The Political and Economic Consequences of Nuclear Energy,* argued that nations would only delude themselves by spending money on nuclear weapons; in due course, the Soviet Union would follow the United States in making nuclear weapons, and then the military usefulness of nuclear weapons would be canceled out. But the first explosions of hydrogen weapons in the early 1950s cast a longer shadow. When four Japanese fishermen were killed by radioactive dust from a thermonuclear explosion in 1954, the world as a whole was given a vivid demonstration of the potential destructiveness of nuclear weapons. Ever since, all discussions of nuclear energy have been colored by the quite proper recognition that full-scale nuclear war could put the future itself in jeopardy. It is no wonder that in 1960, Dr. Herman Kahn found it useful to invent a name for weapons systems capable of destroying all living things—the Doomsday Machine, he called it. It is only fair to add that Dr. Kahn—by choice, one of the most misunderstood of men—was chiefly concerned to show that "the closer a weapons system becomes to a Doomsday Machine, the less satisfactory it becomes."

In the mid-1950s, when the United States had launched an

Is Catastrophe Coming?

international program for making the technology of civil nuclear energy widely available, there were several organized protests at the plans for testing and using nuclear weapons. In 1955, the United Nations held the first of its international conferences on the peaceful uses of atomic energy. The occasion helped to draw attention to the civil as distinct from the military potential of nuclear energy, but the same period saw the beginnings of formal organizations urging the cause of nuclear disarmament on governments in the West and in the Soviet Union. Bertrand Russell's campaign for British unilateral disarmament began in 1955, and with Albert Einstein he issued his declaration that the mere existence of nuclear weapons would entail that at some stage they would be used in anger. By 1956, the alarm of the mid-1950s led to the formation of the Pugwash organization, which has since been not only a pressure group but a valuable channel of communication between East and West. By the late 1950s, however, nuclear weapons tests had become commonplace, and radioactive debris was accumulating in people's food—the discovery of radiostrontium in the skeletons of young children was a more powerful assault on the public conscience than even the discovery of DDT in the liver and fatty tissues of people as well as other mammals a decade later. What with military strategy in Europe still dominated by plans for thermonuclear retaliation, it is no wonder that the 1950s ended with the sense that Doomsday was only just around the corner.

In the United States, the alarm occasioned by the arrival of nuclear energy prompted the emergence of a number of organizations which have since helped to sustain what is called the environmental movement. The Federation of Atomic Scientists functioned principally through its journal. In 1958, however, Dr. Barry Commoner, a biologist at the Washington University at St. Louis, organized the St. Louis Committee for Atomic Information, and aimed to help exercise the public's right under American atomic-energy legislation to take part in public inquiries into the siting of nuclear power stations.

This cause was strengthened by the failure, in 1961, of the

The Doomsday Syndrome

overambitiously designed Enrico Fermi reactor on the shore of Lake Michigan. In New York in 1962, the daring proposal of the Consolidated Edison Company to build a nuclear power station within the city limits, across the East River just north of the United Nations building (see Chapter 7), stimulated the formation of another group of scientists, with Dr. Rene Dubos prominent among them, for providing public information not merely about atomic energy but about other developments in science and technology likely to have lasting social consequences.

It is ironical that the chief dangers to which the public information movement wished to draw attention were defused in the early 1960s. First, the explosion of nuclear weapons in the atmosphere was recognized to be what the critics in the 1950s had proclaimed—a serious hazard to human health—so that the governments of the United States, the Soviet Union and the United Kingdom were persuaded to sponsor a treaty to prohibit nuclear explosions above the ground. Dr. Commoner now says that the partial test ban should be regarded as "the first victorious battle in the campaign to save the environment—and its human inhabitants—from the blind anarchy of technology." For him, at least, there is no doubt where the roots of the environment movement are to be found.

How valid is that claim? Anxiety about radioactive fallout in people's skeletons was undoubtedly an important factor in determining the outcome of the test-ban negotiations, but the nuclear powers of 1964 were the more prepared to sign the test-ban treaty because they had completed the development of warheads for the long-range missiles that were the backbone of the strategic striking forces of the United States and the Soviet Union throughout the 1960s and because they calculated that the partial test-ban treaty would help to postpone the time when other nations became nuclear powers. In other words, they were able to listen receptively to the case against radioactivity in the environment. It is all very well for Dr. Commoner to say that many of those concerned then saw "that fallout was only part of a larger problem—the untoward environmental effects of modern

[16]

Is Catastrophe Coming?

technology"—they were also members of a dedicated army which had tasted blood but which had no further battles to fight.

The environmental movement of the 1970s is not nearly as broadly based as the campaign against fallout, when governments and not merely their critics were aware of the potential hazards. Powerful support for the case against the continued testing of weapons in the atmosphere came from all quarters and a specialist committee of the United Nations was especially influential. By comparison, the efforts of groups such as that of Dr. Commoner (which changed its name in 1964 to the St. Louis Committee for Environmental Information) to deal with other environmental problems than fallout have been necessarily less well supported by the technical community and also less successful. Although the first shots in the battle against DDT and similar insecticides were fired as early as 1962, it is only since 1968 or so, and only in the United States, that the environmental movement has taken on a recognizable shape.

Much of the environmental movement has been institutionalized. The Sierra Club of the United States, for long a consortium of conservationists, natural historians and mountain climbers, became an activist organization under the leadership of Mr. David Brewer, its executive director until the formation of the Friends of the Earth Society (of which Mr. Brewer is the director), of whom it has been said by a United States official with environmental responsibilities, "Thank God for Dave—he makes the rest of us seem like moderates."

The first opportunity to test the support for the new environmental movement in the United States came with the organization of what was called Earth Day on April 5, 1970, and although the legends of that occasion are still mostly concerned with the inconsistencies in the organized events—the litter left behind by the crowds attending rallies, for example—it was at least a vivid reminder to American politicians that there might be votes in the environment. The environment would by now be much cleaner if all the politicians in the United States who have since declared that their hearts are in the right place had also

The Doomsday Syndrome

been prepared to vote the funds or to pass the regulatory legislation that might have helped to prevent the continued discharge of raw sewage into American rivers, for example.

In any event, fallout was eventually replaced by pesticides as a battleground, and the late Miss Rachel Carson became the champion. In 1962, *Silent Spring* provided a new platform for the public protests about the uses to which science and technology were being put. Miss Carson was concerned almost entirely with the way in which insecticides were being used in the United States. Many of her complaints were entirely well-founded—it is absurd that insecticides should have been used to clear insects from inland lakes with such abandon as to kill the fish as well as the insects. Among Miss Carson's many cautionary tales is that of how the use of dieldrin, an insecticide similar to DDT but more powerful, against the Japanese beetle in the cornfields of the Middle West made life easier for another and more dangerous pest, the corn borer, which normally provided food for the Japanese beetle. In this and other ways, she marshaled enough evidence to demonstrate that pesticides should be more carefully regulated and controlled. The most seriously misleading part of her narrative is the use of horror stories of the misuse of DDT to create an impression that there are no safe uses worth consideration.

Why was the influence of *Silent Spring* so great? Much depended on Miss Carson's technique of calculated overdramatization. The silent spring was an apocryphal season in "a town in the heart of America" created by Miss Carson's fertile imagination. Her book begins with what she calls "a fable for tomorrow." Once,

> *all life seemed to live in harmony with its surroundings. . . . But then a strange blight crept over the area and everything began to change. Some evil spell had settled on the community: mysterious maladies swept the flocks of chickens: the cattle and sheep sickened and died. Everywhere was a shadow of death. The farmers*

Is Catastrophe Coming?

*spoke of much illness among their families. In
the town the doctors had become more puzzled
by new kinds of sickness appearing among their
patients. There had been several sudden and
unexplained deaths, not only among adults but
even among children, who would be stricken
suddenly while at play and die within a few
hours.*

The calamity, of course, was caused by too much pesticide.
Miss Carson goes on innocently to reveal that "this town does
not actually exist, but it might easily have a thousand counter-
parts in America or elsewhere in the world." By playing this
literary trick on her readers, Miss Carson provided not merely
a proof of the trivial statement that excessive amounts of pesticide could kill animals as well as insects but also a sense that
excessive use was unavoidable and—more significantly—a
model of calculated exaggeration which has since put its stamp
on the literature of the doomsday movement.

Dr. Paul Ehrlich's book *The Population Bomb* is a splendid
illustration of how the technique has flourished. After a tautly
written account of how "the battle to feed all of humanity is
over," sufficiently vivid to have most of his readers on the edges
of their seats, Dr. Ehrlich finishes with the smug apology that
"any scientist lives constantly with the possibility that he may
be wrong," but that no harm will be done if his argument turns
out to be false, for "if I am wrong, people will still be better fed,
better housed and happier. . . ." The difficulty, of course, is that
alarm does not provide the best atmosphere for finding rational
solutions to the parts of these problems which can be considered
real. Aesop knew what happened to shepherd boys who cried
wolf too often.

Dr. Barry Commoner also uses Miss Carson's technique. He
says in his book *Science and Survival,* for example, that "as
large a body of water as Lake Erie has already been over-
whelmed by pollutants and has in effect died." The truth is now
what it was in 1963 when the book was written, that Lake Erie
has indeed been seriously afflicted by pollution, for such a shal-

The Doomsday Syndrome

low body of water could not be expected to remain unchanged under the assault of such a vast amount of sewage and industrial effluent as the surrounding cities had come to discharge into it. But throughout the 1960s, the lake somehow managed to support a thriving fishing industry. In 1970, it yielded 25,000 tons of fish. Nobody can know for certain why the trout have been replaced by other species—is it the sewage or the influence of the Welland Canal, bypassing Niagara, connecting Lake Erie to Lake Ontario? At last it seems to have been agreed that something must be done to limit the discharge of effluents into Lake Erie, but the proclamation that the lake is already dead, whatever such a phrase may mean, has if anything given Lake Erie more prominence than it deserves. Fair play? In his more recent book, *The Closing Circle,* Dr. Commoner does not say the lake is dead but merely that "we have grossly, irreversibly changed the biological character of the lake and have greatly reduced, now and for the foreseeable future, its value to man." This is a more moderate statement of the position even if the dubious assertion of irreversibility is taken at its face value.

Overstatement is commonplace in the literature of doomsday. Miss Rachel Carson describes the possible hazards to soil productivity from the use of pesticides in the following terms: "As applications of pesticides continue to build up in the soil, it is almost certain that we are heading for trouble. This was the consensus of a group of specialists who met at Syracuse University in 1960 to discuss the ecology of the soil. These men summed up the hazards of using 'such potent and little understood tools' as chemicals and radiation: 'A few false moves on the part of man may result in destruction of soil productivity and the arthropods may well take over.'"

In 1960, it may well have been true that the measurements then available were insufficiently thorough to suggest how long DDT and similar materials would remain in the ground on which they have been sprayed, but is there any reason why fears specifically related to DDT should be extended to the general

Is Catastrophe Coming?

class of "chemicals and radiation"? And was there ever any reason to fear that the whole surface of the earth would be treated in exactly the same way at exactly the same time, so that the insecticides would have had the paradoxical effect of killing off the vegetation everywhere, leaving the insects in charge? What, for example, would the ecologists suggest that the arthropods would feed on when the vegetation had been killed off? And from whom, in any case, would the arthropods in this gloomy scenario take over? From plants? Or from people? Was Miss Carson afraid that too much explanation of these points would make her tale less alarming?

Explanations like these of how particular chemicals or other agencies might function have been generalized, in other hands, into a general sense of cataclysm. Thus C. S. Wallia begins his introduction to a symposium volume *Towards Century 21* with the stern declaration: "It has become a truism of our time that we concurrently face the portents of unprecedented disaster and the potentialities of remarkable fulfillment. Science and technology, it is acknowledged, has brought about this development." Dr. Jack D. Douglas, the editor of a similar symposium *The Technological Threat,* says of the process of technological change that "a growing proportion of us has become aware of the way in which some of these changes pose terrible threats to our cherished values of freedom and individualism and to our democratic forms of government."

The common theme in these declarations owes something to Herbert Marcuse but is made explicit by Dr. Jacques Ellul's book *The Technological Society,* where it is stated that "in the modern world, the most dangerous form of determinism is the technological phenomenon. It is not a question of getting rid of it but, by an act of freedom, of transcending it."

The fallacy in all these generalizations is of course the supposition that the course of development of modern technology cannot be influenced by human beings. However, Dr. Ellul may insist that "there is no choice between two technical methods—one of them asserts itself inescapably," the scope for choice in

The Doomsday Syndrome

technology is if anything now greater than in the past. Nations can decide to manufacture supersonic-transport aircraft, as the British and French governments did in 1971, or they may decide for the time being at least to turn their backs on this line of development as the United States government was forced by Congress to do only a few months earlier. In the great bulk of technological enterprise, the routine developments that rarely make the newspaper headlines but which cumulatively transform the nature of industry and improve its productivity, there is at any time too much to do and not enough money or people to do it.

The way in which so many professional scientists—Drs. Ehrlich Commoner and Dubos for example—have lent their names to the assertion that science and technology are automata in society is a cause of distress to their colleagues. Of course, there are serious social problems to be tackled. To the extent that these have been created by changes that have come about in recent decades, they can be partially laid at the door of technology. The fact that ocean beaches are now so much more crowded than half a century ago is a consequence of the development of motor cars and of the way in which large numbers of people have been enabled to own them privately. But would it ever have been sensible to ask that internal combustion engines should not have been invented for the sake of avoiding overcrowding at the beaches? Is it not preferable to enjoy the other benefits of the invention but to regulate the crowding of beaches by other means? And in any case, where such developments are in question, is it not entirely misleading to suggest that the automobile industry has grown to its present size for reasons connected with the character of technology and not because a need for the products became apparent? On issues like this, the doomsday literature is dishonest.

The environmental literature is also distinguished by its characteristic stand on the nature of living things and their relationship with the environment. Dr. Commoner's book *Science and Survival* has a chapter with the title "Greater Than the Sum

Is Catastrophe Coming?

of Its Parts" which sets out unsuccessfully to demonstrate that the properties of living things cannot be explained solely in terms of the properties of the molecules of which they are made:

> There is, I believe, a crisis in biology today. The root of the crisis is the conflict between the two approaches to the theory of life. One approach seeks for the unique capabilities of living things in separable chemical reactions; the other holds that this uniqueness is a property of the whole cell and arises out of the complex interactions of the separable events of cellular chemistry. Neither view has, as yet, been supported by decisive experimental proof. The molecular approach has not succeeded in showing by experiment that the subtly integrated complexity and beautiful precision of the cell's chemistry can be created by adding together its separate components. Nor has the opposite approach, as yet, discovered an integrating mechanism in the living cell which achieves the essential co-ordination of its numerous separate reactions.

In its essence, this argument is an echo of the old nineteenth-century belief in what was then called "life force"—a special quality of living things whose credibility has steadily diminished ever since the first synthesis a century and a half ago from ordinary chemicals of substances usually considered as by-products of life.

The more recent equivalent of this neovitalism is that the web of life, as Darwin called the way in which different species are linked together by their dependence on each other, is so complicated that it cannot be submitted to the methods of mathematical analysis. This is one of the arguments of Dr. Commoner's book *The Closing Circle*. In the trivial sense, of course, the point is incontrovertible—who would seriously set out to calculate the weight of a full-grown locust when, if the answer is of any interest, it would be much simpler, and probably safer as well, to measure it? But this does not imply that the weight of a locust is in principle incalculable—that there

The Doomsday Syndrome

are features of the ecosphere that lie beyond the scope of conventional science. Among the environmentalists, there is a temptation to emphasize the unity of the living world in circumstances when it would be more appropriate to consider different parts of it separately. For is it not the special character of science to be able to understand complicated problems by setting out to understand much simpler representations of them? The ecologists are sometimes right, in their roles as environmentalists, to emphasize the complexity of the problems with which they are concerned, but on other occasions, when simplicity should be the goal, their obscurantism is culpable.

Why has the environmental movement flourished in the past few years? One charitable explanation for the present preoccupation with survival is that the first landing on the moon by the crew of Apollo 11 provided the people left on earth with a vivid impression of their precarious foothold in an otherwise inhospitable solar system. But the landing on the moon took place when the environmental movement was well established, so that the Apollo landings cannot be a prime cause of the now common belief that the world is a fragile place which could be brought catastrophically to an end by human fecklessness. The view from the moon has nevertheless made much more graphic the concept of the earth as a kind of spaceship, moving through a hostile vacuum with its rapidly growing burden of humanity and other forms of life. Here again, however, the concept is not new—Mr. Adlai Stevenson told the Economic and Social Council of the United Nations as long ago as 1965 that, "We travel together, passengers on a little spaceship, dependent on its vulnerable supplies of air and soil; all committed for our safety to its security and peace, preserved from annihilation only by the care, the work, and I will say the love, we give our fragile craft."

The principle is splendid, as everybody will agree, and to the extent that the environmentalists have been guided by these principles, they are to be admired. But the questions urgently to be asked are whether they are right in their analysis of the

Is Catastrophe Coming?

potential for catastrophe. Up to a point, the analogy of spaceship earth is helpful. Spaceships are indeed isolated and self-sufficient entities. The crew must have air to breathe and food to eat as well as machinery for removing waste products. Appropriately, the surface of the earth has an atmosphere in which some of the waste products can be regulated or recycled, and in which the potentially harmful influences from interplanetary space—ultraviolet light from the sun and cosmic rays from farther away—are prevented from reaching people. There is also a complicated system by means of which the energy of sunlight is converted by plants into food either for human beings or for domestic animals on which human beings feed. One somber use of the analogy is to point out that the life-support systems of man-made spaceships can be put out of action either by accident or by the failure of the crew to use them prudently. The analogy wears thin when it is used to suggest when and how accidents may happen. Another is that some of the resources with which a spaceship is provided cannot be renewed. What will happen, this train of thought goes, if some essential material on spaceship earth should be exhausted?

There is nothing new in recognizing that, on the scale of the solar system, the earth is small, and remote from the other planets, or even the moon. That has moved the imagination of human beings for centuries. And undoubtedly there are limits to the scale on which people can safely set out to change the environment in which they live, and it is important that these limits should be better understood. But there is nothing in the view of the earth from the surface of the moon to lend extra urgency to the task.

Tiny though the earth may appear from the moon, it is in reality an enormous object. The atmosphere of the earth alone weighs more than 5,000 million million tons, more than a million tons of air for each human being now alive. The water on the surface of the earth weighs more than 300 times as much —in other words, each living person's share of the water would just about fill a cube half a mile in each direction. The energy

The Doomsday Syndrome

released in thunderstorms is comparable with that released by the explosion of nuclear weapons; hurricanes or typhoons are the equivalent of several thousand nuclear weapons. The momentum of the circulation of the oceans and the atmosphere is vast. It is not entirely out of the question that human intervention could at some stage bring changes, but for the time being the vast scale on which the earth is built should be a great comfort. In other words, the analogy of spaceship earth is probably not yet applicable to the real world. Human activity, spectacular though it may be, is still dwarfed by the human environment.

There is a good deal of historical evidence to show how resilient the atmosphere of the earth can be. In 1887, the Pacific island of Krakatoa disappeared in a volcanic eruption which carried more than a million tons of dust into the stratosphere. For years afterwards, people all over the world were impressed by the vividness of the sunsets because of the scattering of sunlight in the stratosphere by the dust left over from the volcano. It is also clear from the meteorological records that this layer of dust reduced the amount of energy reaching the surface of the earth from the sun, with the result that temperatures in many places were abnormally low for four or five years afterwards. Yet now, so far as can be told, the effects of the cloud of dust from Krakatoa have entirely disappeared. This is the yardstick for judging the fear that dust from industrial chimneys may produce climatic disturbances of one kind or another.

The threat of man-made catastrophe must also be measured against the possibility of natural catastrophe. Natural climatic fluctuations are common and pronounced. Cold and warm periods seem to alternate every eighty years or so and it is now well understood that the retreat of the last Ice Age took place only 10,000 years ago, only a short while before the first traces of civilized communities in the Middle East and Egypt. In the past two million years, there have been three or more successive waves of ice in the northern and southern hemispheres, with intervals between these Ice Ages climatically similar to the pres-

Is Catastrophe Coming?

ent. So may it not be that the present period is not so much the beginning of a period free from Ice Ages but, rather, merely an interval between the last and the next? So poor is present understanding of the causes of the Ice Ages that nobody is in a position to predict when or how the ice might return. And is it not easy to imagine that the return of the ice, which would make much of North America, Northern Europe and Northern Asia uninhabitable, would be a more serious interference with the way in which people live than any of the disasters foreseen in the doomsday books?

In the long run, as Lord Keynes put it, we shall all be dead. The catalogue of natural disasters includes equally unpredictable natural phenomena which will eventually be more damaging. Thus the pattern of magnetic forces around the earth, which is among other things responsible for the functioning of magnetic compasses, disappears and is created in the opposite direction every 150,000 years or so. But the earth's magnetism is a powerful shield against a great many hostile influences from outside, especially the atomic particles constantly flung out from the sun which are called the solar wind. The result would be, if it were not for the earth's magnetism, that living things would be exposed to more intense natural radiation than at present, so that genetic changes would accumulate in all kinds of living things. Periods like this, when the surface of the earth is shielded less effectively from outside influences, have indeed been suggested as one of the reasons why the dinosaurs disappeared. Whenever the next magnetic reversal takes place, human beings will have cause to be alarmed.

The ultimate disaster, remote though it may be, will come within the transformation due eventually to take place in the sun. Compared with many other kinds of stars, the sun is at a comparatively early stage of evolution. For the past 5,000 million years its energy has come from the conversion of hydrogen into helium in much the way thermonuclear weapons get their energy. By now, some of the initial stock of hydrogen has been used. At some point, and before its hydrogen fuel is any-

The Doomsday Syndrome

thing like exhausted, the sun will become a different object, much larger and relatively colder on the outside but much hotter at the center. When that happens, the sun will be a much bigger object, not one million miles across but possibly a hundred times as big. Then, of course, not merely will life on the surface of the earth become intolerable but the earth itself will be engulfed. It is certain to be more than a thousand million years before such a catastrophe can occur, yet the length of time for which the sun is likely to continue much as it is at present is likely to be comparable with the time, about 3,000 million years, for which living things of any kind have existed on the surface of the earth.

These are horrendous prospects, but they provide a kind of yardstick with which to assess the durability of spaceship earth. On this scale, the self-destructive potential of terrestrial technology will be puny for a long time to come. The analogy of the spaceship is false simply because the scale of the earth is so different from that of any spaceship that could be constructed artificially.

Even if the environmentalists may in the past few years have made too much of some imagined threats to the survival of the human race, may not their excesses be justified by the results? This is one of the most common arguments in favor of what might be called the crusading point of view. What does it matter, so long as, one way or another, they get things done? This is an echo of Dr. Ehrlich's famous question "If I am wrong, people will still be better fed, better housed . . ."

So what have the environmentalists accomplished? Dr. Commoner, in *The Closing Circle*, provides a list of examples of the kinds of things which have been done. He includes in this the partial test-ban treaty, signed in 1963; the "public victory over the Pentagon over the matter of disposal of nerve gas" in 1971, when his own St. Louis Committee for Environmental Information helped to demonstrate that even such large quantities of nerve gas as the U.S. Army had wished to dispose of in the

Is Catastrophe Coming?

Atlantic could be detoxified safely on the spot; the decision of the United States to abandon the development and production of biological weapons; the "decision to halt the spread of DDT in the environment" in the United States; "the defeat of the SST over the massive persistent opposition of the Nixon Administration, the aircraft industry and a number of labor unions"; and, finally, the way in which a Canadian biology student was able to persuade his government to ban fishing in Lake Erie and to close down a number of chemical factories emitting mercury to the lake on the strength of the discovery of seven parts per million of mercury in a fish taken from the lake.

It is no slur on the environmental movement to suggest that not all of these developments can be claimed as victories. The way in which the United States government eventually gave up the development of biological weapons, for example, owes more to the diligence of those in the United States and elsewhere, officials and private citizens, who have for years been helping to devise some way of dispensing with armaments like these. The military authorities in the United States and elsewhere have been exceedingly circumspect in moderating the immediate risks of the research and development of biological weapons. The case against these developments has been and remains quite different—that biological weapons are an unnecessary and an intolerable complication of the arms race which all governments have a common interest to avoid.

Much the same can be said of the decision of the United States Congress in 1971 not to vote further funds for the development of supersonic air transport. It is true that there have been repeated complaints that supersonic aircraft would be an intolerable environmental nuisance. And it remains to be seen whether sonic booms will be more or less of a nuisance than the noise these aircraft will make at takeoff and whether either of these nuisances will be tolerable, yet the reasons why Congress abandoned the SST were much more familiar—an unwillingness to be coerced by the United States administration into a development whose economic virtue was exceedingly dubious

The Doomsday Syndrome

at a time when all kinds of other more desirable forms of public expenditure were restricted.

If the United States government's policy on DDT is a victory for the environmentalists, it may yet turn out to be a Pyrrhic victory (see Chapter 4). Much the same is true of the way in which public anxiety in the United States about such things as the carcinogenic effects of cyclamates or herbicides has jockeyed the government into hasty and (as it has afterwards transpired) incorrect decisions. Yet in the long run it is valuable that people should play a responsible part in the care of the environment and it is inevitable that in such a role, private organizations will necessarily find themselves acting as pressure groups. The Council on Environmental Quality in the United States, in its second annual report (1971), welcomes the part which non-governmental organizations and individual people can play and, indeed, Dr. Commoner might have claimed as a victory for the environmental movement the way in which new federal legislation provides for the intervention of citizens in matters which concern them. By the middle of 1971, there were in the United States more than 3,000 organizations of private citizens concerned specifically with the environment, either on a local or a national basis. The cumulative interest and activity of the people whose energy is thus engaged is in the long run bound to be beneficial.

This is why the excesses of the extremist wing of the environmental movement should not be allowed to cloud important public issues or even to encumber the proper management of the environment. If the environmental movement is to prosper, it is in particular important that it should cultivate the sense of historical perspective which the extremists conspicuously lack. The most urgent need is that the environmentalists should recognize that the environment has been treated much more badly in the past than would now be permissible. The horrors of the cities of Victorian Britain, with their disease and air pollution, have vanished from advanced cities and are quickly being outlawed elsewhere, while those who are quite properly concerned

Is Catastrophe Coming?

with air pollution should acknowledge that where accurate records have been kept, as in the United States and Britain, urban air pollution has been declining for well over a decade. (In the United States, for example, the average smokiness of air in sixty cities declined by 20 percent between 1957 and 1970, while sulphur dioxide at the same sites decreased by a third between 1962 and 1969.) What these and other statistics imply is that pollution and other assaults on the natural environment are not nearly as novel as those who have recently discovered them pretend. If this were acknowledged more openly, it would be possible to dispense with the sense of drama which the extremists in the environmental movement convey.

Another conspicuous defect in the arguments of the environmentalists is their innocence of economics. In reality, most of the issues which tend to be presented as questions of life or death for the human race are essentially questions of economics. On urban air pollution, the overriding question is not whether cleaner air can be provided but how much taxpayers and in particular the operators of motor vehicles and factories are prepared to pay for that amenity. Exactly the same is true of the noise produced by vehicles and aircraft, the amenities available at coastal beaches, and even the extent to which farmers are allowed to use pesticides. On issues like these there is a need for a better understanding of the economics of the communal good—a discipline that would benefit not merely those who would preserve the environment from assault but also those who wish to exploit it in the interests of human survival.

Because the relationship between communities of people and the environment is at some level determined by economic considerations, it is not surprising that different communities should have different objectives and that they should strike their own balance between exploitation and conservation. This is another way of saying that only prosperous communities will pay as much attention to considerations of amenity as those of the United States and Western Europe. One of the more serious dangers of the extreme wing of the environmental movement is

The Doomsday Syndrome

that by insisting that present tendencies have catastrophic implications, it may alienate the countries of the developing world, not yet rich enough to aspire to the kind of freedom from pollution on which the more prosperous nations have set their sights. This was plain enough at the United Nations in 1971, when it turned out to be extremely difficult to hammer out a common platform for the Conference on the Human Environment arranged for Stockholm in June 1972.

Still more serious is the danger that the extreme wing of the environmental movement may inhibit communities of all kinds from making the fullest use of the technical means which exist for the improvement of the human condition. Insidiously, the suggestion has been advanced that science and technology are the sources of potential environmental hazard. The truth is that the blame, if any, attaches to the decisions that have been made about the uses to which technology should be put. And there is no doubt that as the striking of a comfortable balance between human communities and the environment becomes a more intricate task, science and technology between them have an increasingly important role to play. Worse still, the impression, quite falsely, has got about that prosperity as such is a danger. For is it not that the numbers of motor cars in city streets and the numbers of disposable bottles discarded in the countryside are measures of the amounts of money which people have to spend on these contraptions? To insist on this relationship will of course obscure the incontrovertible truth that prosperity in the sense now common in advanced societies is also the way in which communities of all kinds are able to afford health services, education and the other social benefits of amenities in advanced communities to which less fortunate people still aspire.

The Numbers Game

◻

In the literature of doomsday, the growth of the world's population is the most common theme, and indeed there is no precedent for the speed of growth in the past few decades. Sometimes the phenomenon is called the "population explosion." More misanthropically, it is sometimes kown as "people pollution" or "popollution." There is an extra touch of drama in Dr. Paul R. Ehrlich's title for his best-known book, *The Population Bomb.*

The emotional overtones accompanying these arguments are strong and distinctive. The general idea seems to be that population growth is a chariot wheel to which the human race is bound and which will carry it to disaster unless drastic and painful steps are taken to put matters right. Given that the growth of the world's population has its roots in sexual intercourse, it is no surprise that prophecies of demographic doom are shot through with pleas for self-denial which smack of old-fashioned hellfire and brimstone puritanism. "Man can undo himself with no other force than his own brutality," in the words of Mr. David Brewer, the director of the organization Friends of the Earth, Inc. "The cancer of population growth . . . must be cut out," according to Dr. Ehrlich. Is it possible that some of the emotion with which the issue of population growth has been invested stems from a sneaking suspicion that procreation is a sinful business?

This said, it is no surprise that the growth of population is central to the doomsday movement. The most common assertion is that the population of the world is growing more quickly than the supply of food, with the result that famine will occur. William and Paul Paddock have made the most strident statement of this case in *Famine—1975!*—"The famines are inevitable," they say. But people also imply pollution. The more peo-

The Doomsday Syndrome

ple, especially if they hanker after prosperity, the more smoke there will be in the air, the more DDT in people's fat and the more sewage in the rivers and lakes. People also bring pressures on natural and apparently irreplaceable resources as different as metal ores, energy supplies and beaches from which to swim. More people also imply more crowding, and it is held that the consequences include not merely discomfort but social and personal catastrophes. "Population pressures promote wars," in Dr. Ehrlich's view. "Crowding may lead to types of asocial behavior," according to Dr. Rene Dubos. People seem to be the roots of all these evils.

There is no doubt that the population of the world has recently been growing more quickly than ever before, and it is evident that growth at this pace cannot continue indefinitely. The most gloomy prophecies are, however, unwarrantable. Too often these arguments rely on arithmetic that is misleading in its simplicity, but in any case there are already signs that the most rapidly growing populations in the world will in the next few decades be held in check by natural social influences, such as education, health care, and the opportunities which increasing prosperity provide—not just the machinery of contraception—which have in the past century given Western Europe and North America a measure of demographic stability. The threat of widespread famine can be taken seriously only by choosing to ignore the evidence now accumulating that the next few decades are likely to be decades of plenty, as the Old Testament would say (see Chapter 3). The pressures of the growing population of the world on other natural resources or on the environment will grow, it is true, but there is nothing to suggest that they will be insupportable. Declarations that population density will bring political, social and personal calamities seem to spring from naive understanding of the nature of international relations and from dubious analogies between human and animal populations. The demographic catastrophes which are prominent in the doomsday movement are unreal threats.

It does not follow from this that there is nothing to worry

The Numbers Game

about. Especially in countries where the population is growing rapidly, communities cannot invest as fully as they should in economic and social development because they are compelled to devote resources to feeding and educating growing numbers of children. There are novel questions of principle to be dealt with—should countries which have failed to stabilize their populations be given more foreign aid or less? What are the circumstances in which the sheer mechanics of contraception can be used most efficiently? A certain measure of demographic stability is everywhere desirable. But here as elsewhere in the arguments of the doomsday movement, false warnings of catastrophe may distract people from the work that needs urgently to be done, the efficient use of foreign aid in working towards stability, for example.

The belief that the continued growth of the human population will bring disaster is not, of course, a novelty. The circumstances in 1797 in which Thomas Malthus produced the first edition of his *Essay on the Principle of Population* were in many ways the same as those which have evoked the latest wave of anxiety about population. At the end of the eighteenth century, optimism about the future of society abounded. Science and the application of science seemed to promise great and unexpected benefits. The French Revolution had fortified libertarian and egalitarian spirits. To many people, the perfectibility of human nature seemed almost beyond dispute. In Britain, William Godwin looked forward to a world in which "there will be no war, no crimes, no administration of justice and no government. Besides this, there will be neither disease, anguish, melancholy nor resentment. Every man will seek, with ineffable ardour, the good of all."

Godwin was not a lone dreamer. At the same time in France, the liberal revolutionary the Marquis of Condorcet seems to have been able to shut his ears to the sound of the Jacobin tumbrils for long enough to write an equally utopian account of a world that never came.

The Doomsday Syndrome

Both Godwin and Condorcet acknowledged that these visions would come true only if the population did not grow indefinitely. Condorcet asked: "Might there not come a time when, because the number of people in the world finally exceeds the means of subsistence, there ensues a continual diminution of happiness, a true regression or at best an oscillation between good and bad?" How to escape from that dilemma? Godwin supposed that with the continued refinement of the human spirit, the desire to procreate would wither away. Condorcet put the point another way by saying that people would come to recognize their obligations to the rest of society and would not wish to "fill the earth with useless and unhappy beings."

The utopians were egalitarians to a man. As Condorcet put it, "a state of cultivated equality is most consonant to the nature of man and most conducive to the diffusion of felicity." In Britain, the conviction that progress would necessarily lead to a more equitable form of society helped to inspire the spate of constitutional and social legislation which laid the foundations of Victorian liberalism in the first few decades of the nineteenth century.

The first edition of Malthus' *Essay* was both a general protest against the unreality of the utopians and a particular complaint about the legislation which they had helped to inspire—William Pitt's abortive Poor Law, for example. Like those who now follow in his footsteps, but more eloquently than most of them, Malthus had a sense of the apocalyptic:

> *The great and unlooked for discoveries that have taken place in late years in natural philosophy, the increasing diffusion of general knowledge from the extension of the art of printing, the ardent and unshackled spirit of inquiry that prevails throughout the lettered and even unlettered world, the new and extraordinary lights that have been thrown on political subjects which dazzle and astonish the understanding and particularly that tremendous phenomenon in the political horizon, the French Revolution, which like a blazing comet seems destined either*

The Numbers Game

to inspire with fresh life or vigour or to scorch up and destroy the shrinking inhabitants of the earth, have all concurred to lead many men into the opinion that we are touching on a period big with the most important changes, changes that would in some sense be decisive of the future fate of mankind.

The first version of Malthus' *Essay* is a simple forecast of present prophecies that the growth of population will bring disaster. If food is essential for the support of life and if sexual intercourse is similarly (if regrettably) unavoidable, Malthus observed that a population growing without restraint would increase geometrically, doubling in size every few decades. From this, he argued that the balance between the human population and its supply of food would eventually be struck only by the intervention of one or more unpleasant agencies—starvation, disease, war and what he called moral corruption.

Like many more recent writers on this and related subjects, Malthus appears to have been surprised at the reception which the first edition of his *Essay* received. William Pitt, for example, was persuaded by the tract to withdraw his proposed Poor Law. Malthus himself seems to have been persuaded (as he should have been) that his assumptions were at odds with reality. However unpleasant life may have been in the early nineteenth century, it was better than it had been before. The result was that the second edition of Malthus' *Essay*, published in 1803, contained the admission that what he called "moral restraint" (not by any means to be confused with contraception) could help to regulate the growth of a population. The change of ground, of course, is crucial. Malthus began by ignoring the evidence even then available that human populations can regulate their fertility without the help of external catastrophe, with the result that he became a prophet—a false prophet as it turned out—of doom. He finished up on firmer ground, but with an argument of much less awesome significance. Who needs to be alarmed if disaster can be avoided by fertility restraint of a kind even then widespread?

The Doomsday Syndrome

In spite of the weakening of the doctrine, Malthus was a powerful if negative influence on the nineteenth century. To the extent that his work was a reminder of the dependence of a population on its food supply, he was an inspiration to those who would now be called human ecologists. To the extent that he drew attention to the differences between people and faced the plain truth that the poor and hungry would be more likely than the rich and well-fed to succumb to "misery and vice," he provided some ammunition for those who were later to talk about natural selection. But the reason why "malthusian" became and still is an abusive word is that Malthus quite openly argued that the "misery" of the poor was either unavoidable or preferable to other forms of "vice" that would supervene if poverty were relieved. The poor, he implied, are ineradicable.

It is no wonder that Malthus was condemned by Victorians as different as William Cobbett, William Hazlitt, Benjamin Disraeli, John Stuart Mill and Karl Marx. It was not necessary to be utopians to disagree. One complaint was that he was wrong. Another was that he distracted attention and energy from important social problems by making so much of a distant and abstract calamity. The same complaints can be leveled against the modern prophets of demographic disaster, who share with Malthus his particular blend of pessimism about the future and detachment from the present.

One of the saddest features of the present alarm about the growth of the population of the world is that so little has been learned from Malthus' mistakes. Simple arithmetic is usually given much more respect than it deserves, for example. As Dr. Ehrlich explains, ". . . no matter how you slice it, population is a numbers game." He goes on to say, in *The Population Bomb,* that "Each year food production in underdeveloped countries falls a bit further behind burgeoning population growth, and people go to bed a little hungrier. While there are temporary or local reversals of this trend, it now seems inevitable that it will continue to its logical conclusion—mass starvation." This is a simple restatement of the first version of Malthus' doctrine.

The Numbers Game

The trouble with the numbers game is that no amount of arithmetical accuracy can make up for faulty assumptions. *The Population Bomb*, which has played an exceedingly important part in the doomsday movement, begins with an explanation of how the rate of growth of a population is related to the size which it is likely to reach. For the world as a whole in the 1960s, the average rate of increase seems to have been about 1.9 percent a year. Dr. Ehrlich points out that if this rate of growth were sustained, the population of the world as a whole would double in thirty-seven years, and this is a vivid way of displaying the horrors of the geometrical progressions which alarmed Malthus—if the population of the world doubles every thirty-seven years, then after a century it will have multiplied eight times, and it will not be long before there is no room for people to stand up, let alone grow food for themselves.

Dr. Ehrlich goes through what he calls the "absurd" exercise of assuming that the population of the world will double every thirty-seven years for the next nine centuries and concludes that there would then be roughly a hundred people for each square yard of solid ground. He discovers by *reductio ad absurdum* that the geometric growth of population must at some point be interrupted, and this he says is where the famines come in. The real absurdity, however, is not the estimate of how many people there would be in 900 years but the implication that demography can ever be as simple as this. The rate of increase is the balance between the birth rate and the death rate, both of which are continually changing, differently in different places. For what they are worth, the latest United Nations forecasts of world population suggest that the growth rate will be still faster in the 1970s and 1980s, as medical care is more widely diffused, but that declining fertility will decrease the rate of growth to 1.7 percent a year by the end of the century, corresponding to a doubling time of forty-one years. The uncertainties are so great, however, that the deceleration could come more quickly and more sharply. If demography is a numbers game, it is much more intricate than Dr. Ehrlich implies.

Much of the tension in the population question stems from

The Doomsday Syndrome

the undisputed fact that the most quickly growing populations are those of the underdeveloped countries—the UDCs as they tend to be called. This is no accident. Better hygiene and better medical care have helped large sections of the populations of developing countries to avoid untimely death. Precisely similar changes have occurred in the advanced nations of the world within the past century, and the biblical life span of seventy years has come to be regarded as an attribute of advancement. Why then should the people of countries such as Ghana, Tanzania and Burundi be satisfied with only just over half as much?

For the people most concerned, those living in the developing countries, the changes which have come about are most evident in the lengthening of life expectancy. In Ceylon, for example, partly at least because of the use of DDT against the malaria mosquito, the death rate fell from 2.2 percent a year in 1945 to less than 1.0 percent a year in 1954. Children and young adults have benefited most—in the early 1950s, the teenage death rate in Ceylon was a sixth of what it had been in the early 1920s. But the birth rate has decreased much less, so far at least, in Ceylon and in other developing countries, the populations of which are at present growing at close on 2.5 percent a year, more than twice as quickly as the population of the developed countries (1.0 percent a year).

Although the pace of growth in the developing nations creates serious problems, the chief of which is the diversion of resources from economic and social development, much of the language of demographic disaster is ill-considered and even offensive. Thus Dr. Ehrlich uses the phrase "exported death control" to describe the decrease of mortality in developing countries, discounting by so doing what developing countries have done for themselves through awareness of the causes of disease, by hygiene and simple measures of public health. Dr. Ehrlich says he came to an emotional understanding of the population problem "one stinking hot night in Delhi" when he and his companions were "frightened" by the "people thrusting their hands through the taxi window, begging—people defecating and uri-

The Numbers Game

nating—people clinging to buses—people herding animals—people, people, people." So how is it possible to blame the pharmaceutical exporters of the West for the decline of mortality which there has been? How is the notion of exported death control to be reconciled with the chronic shortage of doctors in the developing world—one for every 4,000 people in India, compared with one for every 650 people in the United States?

Everybody agrees, of course, that ways of decelerating the rate of growth will have to be found—Dr. Ehrlich says before 1975. The only alternative, he says, is the "death rate solution" in which war, famine and pestilence, the old malthusian bogeys, take control. He says that famine is one way, perhaps the most likely way, of bringing about such a solution, for "the world, especially the undeveloped world, is rapidly running out of food." India "makes an obvious target" but "population is far outstripping food production" throughout the developing world. But famine is only one of the awesome prospects—"the progressive deterioration of our environment may in the long view cause more death and misery than any conceivable food-population gap." And then "it is all too easy . . . to discount the potential for population control possessed today by plague." Dr. Ehrlich suggests that there will in due course be plenty of opportunities for the organisms of traditional diseases—"malaria, yellow fever, typhus and their friends are still around"—as well as for more virulent versions of the influenza virus that might kill as many as 500 million people in one epidemic. And over everything hangs the shadow of nuclear war, the ultimate solution.

In the past decade, these arguments have been echoed a hundred times. Some have argued that the present size of the population of the world, and the pace at which it grows, is bound to deplete the natural resources which are not naturally renewed. Pollution and population growth are closely linked, at least in the doomsday literature. One syllogism runs: "More people means more pollution; but more pollution means more mortality; therefore more people means more mortality." Some claim that the pressure of population growth is bound to create

The Doomsday Syndrome

within societies such as that of the United States a tendency towards forms of government which are authoritarian and oppressive. Another variant on this theme is that population growth brings crowding which is necessarily bad for people, and it is true that crowded populations of animals as different as jackrabbits (in Minnesota) and deer (in Chesapeake Bay) have been observed to die off in circumstances which suggest that the adrenal glands have been chronically overstressed. Laboratory rats kept in crowded conditions have been found to suffer ills such as premature birth, infant mortality, abortion and loss of nesting instinct. Will human behavior be similarly corrupted?

For the most part, these arguments have about as much intellectual force as the weaker of the two versions of Malthus' *Essay*. Either there will be disaster or people will exercise "moral restraint"—prudence might be a more modern equivalent—and disaster will be avoided. It is a little like telling a motorist approaching a tight corner that there will be an accident if he does not brake. This is why the question whether population growth will bring disaster to the human race turns not on the numbers, or even on the speed at which they grow, but on a sober assessment of the likelihood that societies which have somehow managed to survive for the best part of two million years will at this stage in their history exhaust their capacity for taking prudent steps for their own survival.

The truth is almost the opposite. The prudence which consists of medical care may not be a certain defense against plague and pestilence, but it goes a long way to that end. Fecklessness and a growing population combined can create pollution, but there are also remedies close to hand (see Chapter 4). Famine is not a threat but a scarecrow (see Chapter 3)—the problem is not so much to feed the growing population as to cure the nutritional defects which have plagued the human race for centuries. And is it sensible in one breath to blame the plight of many cities on the concentration of people there and to bemoan the exodus from the city center to the suburbs which has been the usual pattern in advanced societies for several years? What is

The Numbers Game

the abomination—population growth or the failure to deal with social ills that might have gone neglected without the pressure of people?

One of the curious features of present concern about population growth is that it has managed to avoid or at least to obscure the political conflicts with which the demographic issue has usually been clouded. In part, the causes are irrational. To some people, any argument in favor of reproductive moderation may seem like a restraint of freedom. (To some Roman Catholics, it may seem a kind of blasphemy.) But by now, there is also plenty of evidence that overbreeding tends to be the dubious advantage of the poor. It is no wonder that the running battle between Malthus and his critics was a battle between a conservative and the great liberals of the nineteenth century. By the end, Marx was also on the tail of "the contemptible Malthus." In present circumstances, the movement for demographic stability, predominantly staffed by the middle class, has somehow to persuade poor people to make do with fewer children than would be natural. Is it any wonder that the response is sometimes less than wholehearted? Is it any wonder that the stridency of some of the modern prophets comes across as a kind of elitism?

The smugness which may be suppressed in the advocacy of restraint at home often emerges directly in recommendations for action elsewhere, especially in what are called the UDCs. What is to be done there? According to Dr. Ehrlich, the answer lies in the United States, "the most influential superpower." "It is obvious that we cannot exist unaffected by the fate of our fellows on the other end of the good ship Earth. If their end of the ship sinks, we shall at the very least have to put up with the spectacle of their drowning and listen to their screams."

> *Dr. Ehrlich goes on to say that: besides our own serious population problem at home, we are intimately involved in the world crisis. We are involved through our import-export situation. We are involved because of the possibilities of*

The Doomsday Syndrome

> global ecological catastrophe, of global pesti-
> lence, of global thermonuclear war. Also, we are
> involved because of the humanitarian feelings
> of most Americans.

So the first step is to control the growth of the population of the United States, both for the direct benefits which there would be and as an example to nations abroad. Within the United States, Dr. Ehrlich offers a variety of remedies, from more sex education and abortion on demand to differential taxes biased against large families and even baby-handling equipment. Once all this is done, "we will be in a position to take the lead in finding a solution to the problem on a world scale."

The most alarming of all recipes for the ills of the developing countries is that put forward by William and Paul Paddock in *Famine—1975!* and later blessed by *The Population Bomb*. Addressed to the taxpayers of the United States, this document solemnly advocated that American foreign aid should be made available only to those countries which adopted vigorous population policies and which—since money was in any case scarce— were politically compliant as well. By analogy with the dilemma of military surgeons faced with the need for rules to decide to which casualties to devote a limited amount of medical care, the brothers Paddock solemnly advocated the denial of foreign aid to two categories of countries—those likely to survive through their own efforts and those in some sense or another beyond aid. When the book appeared, in 1967, Libya and Gambia were put in the first category—the "walking wounded." India, Egypt and Haiti were beyond aid. On the other hand, the "tough-minded leadership of President Ayub Khan" seemed to qualify Pakistan, or "at least West Pakistan," for aid.

Dr. Ehrlich has a refinement of this scheme under which aid-giving governments can select "rehabilitation areas" on which to concentrate their efforts, providing television receivers and agents trained in the techniques of contraception and able not merely to decide which regions within nations should be helped but also to control migration to the rehabilitation areas so as

The Numbers Game

"to prevent swamping of aided areas by the less fortunate." To be sure, there would be serious "sociopolitical problems" and a policy designed to discriminate between nations to be helped and those to be allowed to fend for themselves might not be workable within the United Nations, but in any case the United States government should be prepared to act unilaterally by putting pressure on governments like that of India to adopt compulsory sterilization as a means of population control.

To be fair, Dr. Ehrlich has on some, but not all, more recent occasions been more guarded. In *Population, Resources, Environment,* Ehrlich and his wife Anne H. Ehrlich plead more explicitly for foreign aid and less explicitly for draconian methods of control such as contraceptives in people's drinking water—"compulsory control of family size is an unpalatable idea to many, but the alternatives may be much more horrifying." The notion that aid-giving countries should be able to override the sovereignty of recipient nations is replaced by the concept of "semi-development." In particular, "as examples of semi-development, Kenya and Tanzania might be semi-developed as combination agrarian-recreation areas. They and some other African nations can supply the world with a priceless asset—a window on the past when vast herds of non-human animals roamed the face of the earth." The argument continues with a description of how a "Planetary Regime," incorporating the "United Nations into a sort of International Agency for Population, Resources and Environment," could control all international aspects of the control of the "development, administration, conservation and distribution of natural resources" as well as the regulation of all foreign aid, international trade and food exporting.

It is hard to think that the means suggested as stabilizers of the population of devcloping countries can have been fully considered by those who make them. Selective aid-giving is as much an assault on the conventions of international relations painfully developed in the past few centuries as Malthus' remedies were an affront against the ideal of an egalitarian society. And is it politically feasible that aid-giving nations should try to

The Doomsday Syndrome

discriminate between one province and another within a recipient nation? Is it even possible that recipient nations would accept aid on terms like these? Within nations, is there any chance that governments would be allowed to introduce contraceptives into drinking water when they have in the past found it exceedingly difficult to distribute fluoride, recognized prophylactic against tooth decay, to their own people? Is it realistic, let alone consistent with good government, to think of programs of compulsory contraception—"involuntary contraception" as it is called? The most charitable view of these suggestions is that the people who make them have been panicked. No excuses can, however, remove the unfortunate impression which these statements make outside the comfortable communities in which they originate. Is it any wonder that the cry for population restraint seems like neocolonialism in many developing countries?

Extreme statements of the case for controlling the growth of poor populations may yet undermine a good deal of what has been done in recent decades to improve relations between developed and developing nations.

There is no doubt that the human population is now growing more rapidly than ever before, but this unprecedented growth is just as explicable as are the times in the past two million years of human history in which the human population has grown quickly. What has happened is that the natural restraints that kept the population in check in the years before the Second World War have been removed. The chance that a newborn child in an underdeveloped country will grow to maturity is now much greater than in the 1930s; inevitably, the same surviving adults themselves produce more children. There is also no doubt that growth of the population cannot continue without check, so that the question is how and how soon the rate of growth will decelerate. Thanks to the steady and accelerating improvement of agriculture (see Chapter 3), starvation is not a serious worry. And even in the developing regions of the world, where the pace of growth is fastest, there is every reason to

The Numbers Game

expect that in the next thirty years the rate of growth will be contained by exactly the processes which have given advanced societies a large measure of demographic stability.

How will this come about? By what means have advanced societies, more able to put up with rapid population growth than less fortunate regions of the world, managed to exercise some measure of what Malthus would have called "moral restraint"? And how can advanced societies help others to learn the same tricks? These are questions which the prophets of demographic disaster should be asking.

Looking back is essential. Overpopulation is by no means a novelty. The million or so Indians in North America when the first European settlers arrived were seriously and chronically short of food. Three hundred years later, the same continent can support more than two hundred times as many people and yet manage to have a large surplus of grain. What has happened is that the farmers of the Middle West have an agricultural technology which is a vast improvement on that of the old Plains Indians. The lesson to be learned from this transformation is that there can be no absolute yardsticks for calculating how many people can be comfortably supported on the surface of the earth. The more skill, the greater the population may be. The steady increase of the human population in recent centuries is a measure of the steady improvement of the technology of survival—agriculture and health care in particular.

The first creatures with distinctively human characteristics probably appeared in East Africa nearly two million years ago. Most probably, they moved about in family groups, living off vegetation, small animals and such things as birds' eggs (in season). They themselves would have been attacked and killed by larger or stronger carnivores, lions or hyenas, for example. Even if, at the beginning of the Ice Ages, the high uplands of Africa were more lush than they are now, the ancestors of human beings would have been safely established only where conditions were especially suitable for the particular kinds of hunting and gathering on which they depended for food. Like

The Doomsday Syndrome

the communities of baboons which still survive in Africa, the ancestors of the most primitive human beings would have been prevented by their need for shelter (from predators as well as the climate) and by the long infancy of their young from roaming about in huge herds as if they were zebra or buffalo. For them, there would have been no safety in numbers. The largest of the primitive communities can hardly have numbered more than a hundred or so.

The survival of these pre-human communities must have been exceedingly chancy. Entire communities would have been carried off by natural disasters of one kind or another—climate, disease or war. Even then, however, the safest communities would have been those with some method of restricting growth. After all, if the population grows without restraint, the amount of food available for each person is decreased, health is undermined and the chances of survival for all are diminished. Even now, one of the chief consequences of undernourishment in countries such as India is not starvation but a greater risk of death by cholera. Although fertility is evidently a prerequisite of survival, methods of regulating the sizes of communities must a. have been an advantage in the long history of the human race.

The same harsh conditions must have imposed themselves on the communities of recognizably modern man which first emerged half a million years ago. The aboriginal communities that still survive in New Guinea or the South African bush are frequently dominated by devices such as taboos on sexual intercourse or marriage ceremonies, which help to ensure that the population does not grow to the point at which food shortage would undermine communal health. In other words, the social function of much of the primitive ritual in which anthropologists now delight may have been to ensure that communities live well within the resources available to them. Moral restraint is much older than Malthus thought.

Until 10,000 years ago, the surface of the earth was only sparsely populated by human beings. Paleolithic France is

The Numbers Game

thought to have been so thinly occupied that there was only one person for each twenty square miles, which implies that the population of what is now France cannot have been more than 10,000. In Britain, at the same time, the population may have been only a tenth as much. The first population explosions, as the Ehrlichs of the time would no doubt have called them, were made possible by the first developments of primitive agriculture—the domestication of animals, and techniques for clearing land by setting fire to the bush. The domestication of animals brought with it two important changes—greater productivity for the land and a measure of mobility—sometimes enforced mobility occasioned by the need to find fresh grazing. It seems that hunting and food gathering required four square miles for every person. With grazing animals in good natural grassland, on the other hand, a whole family might be able to support itself from less than a square mile. Primitive cultivation of the land made possible still more densely packed communities, and these are the technological reasons why the population of Britain increased from 1,000 or so in paleolithic times to 20,000 in the neolithic period and to 400,000 by the Iron Age.

Although the population of the world has grown with the passage of time, growth has been however, neither uniform nor assured. In primitive communities such as those of the Australian aborigines or the South African bushmen, the chances that an individual will reach the age of twenty are one in three or less. Survival of the community requires that the few women who survive to childbearing age should begin to produce children at an early age and that they should aim at large families. Even so, natural calamities of various kinds may easily put the community as a whole in jeopardy, and it is not surprising that many populations have been seen to shrink as well as grow. England was depopulated by the Black Death in the fifteenth century. The population of Russia seems to have been declining in the eighteenth century. That of Ireland declined sharply a century later and continued to do so until 1961.

The coming of the technology of primitive agriculture had

The Doomsday Syndrome

a profound effect on the population of the world as a whole. By 7000 B.C., when a good many steps forward had been taken, the population of the world was between 5 million and 10 million. By the beginning of the modern era, the population had multiplied fifty times, so that it may have been just greater than 250 million by A.D. 1. This increase is as dramatic as any more recent cause of discontent. Compared with the pace of growth in recent decades, however, the population growth following the development of neolithic agriculture was leisurely—the world's population doubled every 1500 years or so. This no doubt is why the early populations were able comfortably to develop the social institutions necessary to regulate this growing population—cities, mercantile systems and the law. The complaint about the growth of the world's population stems not from its sheer size, but from the pace of growth.

For the world as a whole, the rate of growth is 1.9 percent a year. In countries such as India, the pace of growth has been even faster—2.5 percent a year in the 1960s, for example. Even in the heyday of the growth of Victorian England, where the population multiplied four times in a century, the average rate of growth did not exceed 1.3 percent a year. And for Europe as a whole, in the nineteenth century, the onset of growth occurred at different times in different countries, with the result that the average pace of growth was much less than that of the fastest growing country at any time. What is happening now in the developing world is that rapid growth has begun at more or less the same time everywhere, and that the pace of growth is more rapid than in the advanced nations in the nineteenth century, chiefly because the impact of modern medicine on mortality has been more dramatic than it could have been a century ago. All this is common ground between the Ehrlichs and the moderates.

Where will it all lead? The best keeper of statistics is the United Nations, but the hazards of forecasting are immense. If the population of the United Kingdom has been discovered (in the 1971 census) to be as much as 1 percent in error, who will believe that the United Nations estimate of 3,552 million

The Numbers Game

for the world's population in 1969 is accurate to within 100 million? And there are certain to be immense uncertainties about the compositions of the population of the world. How many women of childbearing age are still alive? How many are too old to contribute further to the population? How many children are there clamoring for schools? It is a great surprise that the prophets of demographic disaster, for all their professions of humility, appear frequently to overlook the warnings of error with which the official presentations of the statistics are laden. The most serious uncertainty in forecasting bears on precisely the point with which Dr. Ehrlich and his followers are concerned—what will be the childbearing habits of women in the decades ahead? It is always possible to predict disaster by supposing there will be no change; serious forecasters are much more inclined to ask how great the change will be.

This is part of the reason why the estimates of the United Nations for the population of the world by the end of the century consist not so much of a prediction as a range of predictions. The best guess (in 1971) is that the population of the world as a whole will increase from 3,630 million in 1970 to 6,490 million in A.D. 2000, but there are also higher and lower estimates based on different assumptions about the extent to which the child-bearing habits of people will change. The higher and lower figures are 7,000 million and 5,790 million respectively (see Table 1), which is another way of saying that the

Table 1—United Nations estimates of world population in A.D. 2000 with different assumptions about fertility (millions).

	Present	Low Estimate	Medium Estimate	High Estimate
Developed countries	1,090	1,450	1,450	1,450
Developing countries	2,540	4,520	5,040	5,650
Total	3,630	5,970	6,490	7,100

The Doomsday Syndrome

best estimates of the world's population ten years from now may easily be ten percent in error. Professional demographers will not be a bit surprised at this spread of uncertainty. And there is a good chance that even the lowest estimate will not be realized.

Whatever happens, there is certain to be rapid growth between now and the end of the century. Most probably, the population will have increased between A.D. 1970 and A.D. 2000 by at least two-thirds. This, as it happens, is a little faster than the pace of growth in Western Europe in the last thirty years of the nineteenth century. To be sure, the numbers are larger, for they apply to the whole world, but only determined pessimists will believe that they necessarily spell disaster.

Why has the pace of growth been so rapid? In what ways do modern populations differ from the aboriginal communities? The simple and appalling truth is that for most of human history, and until quite recently, the most powerful regulator of population growth has been death in childhood.

Burials in Stone Age graves are eloquent proof of the hazards of childhood in primitive communities—well over half of all children born would be dead by the age of fourteen. More recently, it seems, more than half of all children of nineteenth-century slaves in the West Indies died before puberty, and the same was true of the population of China in 1930 and certain African tribes even in the past few years. In the Philippines as recently as 1967, deaths of children younger than fifteen were 48 percent of the number of registered births. If such communities are to survive, each woman must on the average produce more than four children—two for the grave and two for adult life. Given the relative infertility of women in primitive populations (often the consequence of venereal disease but sometimes of practices such as polygamy) and the high rate of death among young adults (especially women at childbirth), the women capable of childbirth might have to produce an average of six or more children simply to keep their communities alive. It says a great deal for the malleability of human traditions

The Numbers Game

that such a primitive instinct as high fecundity has already been abandoned in most advanced societies.

Primitive communities have high proportions of childhood deaths and high birth rates in compensation so that improvements of living conditions are bound to have important consequences. The demographic history of the past two centuries is largely the tale of how the decrease of mortality among children and young adults has provided the driving force for a rapid increase of population, first in the advanced communities of Europe and now in the developing countries of the world.

Statistics show quite clearly what is happening. In Sweden in the 1760s, only six out of every ten children survived to the age of fifteen—a small improvement since the Stone Age but a risk that would now be quite intolerable. By the 1830s in Sweden, seven out of ten children survived to the age of fifteen, and the proportion had increased to more than eight out of ten by the end of the nineteenth century. By 1968, the risk of death in childhood had decreased to such an extent that only about two children in a hundred failed to reach childbearing age. Given that the compulsory sterilization of unwanted young is unlikely ever to be acceptable, reductions of mortality in childhood are bound to be followed by population growth. There can be stability again only if fertility settles at a lower level— if there are fewer children for every woman of childbearing age. Most of the countries of Western Europe have gone through a period of rapid growth in the past century or so. In all of them, this has been followed by a compensating decrease of fertility.

Historical evidence of fertility restraint is commonplace. The population of the United States grew much less quickly than it might have done in the nineteenth century, and bourgeois conventions of late marriage seem to have been as much responsible as the exertions of the Civil War and the expeditions to the West. In Catholic Ireland, rules for the inheritance of land have been restraining influences much as if they were rituals in a primitive society. What this implies is that even without the apparatus of modern birth control, it is not beyond the wit of

The Doomsday Syndrome

societies to devise methods of regulating the birth rate, usually for the sake of stability. Sometimes a community will go the other way and lift self-imposed restraints, as seems to have happened in Britain in the early nineteenth century.

The population of England and Wales was ten million in 1800 and had grown to just over twenty million by 1850 in spite of vigorous emigration. Growth was in its way as rapid as any that is happening now in developing countries. Throughout this period, however, the death rate for the country as a whole appears to have remained substantially unchanged. The most conspicuous change was the growth of the large industrial cities, and a comparison of birth and death rates in town and country shows that the beginning of industrialization made it possible for the rural population to relax its previous restrictions on population and to export large numbers of young people to the cities. People seemed glad of a chance to breed so long as there were places in which their children might find jobs.

A sharp reduction of death rate is a much more common spur to demographic change. This is what happened in Britain and the rest of Western Europe in the second half of the nineteenth century. This is what is happening now in the developing world. In the space of a few decades, the death rate can easily be reduced from between 3 and 4 percent a year to about 1 percent a year or even less. In the Netherlands, for example, the death rate fell from 3 percent a year in the 1870s to less than 1 percent a year in the 1920s. In many developing countries, the pace of change has been faster—the death rate in Ceylon fell from 2.2 percent a year in 1945 to 0.8 percent a year in 1969. Such dramatic changes are bound to cause upheaval. The experience of the advanced countries of Western Europe in the past century has been that there is first of all a period during which the new low death rate and the old high birth rate coexist, which means that the population grows rapidly in numbers. But then comes a time when the birth rate also decreases, so that a fresh demographic balance is struck on

The Numbers Game

the basis of a low birth rate and a low death rate. This phenomenon, by now as familiar a part of social history as the disappearance of feudalism, is called the demographic transition.

One of the strangest features of the present excitement about the population explosion is that those who prophesy demographic disaster appear to assume that the social forces which have given the developed world stability are inapplicable elsewhere. Is it any wonder that they give offense to the people they set out to help?

The decline of the birth rate necessary to stabilize a population can set in quite early. Thus the birth rate declined steadily in Western Europe and North America between about 1875 and 1960, from just over 3.5 percent a year to between 1.1 percent and 1.7 percent a year. Even so it is clear that, even in some parts of Western Europe, the demographic transition is not yet complete—in the Netherlands, for example, it began late and is not yet fully worked out. Is it in the circumstances sensible to complain that the developing countries have not yet come to terms with a problem that is more recent and more dramatic?

Just what is meant by demographic stability? The slogan "Zero Population Growth" is not much help, as can be told from what is now happening in Western Europe. The number of births each year is for practical purposes the same, but the population continues to grow. In Europe as a whole, East and West combined, there were 8.85 million births in 1950 and 8.95 million in 1968—the number of births each year is essentially unchanged. During the same period, the population had grown from 380 million to 455 million. In other words, more than 70 million people have failed to die in childhood or early adulthood, but instead have survived to contribute to the economy of Europe. Does such an increase, for such a benign reason, justify the name population explosion?

The transition from primitive to sophisticated demographic stability can also be measured by counting the average number of girl children born to each woman during a reproductive

The Doomsday Syndrome

lifetime. Stability is a condition in which each fertile woman produces enough girl children to carry on the work of procreation, to compensate for the childlessness of others and to make good losses due to the death of women before the childbearing years are over. Whether or not the actual number of people in a community is growing, if the gross reproduction rate is just a little more than 1.0, the population is stable. The history of the past half century shows what can happen. In Sweden, for example, the reproduction rate was just under 1.9 girl children for every woman in 1900, but had decreased to less than 1.0 in the thirties and has fluctuated in the 1960s between 1.1 and 1.2. Older people are living longer, so that the population of Sweden is still increasing, yet for practical purposes the country is demographically stable. In exactly the same way, the gross reproduction rates in Bulgaria, Hungary and Japan decreased from well over 2.0 at the beginning of the century to 1.0 or thereabouts by the 1950s. Rapid growth had given way to demographic stability within roughly half a century.

The demographic transition which has already happened in advanced countries has several important lessons for those who fear demographic disaster. First, the simple birth and death rates are only crude indications of underlying changes. Those who complain of population growth on the scale now found in Britain are really complaining that fewer people are now dying in early adulthood or middle age than used to be the case, for example. What this shows is that a population can continue to grow long after stability has been attained as people in middle life reap the benefits of medical techniques not available when their grandparents died. Finally, it is clear that the demographic transition can be a rapid process. In countries as different as Sweden, Bulgaria and Japan, the demographic transition has been completed in just about half a century.

What is happening in the developing countries, where the population is still growing rapidly? The decrease of mortality has been much more rapid than it was a century ago in the more advanced communities, but there are unmistakable signs

The Numbers Game

of the deceleration of growth that will eventually bring demo-graphic stability. Indeed, the rapid decrease of mortality is being followed in some communities by a more rapid decline of fertility than ever took place in Europe and North America. If these trends are confirmed by the experience of the next few years, it could easily be that forecasts of future population will turn out to be much too high.

There is no mystery about the reasons why the developing countries are growing more quickly than Europe and North America half a century ago. Mortality has declined more quickly. Changes which used to take a century or more have been accomplished in a few decades. In the Netherlands, for example, it took the best part of a century—between the 1850s and the 1940s—for the annual death rate to decline from 2.5 percent a year to 0.8 percent a year, but in eleven countries in Latin America, by contrast, the death rate had declined from 3.3 percent in the early 1930s to 1.4 percent in 1960s. Yet there is still some way to go. Infant mortality in particular leaves much to be desired—in Chile in the 1960s more than 9 percent of all children died in their first year—roughly four times the rate of infantile death in the United States and eight times that in some of the countries of Western Europe.

Is medical research to be blamed for the pace of growth of developing countries? Medicine as such has been less important than deliberate care for public health and the improvement of diet. The use of DDT and similar insecticides against mos-quitoes made possible dramatic reductions of death rates from malaria in Asia and Latin America. In British Guiana in the early 1940s, for example, three out of a thousand people died each year from malaria, but this rate had been reduced to one in a thousand by 1947 and 1948 and has since been entirely insignificant. At the same time, diet and hygiene have between them brought similar if slower decreases of the death rate from tuberculosis and kidney infection. The death rate from cholera has declined because better-nourished people are more resistant to the disease. And there are many circumstances in which mere

The Doomsday Syndrome

understanding is almost as powerful as medical treatment in fending off disease. Who knows what the knowledge that typhoid is a water-borne disease has done to keep that disease in check? To describe the decline of mortality in developing countries as "exported death control," as Dr. Ehrlich does, is in the circumstances not merely inaccurate but offensively paternalistic. The developing nations are merely following half a century or so behind the now advanced societies, in public health and public nutrition.

What of the future? In many developing communities, the decline of fertility needed to complete the demographic transition is already clearly apparent. There is always a time-lag between the decline of mortality and fertility, but it seems that the later the process begins, the more rapidly it gets under way. One of the most decisive decreases of fertility has taken place in the Soviet Union, where the annual birth rate has in the past seventy years decreased each decade by about 4.7 births per thousand. In many developing countries, the birth rate appears to be falling even more quickly. Since the mid-1950s, there have been dramatic decreases in Taiwan (Formosa), Hong Kong, Singapore, many of the islands of the Caribbean and also in Albania. In Singapore, for example, the annual birth rate has decreased from 4.7 percent per year in the late 1940s to 2.2 percent in 1969. In Puerto Rico, the annual birth rate has decreased from more than 40 percent in the early 1930s to 2.4 percent in 1969, and the decrease has been especially rapid in the late 1960s. To be sure, there is still some way to go, but the statistics are moving rapidly in the right direction.

In many countries, the actual number of births each year has been decreasing steadily for some time. What this means is that stability of a kind has already been reached even though the population may grow because youths and adults are now better equipped to cheat death. Table 2, based on United Nations statistics, shows for a selection of countries in which fertility is decreasing the year in which the number of births appeared to have reached its peak and the number then and

The Numbers Game

TABLE 2: Decreasing numbers of births in selected countries.

Country	Peak year	Births then	Births 1969 (or latest available figure)
ASIA			
Ceylon	1962	370,762	269,531 (1968)
Hong Kong	1962	119,166	82,666
Jordan	1966	94,299	69,423 (1968)
Korea	1966	896,721	498,236 (1966)
Pakistan	1963	5,103,000	4,950,000 (1965)
Singapore	1959	63,720	44,738
Taiwan	1963	424,250	352,762
Thailand	1964	1,119,715	1,116,427 (1967)
AFRICA			
Algeria	1966	561,528	529,806 (1968)
Equatorial Guinea	1962	7,366	4,966 (1966)
Mauritius	1963	28,156	21,718
UAR	1966	1,234,976	1,194,585
AMERICA			
Barbados	1960	7,833	5,474 (1968)
Canada	1959	479,275	371,365
Cuba	1964	264,300	232,027 (1967)
Jamaica	1966	71,364	65,400 (1968)
Puerto Rico	1965	79,608	67,903
Trinidad & Tobago	1962	34,107	28,107
USA	1961	4,268,326	3,571,000
Chile	1963	291,731	282,743 (1967)

more recently. The table omits all the communities of Western Europe, where the population has been stable for decades. And although these hopeful tendencies may occasionally be reversed when girl children born in the 1950s and early 1960s reach childbearing age, there is no shortage of hopeful pointers in the right direction.

Even when the birth rate remains high and the number of

The Doomsday Syndrome

births is still increasing from year to year, there may be signs of incipient demographic change. In Colombia, for example, where the number of births each year appears to have been roughly 670,000 between 1963 and 1967, the number of births to women in their early thirties decreased from 107,000 to 101,000 at a time when the number of potential mothers increased substantially. In Guatemala, where the number of births each year is still increasing, the statistics show a tendency towards later marriage and towards smaller families in the middle years. In due course, these changes will contribute to demographic stability as they have done in Western Europe. The question to be asked is not whether they will come about or even when, but how best to encourage movement in the right direction.

What is to be done? Instead of pleading for variations on the old-fashioned Malthusian remedy of moral restraint, the prophets of disaster would be well advised to look for an understanding of the reasons why fertility seems inevitably to decline in the course of demographic change. The technology of contraception is essential but certainly not sufficient. The past two centuries show clearly that social behavior plays an overwhelming part in helping to bring births and deaths into some kind of balance. The social conventions in primitive communities that kept young women chaste unnaturally long had parallels, after all, in the devices that made the fertility of settlers in North America less than it might have been—celibacy and late marriage. The tendency towards later marriage which helped to reduce the birth rate in Britain in the nineteenth century is now also an important influence in Ceylon. Even in countries where the influence of the Catholic Church has been opposed to the technology of birth control, populations such as that of France have been remarkably ingenious at the invention of social conventions which keep fertility within bounds. The fertility of French families seems at present independent of their religion, although Catholic families were producing 20 percent more children than Protestants half a century ago.

The Numbers Game

Even before the Pill, as it is called, it was plainly possible for communities to regulate their numbers.

Population restraint depends on the private decisions of individuals or couples. What are the influences which bear on these decisions? Plainly there must be great differences between countries such as India and countries such as those of Western Europe. Where the risk of infant mortality is high, as in the developing countries, individual couples will usually set out to produce enough children to ensure that some of them at least will survive to adult life. In advanced societies, the instinctive drive to produce living descendants is tempered by an awareness that most children will survive and that large families are harder to care for. This is the mainspring of the demographic transition, conveniently overlooked by the prophets of disaster.

In the past few years, social surveys in Western Europe have shown that on the average, women want families that range from 2.0 to 2.8 children, but women in India say that they will aim for roughly four children on the average, and the desired family size appears to be even greater in Ghana and the Philippines. The simple truth is that when childhood mortality is high, the average woman's ideal family is a large one. Who will be surprised at that? But the consequence, paradoxical though it may seem, is that one of the most powerful ways of keeping the birth rate low may be a vigorous attempt to keep children alive.

Education also plays an important part in helping restraint. In Latin America and in Taiwan, as throughout the developing world, people with several years experience at school or university tend to produce smaller families. At the very least, education postpones the onset of childbearing and makes family planning advice more accessible. Its more positive tendency is to demonstrate the social advantages of smaller families. For better or worse, social advancement and educational ambition have been powerful influences in stabilizing the population of advanced societies. Why should the developing countries not be similarly sensitive?

The Doomsday Syndrome

Prosperity, now much maligned, is another restraining influence. There is now a wealth of evidence that in developing nations, richer families tend to be smaller families. Among developing nations, fast growth of gross national product goes with slow growth of population. One of the contradictions in the doomsday literature is that it deplores many of the appurtenances of civilization with which declining fertility is plainly linked. Whichever comes first, it is hard to think that populations of developing nations will find stability without adopting, sometimes with great speed, some of the industrial and commercial institutions that have made advanced societies prosperous and which now assure their stability.

What will the outcome be? Although the demographic transition has only just begun in large parts of the developing world, there is every reason to expect that it will produce demographic stability entirely comparable with that which now exists in Western Europe and elsewhere in the industrialized world. To pretend otherwise is to ignore a great deal of the evidence to the contrary which has become available in the past decade, to neglect instruments such as medical care and education which can help to induce stability and, at the same time, to imply that the communities in developing countries are somehow immune from the influences which have helped to stabilize the population in advanced societies within the past century. Is it any wonder that hand wringing about the population explosion, however well-intentioned, seems to the people on whom restraint is urged to be a patronizing plot? Certainly it is wrong to claim, as Dr. Ehrlich does, that no harm will have been done if his gloomy predictions turn out to be exaggerated. The population explosion has all the signs of being a damp squib, but it will be harmful if it distracts attention—as it might —from problems that really matter.

Although population stability is the most likely outcome of the present rapid growth, it does not follow that there are no demographic problems to be tackled. To be sure, if the population

The Numbers Game

of the world does grow to 7,000 million by the end of the century, the high estimate of the United Nations, that will not imply disaster. There will be enough food and other natural resources (see Chapter 3). Side effects such as pollution are not so much consequences of the size of the population of the world as of the nature of industrial activity in advanced societies. But with these reservations there is work to be done.

One important need is that communities should somehow recognize how volatile can be the rate of growth of a population, and how uncertain may be estimates of its future. There is no scandal in this, but the government of Britain and the United States have been awkwardly caught out in the past few years, even though their statistics are as good as anybody could ask. In the United States, for example, the Bureau of the Census published in 1967 a forward projection of the population of the United States in which four sets of assumptions about the fertility of women of different ages were used to form different estimates of the population in the remainder of the century. Three years later, in 1970, the bureau found it necessary to issue a second report which omitted the highest of the four earlier estimates and substituted a fifth based on even more conservative assumptions about the childbearing proclivities of American women. By 1971, the estimated rate of growth was still further reduced, although it turned out that earlier predictions had underestimated a recent tendency towards earlier childbirth among married women.

The moral is not that demography should be lumped with astrology but that the prediction of human fertility has become exceedingly difficult, at least in advanced societies. This is why it would be a public service if governments, their servants and their critics were to direct attention from the thankless task of predicting the size of a whole population to the more certain task of estimating those features which can be determined accurately—numbers of old people, for example.

Whatever the amateur demographers may say, the growth of the population in many advanced societies does not merit the

The Doomsday Syndrome

status of a social problem. Where a low death rate is more or less balanced by a low birth rate, there is plenty of scope for rapid fluctuation of the number of births from one year to another. In the United States, the birth rate has fluctuated in the decades since the Second World War between 2.7 percent and 1.7 percent, and there is continuing dispute about the reasons. Did the Korean War and then the Cold War sustain the American birth rate in the 1950s? Was the sharp decline in the 1960s a prelude to the movement for Zero Population Growth or were they both products of the same cause? Whatever the reasons, these changes from year to year are great sources of inconvenience to public authorities who must plan accommodation for children in schools and recruit teachers as well, but there is nothing in the recent demographic history of countries such as the United States and Britain to suggest that population growth threatens survival or even comfort. Moreover, there is nothing in the forward estimates of growth to suggest that the sheer size of the population or the numbers of particular age groups will be more than an embarrassment to those in charge.

The demographic problems which need to be taken seriously are all to be found in the developing countries of the world, and this is no accident. One obvious penalty of rapid growth is that it brings large numbers of economically unproductive dependents, mostly children. In Zambia in 1969, 51 percent of the population was under twenty but in France in the same year, only 33.6 percent of the population was in the same age group. Although in primitive communities children may cost comparatively little to rear, and may even be a help around the farm, in societies with ambitions for economic and social advancement, children are an economic burden to the extent that they must be provided with education and health care. What this implies is that the burden of dependency is more keenly felt once subsistence agriculture has been left behind.

The scale of these burdens is obvious. In 1960, children between five and fourteen inclusive accounted for 16 percent of

The Numbers Game

the population of Europe but 26 percent of that of Africa. The communities in developing countries know that education is one of the most fruitful avenues for escape from poverty, but when the childhood population is growing quickly, large capital investments are necessary and large proportions of the educated labor force must be induced to work as teachers. Is it any wonder that in Ghana, teachers' salaries are on the average five times the national average, while the corresponding ratio is less than 1.5 in the United States? Some of the poorest communities in the world are forced to spend more than 8 percent of their national income on education, more than the nations of Western Europe and North America spend on military defense. Zambia, with a gross national product of $200 per head, spent 6.2 percent of that on education in 1969. In the same year, the much more elaborate educational system of the United States consumed only 5.8 percent of the gross national product.

In the face of such obstacles, the progress that has been made in education in developing countries is a great triumph. Between 1965 and 1970, the rate of primary school enrollments increased by 4.6 percent a year in Latin America, 5.9 percent a year in Africa and 6.2 percent in the developing nations of Asia. Yet there is a long way to go before the pace of growth of the population will allow each child to be given a full primary education, while secondary education is still some seventy years behind that of Western Europe and North America. The irony, in education as with many other forms of social service, is that the development of education services is hampered by the pace of population growth, and that the restraint of population growth is hampered by the inadequate education.

What applies to education also applies to economic development and to welfare. The commitment of resources to the needs of the rapidly growing younger section of the population limits the extent to which developing nations can invest in other social services or industrial development. Yet in the past two decades, the pace of economic growth in the developing world has

The Doomsday Syndrome

been more rapid than that of the population, so that for the developing world as a whole, there is a prospect that individual prosperity (measured as gross national product per head of population) will double in twenty-five years. The complaint is not that economic development is being prevented by a flood of children, but that the developing countries could improve their lot even more quickly if only fertility could be reduced. It may be important that when fertility is eventually reduced significantly, in the 1980s and thereafter, the now developing countries will enjoy a rapid improvement of living conditions even more remarkable than the sudden prosperity that has made Victorian England a century ago seem something of a legend. It follows that the incentive for population restraint is not so much that it is necessary to fend off imminent disaster as that the sooner the growth of population can be contained, the sooner these benefits will be enjoyed.

Among the dire warnings that have been uttered about the dangers of rapid population growth, the most nebulous is that simple crowding may by itself have serious and undesirable effects. Somber speculations on this theme have been inspired by laboratory experiments carried out to test the behavior of animals, usually rats, kept in crowded conditions as well as by attempts to account for some of the problems that have arisen in large cities. And there is no doubt that overcrowding will induce pathological behavior as well as high infant mortality (aided by infanticide) in crowded rat cages. The trouble is that much depends on what the animals have been used to. This is why the social problems of rats and mice in cages are poor analogies for knowing how cities function. The problems of modern cities are problems in their own right.

Unfortunately, however, this has not prevented the prophets from following the analogy. Dr. Rene Dubos considers that crowding itself may undermine the character of civilized life.

> *Complete surrender to overcrowding in a highly technicized society is not likely to destroy mankind, but it will mean an increasingly organ-*

The Numbers Game

ized world. The environment will favor the selective reproduction of people best suited to a regimented life. Many people today are maladjusted to crowded life, but as long as there are uncrowded places and social control remains ineffective those who really want to enjoy a free life can still find a world of their own choosing. If crowding and regimentation continue to increase, however, the descendants of such maladjusted people will be progressively eliminated. When they disappear, many of our present human values will become meaningless and will eventually be forgotten. There will be no place for sensitive literature, intensely personal art, or unorthodox science in the human ant hill of the future; not even room for primitive Christianity. What meaning can the parables and poetry of the past retain if there are no lilies in the field? We must hope that there will still be rebels to champion freedom.

Dr. Ehrlich takes the view that increasing population and population density will increase the risk of war—"population-related problems seem to be increasing the probability of triggering a thermonuclear Armageddon."

Luckily, the evidence for this view is at best confusing and contradictory. Some, like Dr. Robert C. North, argue that "pilot statistical studies of war involvement of major European powers in modern times have revealed very high correlations among rates of population growth, rising GNP, expanding military budgets and involvement in wars." The trouble, of course, is to know what may be the cause of the trouble. The most crowded country in Europe, the Netherlands, is neither the most aggressive nor the most disturbed. In Africa, Tunisia is comparatively stable with thirty-three people to the square kilometer—more so than Syria, with twenty-six to the square kilometer. In short, in the search for demographic correlates in international relations, such evidence as exists can be used in both directions.

Within countries, to be sure, demography may be more

The Doomsday Syndrome

disturbing. In the United States, the fact that the Negro population is growing more quickly than the white has been widely resented, while the comparatively rapid growth of the Catholic population of Ulster has offended many Protestants. In both sets of circumstances, as it happens, the aggrieved majority has been slow to bring the rates of population growth into correspondence by improving the economic lot of the poorer community. In the United States, blacks are by no means conspicuous among those who advocate rigid control of population growth. Is it possible that the benefits of Zero Population Growth would be more apparent if there were more obvious opportunities for economic advancement?

Even if the present pace of population growth cannot remotely spell disaster, may it not be sensible to define the ideal population for the earth—the optimum population? This concept is frequently advanced, but the issue is unsettled. If most of the consequences of a large or growing population are inconveniences, there are also arguments that work the other way. The way in which Britain in the nineteenth century was able rapidly to populate several rapidly growing cities and thus to provide the basis for the Industrial Revolution is one benefit of rapid growth. A rapid increase in the proportion of young people may also help to break down conventional social structures which are in themselves impediments to economic development, particularly if for some reason educational services can be provided without too much difficulty. Especially in developing countries, which cry out for social and technical innovation, there may be some temporary benefits of rapid growth to offset, in part at least, the economic penalties of growth.

In the long run, the exact size of the world's population is probably unimportant. Obviously it would be a great cultural deprivation for the world as a whole if the population were not great enough to support a variety of nation states with a variety of metropolitan cities, but there is no danger of such a plight. By the same test, it would be a great misfortune if the population grew to such a point that the pressure on resources

The Numbers Game

such as land became intolerable but that is also almost equally improbable. What matters, therefore, is how a community decides to apportion resources between population growth and the other benefits which it might enjoy. Since there is no virtue in numbers as such, obviously it is prudent to grow as little as may be necessary. But there is nothing in demography nor in the record of the past few years to suggest that temporary lapses will bring catastrophe.

The End of
the Lode

□

In the proclamation of doomsday, one of the most common components is the assertion that the resources of the earth will prove to be inadequate in some sense or another. The threat of famine is continually pronounced, paradoxically when many of the hungry nations of the world are on the threshold of unaccustomed plenty. The prospect of exhaustion of energy supplies is repeatedly held to be a simple consequence of the growth of the world's population and the spread of industrialization, yet the outlook is now much brighter than it has been since the Industrial Revolution began. The limited stock of minerals on the surface of the earth is offered as yet another serious limitation of the freedom to grow, yet the prices of the raw materials which are supposed to be at risk do not increase as would be expected if the threat of scarcity were as immediate as it is said to be. Are the environmentalists just bad at arithmetic, or are there other issues to be decided?

Nobody will pretend that there are no problems to be solved, yet the threat of scarcity has been a part of the human condition since the beginning of the human race. The aboriginal populations of North America and Australia were, after all, compelled to live near the limits of the food available. The Industrial Revolution of the nineteenth century was founded on the discovery that the productivity of labor can be enormously increased by the use of fuels more efficient than wood and charcoal and by the use of metals more versatile and more efficient than wrought iron, the workhorse of medieval metallurgy. From this point of view, the question to be decided is not whether the threat of scarcity is real but what steps need to be taken, in the decades ahead, to ensure that life goes on.

The fear that natural resources would be exhausted has in the past few years been inflamed by speculations about the

The Doomsday Syndrome

future population of the earth. For if the population doubles, between now and the end of the century, does it not follow that food production must also be doubled? And if in recent decades the threat of famine has come too close for comfort, how can it be that an essentially fixed amount of agricultural land can yield twice as much food? The flaw in this simple argument is the neglect of the way in which agricultural productivity, acre for acre, can be enormously increased by modern methods. Since the agricultural revolution of neolithic times, the amount of land needed to support a single person has decreased from some tens of square miles to roughly an acre, a ten-thousand-fold improvement, but there is still a long way to go before the productivity of agriculture bumps up against the theoretical limit, food enough for one person from each five square yards or so of the surface of the earth.

In making catalogues of scarcity, it is conventional to distinguish between resources which are renewable and resources which are nonrenewable, but this distinction is often sharper than it needs to be. To be sure, all kinds of food ultimately depend on sunlight for their energy. Without light energy, plants will not grow. Without plants to eat, herbivorous animals cannot survive. And without herbivorous animals, carnivores cannot live. In short, the complicated food chain on which the survival of the human race depends is ultimately dependent on the energy from the sun. Each year, there is a new cycle of plant growth and a fresh food supply for the human race or for the domesticated animals on which it depends for protein, so that the supply of food is a renewable resource—each year brings its own new harvest. The complaint of those who fear famine is that the amount of this renewable resource will eventually be insufficient to keep a growing population fed. If the population were to grow indefinitely, there would certainly come a time when the apparently vast supply of solar energy would be insufficient to keep everybody alive. Luckily, this point is much further off than the catastrophists declare. In any case, there is no reason to suppose that the recent growth of population will persist indefinitely.

The End of the Lode

The nonrenewable resources are the minerals of the earth's crust. Dr. Barry Commoner says, in his *The Closing Circle* (1971), that:

> *mineral resources, if used, can only move in one direction—downward in amount . . . Fossil fuels such as coal, oil, and natural gas were deposited in the earth during a period of its evolution that has not since been repeated . . . Once fossil fuels are used, solar energy trapped within them millions of years ago is dissipated irrevocably.*

On the face of things, the argument is convincing enough. As every puritan will acknowledge, you cannot have your cake and eat it. The fallacy is that the human race is so ingenious that it is not compelled to depend for its survival on one kind of cake. The past few centuries have seen an enormous change in the pattern in which natural resources are used. As recently as half a century ago, neither synthetic polymers nor even aluminum were commercially available. Few at this stage would venture to predict what innovations there may be in the decades ahead. The minerals with which the surface of the earth is endowed may be fixed for all time, but there seems to be no easily foreseeable limit to the ways in which even the most unlikely substance may be put to useful ends.

Anxiety about mineral resources is reinforced by fears of what might happen if the affluence of the industrialized world were to spread to developing countries. Vance Packard begins a chapter called "The Vanishing Resources" in his book *The Waste Makers* with the observation that "the average American family throws away about 750 metal cans each year—in the Orient, a family lucky enough to gain possession of a metal can treasures it and puts it to work in some way, if only as a flower pot."

Does not this imply that affluence for all will mean that an extra 750,000 million tin cans are discarded each year? That is how the gloomy arguments tend to go. Luckily, there is every reason to think that countries now developing will be able to

The Doomsday Syndrome

emulate the prosperity of affluent countries without repeating their mistakes.

In all these arguments, the distinction between renewable and nonrenewable resources should not be made too sharp. In modern agriculture, for example, sunlight is by no means sufficient. Artificial fertilizers are also necessary, and these require energy to manufacture. Irrigation water is also necessary in tropical agriculture, which implies that food production depends in part on investment in water-impounding dams, pipelines and other instruments of rural engineering. In the extraction of minerals, on the other hand, it is often more important to know what price it is worth paying to extract coal or iron ore from a mine than to decide precisely how much there may be in some deposit. Natural resources such as fisheries are different again. For many purposes, the stock of fish in the sea can be thought of as a natural resource which renews itself each year because of the solar energy trapped by the plant cells lying near the surface, but if hunting for fish of some particular kind is too vigorous, or too successful, the result may be that a whole stock of fish may disappear, so that the natural resources cannot be renewed.

The usual distinction between renewable and nonrenewable natural resources is unfortunate because it is clear by now that the proper exploitation of natural resources is governed much more by economics than by the simple arithmetic of how much food can be grown with how much sunlight, or how great (or how small) may be the amounts of particular minerals locked up in the earth's crust. This is yet another illustration of the oversimple way in which calculations of calamity are carried out.

The view that natural resources are in danger of exhaustion is now often dramatized with the help of the concept of spaceship earth. The idea is that the world is a self-contained living space, a closed place, provided since the beginning of time with a certain stock of supplies and able to gather a limited amount of energy from the sun. As in a real spaceship, it is implied,

The End of the Lode

once the available resources have been consumed, life will be at an end. Luckily, the analogy between the earth and a spaceship is misleading. However small the earth may seem from the moon, it is still vast compared with the scale on which human beings live.

The scale of the earth's oceans is a telling illustration of the durability of spaceship earth. With the present population of 3,500 million, there is the equivalent of one tenth of a cubic mile of sea water for every person. There are more than seven million tons of gold in the waters of which the oceans are made, 5 pounds or thereabouts for every person now alive. The amounts of other materials in the oceans are much larger still—there are, for example, about 50 tons of iron in the sea for every living person. To be sure, the cost of extracting minerals from the sea, and the difficulty of doing so, is enormous, so that the oceans cannot be thought of as more than a resource of last resort for materials other than magnesium, potassium, bromine, iodine and some of the other metals for which economical extraction processes have already been developed, but the minerals in the sea consist merely of those chemicals which have been extracted from surface rocks by erosion and other processes. The crust of the earth is much more lavishly supplied with minerals. Sheer physical exhaustion of the resources of spaceship earth is obviously an exceedingly remote possibility. So too is the more subtle danger that the integrity of spaceship earth might be upset by some accidental interference with a part of what is called the ecosphere (see Chapter 4).

Paradoxically, the United States, on the continent most lavishly provided with natural resources, has become the chief source of concern about scarcity. The conservation movement is almost as old as American industry itself and has been as much concerned with minerals as with the landscape. From the start, American preoccupations with natural resources have been part of the concern about the strategy of national survival as such. In 1908, a conference of state governors at the White House set in train an attempt to compile an inventory of the

The Doomsday Syndrome

natural resources available to the United States. There have since been several more up-to-date, but similar, compilations. In 1952, for example, the President's Materials Policy Commission, otherwise known as the Paley Commission, published under the title *Resources for Freedom* an assessment of, and a warning about, the speed with which nonrenewable natural resources were being consumed. In the early sixties, an independent organization, Resources for the Future, Inc., produced an account of the problem which was much more clearly informed by economic considerations.

More strident expressions of these views, now to be heard on every side, are an integral part of the doomsday syndrome. Dr. Ehrlich's views about the prospect of famine are familiar. Dr. Stephen Spurr, dean of graduate studies at the University of Michigan, has said at a conference on the management of natural resources that "the overwhelming impression . . . is that time is running out." Dirck Van Sickle in his book *The Ecological Citizen* says that:

> We must cut consumption because its future simply isn't there; if it were there, it would be an ecological disaster to consume it; and it would be immoral to gobble nonrenewable resources of hungry nations to satisfy our short-term dreams. Even if the vast majority of the human race avoids famine and dieback, it will never be able to develop if its mineral wealth has disappeared years before into American trash.

The same point is echoed by Dr. Barry Commoner, who says:

> our technological society has committed a blunder familiar to us from the nineteenth century, when the dominant industries of the day, especially lumbering and mining, were successfully developed—by plundering the earth's natural resources. These industries provided cheap materials for constructing a new industrial society, but they accumulated a huge debt in de-

The End of the Lode

*stroyed and depleted resources, which had to
be paid by later generations. The conservation
movement was created in the United States to
control these greedy assaults on our resources.
The same thing is happening today, but now
we are stealing from future generations not
just their lumber or their coal, but the basic
necessities of life: air, water, and soil. A new
conservation movement is needed to preserve
life itself.*

In these declarations, the new ambivalence of the United
States towards consumption as such is plain for all to see. The
old-fashioned waste-not–want-not virtues of the first European
settlers in North America were replaced in the twentieth century
by the view that consumption, even conspicuous consumption,
is an economic necessity. The ambivalence which led to the prohibition of alcohol in the 1920s may yet lead to the prohibition
of the disposable bottle in the 1970s. Unfortunately, the great
energy devoted to these causes has comparatively little bearing
on the management of the natural resources of the earth.

The threat of famine is unfortunately too easy to pronounce.
Dr. Paul Ehrlich is, for example, eloquent on the subject:

*There is not enough food today. How much
there will be tomorrow is open to debate. If the
optimists are correct, today's level of misery will
be perpetuated for perhaps two decades into
the future. If the pessimists are correct, massive famines will occur soon, possibly in the
early 1970s, certainly by the early 1980s.*

Elsewhere he says, "We have too many people and a ridiculously
high growth rate and we are running out of food." Ironically,
there has hardly ever been a time when this prediction has been
less apt.

The Food and Agriculture Organization of the United Nations, once described as "a permanent organization intended
to demonstrate that the world is short of food," has in its time
done as much as anybody to cast a baleful influence on public

The Doomsday Syndrome

discussion of food supply. Thus the then Director General of the FAO, Dr. B. R. Sen, in his introduction to the *Third World Food Survey,* said that in the less developed countries "at least twenty per cent of the population is undernourished and sixty per cent malnourished." In successive annual reports, the FAO has recorded steady improvements in the supply of food in the past few decades and yet has repeated its dire warnings that nutrition as such remains substantially unchanged. Throughout this time, the FAO has done very little to rebut the charge that the yardsticks which it uses to determine the food requirements of an individual are unrealistically high.

More recently, and with the benefit of new management, the FAO has fortunately been more willing to look its own facts (which are not disputed) in the face. Thus the annual report for 1970 is introduced by the Director General, Dr. A. H. Boerma, with the plain statement that "at long last something of a turning point may have been reached in the difficult struggle of the developing countries to achieve a sufficiently rapid increase of their food production." Would the FAO have been quicker to claim this success if it had appreciated more clearly that its own existence does not inextricably depend on the penetration of hunger?

The truth is that food production in the world is now increasing much faster than the population. For most of the sixties, for example, the population of the world has been growing at 2 percent a year, but total agricultural production in the same period has grown by 2.7 percent a year. Over the same period, according to FAO statistics, there has been a particularly rapid increase in the production of fish, which increased by 57 percent in the ten years to 1968. In the past few years, there has been especially encouraging progress in the countries where progress is most needed—Southeast Asia and India. In the sixties, food production in both regions increased by 4 percent a year, nearly twice as fast as the population, and further improvements are already in prospect. And although in the world as a whole the population grew more quickly in the sixties than

The End of the Lode

in any previous time in recorded history, the production of food increased still faster. Moreover, there is no reason why this increase should not continue for a long time to come.

There are several ways in which food production may continue to increase so as to better the pace of growth of population. Making fuller use of the land is an obvious place to start. In 1967, a committee of the President's Science Advisory Committee in the United States estimated that only something like 44 percent of potentially arable land is at present cultivated. In many parts of the world, but especially in the tropics, vast areas of land are given over to unproductive tropical forests. The Amazon and Congo rivers, for example, include enough land at present not used for agriculture to provide 1,000 million acres of cultivable land, enough to feed 1,000 million people or more (given that, with present techniques, one acre of cultivated land is needed to keep each person alive).

Bringing cultivable land under the plough should be enough to support 7,500 million people, but this is plainly an underestimate of what might be done. The past few years have shown how rapidly the yield of cultivated land can be increased by irrigation, fertilizers, and improved varieties of plants. For the immediate future, there is a more profitable line of attack.

In the United States, for example, the production of corn (maize) from an acre of cultivated land increased nearly threefold between the early thirties and the early sixties. Between 1950 and 1965, the average yield of rice per acre increased from just under 1 ton to 1.53 tons, an increase of more than 50 percent in fifteen years. During the same period, the yield of wheat increased by roughly the same proportion. In Japan, however, with more intensive methods of cultivation, the production of rice was close on 1.5 tons per acre in 1950 and, on the average, had increased by close on a quarter, to 1.75 tons per acre, by 1965.

During these same years, production elsewhere, especially in the developing countries, was substantially less than that in the United States and Japan. In 1965, for example, wheat produc-

The Doomsday Syndrome

tion per acre in India was less than a half of that in the United States and less than a third of that in Japan. But in more recent years, there has been a dramatic change. With the introduction of new strains of wheat and rice in the Philippines, India and Pakistan, the yield of the land has been increased enormously. And the green revolution, as it is called, is only just beginning. In due course, it is bound to have an even more profound effect on the developing world than the agricultural revolution in Europe at the end of the eighteenth century.

The process of change in the agricultural economy of Southeast Asia is apparent in the United Nations *Economic Survey of Asia and the Far East 1969*. The introduction of new, highly productive strains of rice, wheat and maize is only the most recent innovation in a long chain of improvements stretching back for fifteen years. Since the early fifties, the acreages given over to agriculture in Ceylon, India, Indonesia, Malaysia, Pakistan, the Philippines and Thailand have steadily increased. So too has the intensity with which the land is cultivated, either by the use of irrigation water to produce more than one crop a year from the same land or by the more intelligent choice of crops. The new high-yielding strains of wheat, rice and maize have begun to make felt their influence only since 1965, and will yield their full benefit only in the 1980s.

Thailand has been the most spectacular success in Southeast Asia. Since 1960, agricultural production has grown by 1.5 percent a year, so that the country is now an exporter of food. In Pakistan, agricultural production has increased by 4.5 percent a year and the rate of growth is still accelerating. Several different influences have contributed to these changes. In Ceylon, for example, the area of land given over to rice increased by a fifth between the mid-fifties and the mid-sixties, but in West Pakistan the use of irrigation water produced by tube wells has been more important. Throughout Southeast Asia, fertilizers have been used much more widely—in 1969, for example, Indian agriculture used more than four pounds of fertilizer for each acre of land under cultivation.

The End of the Lode

What is the outlook? Experience so far with the new varieties of cereals, combined with sufficient fertilizer and irrigation water, is exceedingly encouraging. In India, the new varieties of rice may yield anything between 46 percent and 75 percent more than the traditional varieties. Wheat production, measured in tons per acre, may be increased by anything between 60 percent and 400 percent. Similar successes can be expected in Pakistan, the Philippines and throughout Southeast Asia, although it is too soon to calculate what the results will be.

Much will depend on the skill with which farmers are helped to understand the difficulties of managing these new crops, with their need of extra fertilizer and with their more rapid growth cycle. In West Pakistan, for example, each acre of land under Mexi-Pak wheat, one of the new strains, was yielding one ton of grain in 1966 but only four-fifths of a ton a few years later, chiefly because the new strain had been introduced to unsuitable land. In spite of such diminishing returns, however, there is still a great deal of room for further development. In India, for example, it is reckoned that even in 1973, less than a third of the rice under cultivation will be one of the new varieties, and that less than half the acreage under wheat will consist of improved strains.

Instant revolution in agriculture is impracticable. It is necessary first to educate farmers and to provide the ancillary materials necessary for the new agriculture. But at the present pace, it should be entirely feasible for the production of cereal from the acreage now under cultivation in Southeast Asia to be increased by well over 50 percent during the 1970s. In short, food production should grow more quickly than even the highest estimates of population growth.

It goes without saying that the new agriculture is a more risky agriculture than the old. Dependence on highly specialized strains of cereals carries with it the risk that plant disease may create havoc with a crop in much the same way that, in the United States, corn blight has fiercely attacked the highly productive strains of maize under cultivation. This is why there

The Doomsday Syndrome

will be no cause to cry calamity if a decade or so from now some of the new varieties of wheat and rice, in some of the countries in which they have been introduced, should turn out to suffer from plant diseases of various kinds. Just as in the United States and Canada, the plant breeders know that the struggle against plant disease is never-ending, but need never be lost.

The plant breeders have been almost solely responsible for the development of the new strains of cereal crops. The development of the new wheat strains used in India and Pakistan was carried out in Mexico in the late fifties and early sixties, but can be traced back to plant breeding in the United States immediately after the Second World War. There has rarely been such a clear illustration of how scientific research can be used to help with the solution of urgent social problems.

The social consequences of the new agricultural revolution will be harder to accommodate than the technical problems it will create. Indeed, the problem of how best to market the farm surpluses which have appeared in Southeast Asia has already emerged and there are dangers that farmers will be discouraged if they cannot be assured of a reasonable price for what they produce. It will also take time before the supply of seed and fertilizer can be organized in a way that farmers understand, and before sources of agricultural credit can be organized. And then there are structural problems in the agriculture of Southeast Asia. In 1969, in West Pakistan and in the Philippines, four farms out of every five consisted of less than five acres. In most of the rest of Southeast Asia, the holdings were even smaller. This fragmentation of the land cannot long survive in the face of agricultural innovation, but the social upheaval will be slow and like all changes will seem to be painful.

Governments in developing countries will have to play an active part in the management of the transformation. Irrigation works must be built, responsibility has somehow to be accepted for the attestation of new varieties of seed and the training of the people who will use them. Fertilizers must be manufactured or imported. And it is clear, as the harrowing experience of East

The End of the Lode

Bengal in 1970 indicates, that the existence of an agricultural market requires roads for carrying the crops away from the land. Providing the framework for this new agriculture must seem to the people on the spot to be a formidable undertaking, but the results will not be merely a supply of food which is plentiful enough to meet the needs of the growing population (and occasionally sufficient to provide a surplus for export), but also an incentive to develop the kind of social framework within which other changes will be easier.

What is happening in Southeast Asia has yet to happen in Africa and Latin America where the record of the past few years is less encouraging. To be sure, food production has kept ahead of the growth population, but only just. In this sense, however, the great success which there has been in providing cereal crops for Asia is likely to be a powerful spur to further change. According to the FAO report *The State of Food and Agriculture, 1970*, there are in Africa "encouraging signs of a progressive introduction and adaptation of more modern techniques." Plant breeding, so far chiefly confined to the cash crops such as cotton and coffee on which many African countries base their export trade, has now been extended to the cereal crops, especially in North and East Africa. Locusts are under better control. African livestock farming remains spectacularly inefficient, but it remains a simple fact that no fewer than ten African countries were able to double their total production of food between the mid-fifties and 1970.

If food production is increasing more quickly than the population, it does not follow that the prospect of undernourishment, and even of famine, can be relied upon to go away. Crude numbers are misleading. And there is plenty of evidence that within regions of the world such as Africa and Latin America, some countries are moving ahead faster than others, that within most countries food is not distributed equitably and there is certainly no assurance that diet is always the best suited to survival. Questions like these rather than questions of whether the world supply of food will match the size of the population

The Doomsday Syndrome

are those to which managers of natural resources should pay attention. What is being done?

The development of an international market in foodstuffs is in many ways as important as the development of new varieties of cereals. In the past two decades, the United States has functioned as a prolific source of food. Since the early 1950s, exports of grain from North America have grown to between forty and fifty million tons a year, close on 8 percent of the production of grains other than rice in the world as a whole. Although there is no absurdity in the notion that North America should become a kind of granary for the developing world (an argument originally put forward by Dr. W. Arthur Lewis), there are obviously advantages in the development of a market in foodstuffs by means of which commodities could be exchanged between countries such as Thailand and India. This is a point which the United Nations has been trying to impress on the governments concerned, but there is a long way to go.

Within nations, it is obviously hard to arrange that food should be shared out on egalitarian principles. Poverty and hunger go together, after all; food costs money and poor people can usually afford less of it. Even in the United States there has been consternation in the past few years at the discovery that poor families in states such as West Virginia and Kentucky have been undernourished, at least by the standards which it seems appropriate to apply in North America. One of the problems in predicting how much food the growing population of the world will need stems from the certainty that prosperity as well as population will grow in the course of development. This implies that larger proportions of people in developing nations will be able to afford more and better food—meat, for example—so that general economic development of the developing world will add to the requirement of food production necessary to feed the growing population. It is hard to calculate precisely how much extra food will be necessary for reasons such as this, but it is unnecessarily rigorous to assume that every member of the world's population will eventually consume food and drink on

The End of the Lode

the scale now regarded as normal in the advanced countries.

In spite of a great deal of study since the Second World War, it is not clear precisely what is a sufficient diet. The yardstick most commonly in use is that promulgated in the early 1950s by the FAO. Part of the difficulty is that the amount of food that a person needs depends on his age, his weight and the work he does. There are some reasons to fear that the FAO standard is too generous—in Japan, for example, food consumption does not reach the standards laid down by the FAO even though there is neither a shortage of food as such nor serious shortages of money with which to buy it. The importance of this question is that a proper definition of what represents an adequate level of nutrition is a necessary preliminary to any attempt to calculate the proportions of people who may at any time be undernourished. One of the now widely held suspicions is that the FAO's own estimates of the numbers of people who are undernourished are in error.

Unbalanced diets are much more serious and widespread, and this is what people should mean when they talk of starvation. In developed parts of the world, it tends to be forgotten that nutritional deficiency diseases were common as recently as the 1930s. Rickets, caused by a lack of vitamin D in food, has left its mark on some of the most sophisticated populations. Out-and-out protein deficiency is still a serious cause of stunted development and mental retardation among poor people even in advanced societies. Skeletons from medieval graves in Europe, or from aboriginal burial grounds in North America, show that nutritional diseases of the several common kinds were widespread in antiquity, and protein deficiency has been for centuries endemic among the rice-eating communities of Southeast Asia and those in West Africa which depend on other kinds of cereals such as millet. The chances are that unbalanced diets go back to the Garden of Eden.

At present protein deficiency is most apparent in developing countries. Experience has shown that growing children and pregnant women are especially vulnerable to lack of protein. In strictly arithmetical terms, the actual production of protein in

The Doomsday Syndrome

the world as a whole is probably more than enough to keep everybody properly nourished. Even on the somewhat generous standards promulgated by the Food and Agriculture Organization, the average protein need amounts to about twenty-five grams—an ounce and a quarter every day. In India even in the 1960s, protein foods of the kind found in the average diet were enough to have provided 20 percent more than the minimal standard. So how can it be that protein malnutrition is plain for each trained eye to see in the larger Indian cities as well as in the country? Some people eat more protein than they need, which means that others have too little. But it is especially difficult to meet the needs of growing children and pregnant women with traditional cereal diets and, in any case, there is only a fitful recognition that the consequences of malnutrition are not simple hunger nor out-and-out starvation but, more commonly, stunted growth and development in young children and abnormal susceptibility to diseases such as cholera at all ages.

In Africa, the name for the disease as it affects children is kwashiorkor, a West African word to denote children weaned because of the arrival of a younger sibling. Kwashiorkor and the other diseases caused by protein deficiency are puzzling and may turn out to be more complicated than they seem. There seems, for example, to be a strange link between kwashiorkor and measles. Malnourished populations are especially susceptible to measles—the measles epidemic in India in 1959 killed two people in every 10,000, a death rate at least a hundred times as great as any recorded during a measles epidemic in more advanced countries. But the relationship between measles and kwashiorkor seems also to work the other way. In Peru in the late 1950s, between a quarter and a half of those reporting to hospitals with kwashiorkor had suffered from measles within the previous three months. Is it possible that while protein deficiency increases the chance that an attack of measles will be fatal, an attack of measles may also bring on (or bring out) kwashiorkor? Certainly those who suffer from kwashiorkor are

The End of the Lode

less able to make use of protein in their diet than healthy people. In short, kwashiorkor and the other deficiency diseases may yet turn out to be as much matters of public health as of diet. This is why organizations such as UNICEF are to be applauded for recognizing in the early 1950s that public education is as important as the supply of adequate food. Instinct may be enough to ensure that people fill their bellies with enough food to give them energy, but eating a balanced diet is possible only if people know what proteins are and why they are important. Malnutrition is as much a consequence of ignorance as of food shortages.

Much can and should be done to make better use of the protein and the agricultural resources which at present exist. In developing countries, the most urgent need is for welfare programs to allow poorer families to buy the food they need to keep alive. A survey in India in 1958 showed that poor families were not merely less well supplied with calories than rich families but were also compelled by poverty to eat less balanced diets. Schemes for fortifying the cereals which the populations of the developing world rely on for food have an essential part to play in the years ahead. Even in countries such as Britain and the United States, there are regulations which prescribe the minimum quantities of calcium and certain vitamins in bread sold for human consumption. Wheat flour supplied by the United States as aid to developing countries was artificially enriched in vitamins in the 1960s. More recently, there have been schemes for fortifying wheat flour by a protein concentrate obtained by drying and grinding fish, as well as by the addition of the chemical called lysine, one of the nine essential amino acids found in a complete protein diet which happens to be deficient in wheat protein. The cost of these additives is surprisingly small—fully enriched flour can be produced for something between two and seven dollars per ton, which works out at a fraction of a dollar for the cereal consumed by a child in a developing country in the course of an entire year. In short, food technology has an important part to play in the prevention of

The Doomsday Syndrome

protein deficiency. Too little has been done so far to exploit known techniques to improve the quality of the world's food supply.

Further ahead, there are more radical steps to be taken to combat protein deficiency. Rice contains only two-thirds as much protein as wheat flour, and in due course it will be necessary to breed strains of rice that yield larger amounts of protein. The wheat breeders have already shown what can be done—strains which are much better supplied with the amino acid called lysine are being developed in the United States. The Food and Agriculture Organization is excited at the potential benefits of a piece of genetic engineering, as the phrase goes, which has led to a hybrid of wheat and rye, called triticale, now being tried out in the Near East—these plants yield grain containing 20 percent of protein, equivalent in quality to that of skim milk.

There are also more unconventional devices for improving the supply of protein, not the least of which is simple chemical engineering. And if it has been possible for the chemical industry to increase its production of synthetic plastics and resins to twenty-five million tons a year, by weight a third of the world's production of meat, is it not sensible to think that the manufacture of the essential amino acids which are inadequately supplied by cereal protein might grow quickly to be of economic importance? There are also techniques for manufacturing protein by growing microorganisms, themselves rich in protein, on hydrocarbons produced as by-products of oil refineries—these could easily yield millions of tons of protein concentrates in the late 1970s. The potential usefulness in human diet of crops such as soya beans, traditionally used in animal feedstuffs, has yet to be exploited. Here again, it seems, it is easier to cry disaster than to take the sensible steps to implement the technology which is already available and which is entirely sufficient to provide protein for the world's population even if it should double between now and the end of the century.

None of this implies that the need for food in the decades ahead will be met by the chemical engineers, but the chemical

The End of the Lode

industry should become a useful complement to agriculture in keeping people well nourished. In any case, the prospect of increased productivity in conventional agriculture is much more important.

It is therefore quite mistaken to ask how many people the earth might be made to support. It is more important to know how much governments and farmers can be persuaded to invest in new agricultural techniques—seeds, machinery, the recovery of underexploited land or irrigation. But these technical opportunities, important though they may be, may in the long run be less important than arrangements for making sure that farmers in the developing world, now being blessed for the first time with food surpluses, will be able to win a just reward for the trouble. Nobody should think that these problems will be solved easily, but they are far different from the problems of absolute shortage with which most prophets of calamity are preoccupied. There is no doubt that the world could support 7,000 million people or even twice that number. The question is whether people will take the trouble to do so.

The idea that the sea could be made to yield very large amounts of food has been widely canvassed in the past few years, but the outlook here is much less cheerful than with conventional agriculture. The oceans are an important source of protein, and they will no doubt be made to yield more of it, but there are serious limitations to what may be done. Until 1970, the production of fish in the world as a whole had steadily increased (by an average of 6.8 percent a year between the late 1950s and the late 1960s). The total catch of fish now amounts to more than sixty million tons a year, an average of one pound of fish a week for every person in the world.

So why should not the oceans be made to yield continually increasing quantities of fish? Ingenuity and the will to invest in such things as fishing vessels sometimes seem to be the only requirements, but there has also been a great deal of optimistic talk about farming the sea, by which is meant a deliberate

The Doomsday Syndrome

attempt to increase the catch of fish of various kinds, by providing some parts of the sea with suitable nutrients. Unfortunately, enthusiasm has leaped ahead of practice.

In the oceans as on land, living things depend on energy from sunlight, which is first absorbed by single-cell plants called plankton or by more visible organisms such as seaweeds or algae. Just as grass is eaten by land herbivores, so the marine plants are grazed by marine herbivores. Then there are carnivorous fish which live on the herbivores but which may then be caught either by larger carnivores or by fishing nets. Although the oceans cover two-thirds of the surface of the earth, microscopic plant life grows luxuriantly only where the water contains substantial amounts of the simple chemicals, chiefly phosphates and nitrates, which function as body-building nutrients. The result is that most of the surface of the ocean is not particularly efficient at converting the energy of sunlight into organic chemicals which can become the basis of a chain of food production. The comparatively shallow waters around the edges of continents—the continental shelf as it is called—are the best places, but the whales of the South Atlantic owe their existence (such as it is—see below) to the way in which nutrients are carried up from the ocean bottom by a series of submarine currents running a thousand miles or so northwards from the edge of the Antarctic ice shelf.

Estimates of how much fish the sea could yield range widely from a figure which is not much greater than sixty million tons of fish which the oceans yield at present to figures which are several times as big. So long as fisheries are based, as at present, on the continental shelves, and in the absence of radically new techniques for increasing productivity at a reasonable cost, the yield of the fishing fleets of the world is unlikely to be dramatically changed. It is possible that economic ways will be found of exploiting the resources of the deep oceans, but land-based agriculture promises to be much more buoyant in the decade ahead.

Another difficulty in relying on the sea as a source of protein

The End of the Lode

is that fishing is a necessarily chancy business, still imperfectly understood. Although fishing vessels and their equipment have become steadily more efficient, fishing vessels still operate most confidently in those parts of the ocean in which they have caught fish before. It is exceedingly hard to tell whether there is a rich harvest to be won from the deep seas off the edges of the continental shelves.

Efficiency may even damage the long-term health of the fishing industry itself. There are already signs that some fisheries are being exploited too vigorously. In the past few years, the rate at which fish are caught seems to have leveled off, even though the efficiency of fishing vessels has improved and their number has increased. For fishermen, there seems no prospect of a return to the palmy days immediately after the Second World War when stocks of fish, which had been undisturbed for more than five years, were prepared to surrender to the nets. And it is known that some species of commercial fish, haddock, for example, are at present being fished off Newfoundland to the fullest extent compatible with the survival of the species, and that herring are now almost rarities off the English coast, as are sardines in the Bay of Biscay. To be sure, since the early 1960s, there have also been increases in some of the populations of fish which provide the foundation of commercial fisheries—haddock and whiting in the North Sea have increased as the herrings have declined, and the reasons for these trends are not at present understood. In fisheries, the most urgent need is to devise machinery to make sure that fishing does not kill the goose that lays the golden eggs.

The scandal of what has happened to the whales in the southern seas is miserable proof that folly can make its way even in a reasonable world. Since the Second World War, it has been clear that the whaling industry was in danger of fishing itself out of existence, which is why it seemed sensible to everybody concerned that there should be an International Whaling Commission to regulate (but not directly to enforce) the annual catch of whales. Under pressure from nations anxious to catch

The Doomsday Syndrome

as many whales as possible as soon as possible, the commission has consistently set annual quotas which are too large and has at the same time allowed that the annual catch should be defined in terms of a so-called blue-whale unit, but that whalers failing to find blue whales should be allowed to substitute larger numbers of other species instead. The result is that the total population of blue whales is probably no more than a few hundred, and the hunters have turned their attention to the fin whales. The United States government did well to declare in 1971 that whale products would no longer be imported into the United States, but fishing vessels from other nations, especially Japan and the Soviet Union, will keep up the hunt. The failure of the International Whaling Commission to do the job for which it was set up is a poor augury for the international organizations which are probably already overdue if the stocks of valuable commercial fish (whales, of course, are mammals) are not to be depleted by overfishing.

The output of the oceanic fisheries is therefore most likely to be sustained if there can be sensible programs for the control of fishing vessels. This is yet another proof that mere technical innovation and the fishing of previously unexploited parts of the ocean are insufficient. Luckily there are signs that some governments are moving in the right directions. The meeting of the North-East Atlantic Fisheries Commission in December 1971 agreed to extend the present fishing restrictions on herring in the North Sea, which consist of minimum dimensions for the mesh openings in fishing nets, to include limits on the permissible catch. Similar steps were taken to protect the Icelandic cod, recently under severe pressure from overfishing. But it remains to be seen whether organizations like the North-East Atlantic Fisheries Commission will be consistent enough and vigorous enough to prevent the destruction of important fisheries.

If fish are to contribute substantially to the protein supply, the further exploitation of the oceanic fisheries is less important than the development of freshwater fisheries in which fish can literally be farmed. The present yield of fish from the most pro-

The End of the Lode

ductive oceans, the Atlantic and the Arctic, is about two-thirds of a pound per acre per year, but untended freshwater fish ponds can yield twenty-five pounds of fish per acre per year, while carefully cultivated ponds in the tropics can yield 500 or 1,000 times as much. Such large yields can be obtained by fertilizing the ponds or even deliberately feeding the fish. In traditional Chinese fish farming, weeds, grasses and animal wastes are used to provide the water with nutrients and the fish with food. Elsewhere, it has been possible to use cereals fortified with vitamins to produce trout with such efficiency that something like two pounds of food would on average produce a pound of fish.

In this sense, fish are among the most efficient converters of foodstuffs made from plants into edible foods. In cattle ranching, six pounds of food are needed to produce one pound of animal, but in fish culture rather less than one and one-half pounds of food will produce one pound of catfish—the most efficient fish. But simple methods can be used for catching fish grown in artificial ponds, so that if fish farming has a bright future, it is more likely to be centered on freshwater ponds or shallow brackish-water lagoons than on the open sea.

With these reservations, there is no doubt that fish can be made to contribute in important ways to the world supply of protein. At present, ocean fisheries provide about a third of the minimum requirement of protein of the world as a whole, but fish farming contributes only a small fraction of this. There is no reason why that should not be enormously increased.

Fears of a shortage of energy have been another powerful preoccupation in the past few years, and the problems of energy supply are in many ways typical of the management of all kinds of natural resources. The starting point for most complaints is that the traditional fossil fuels appear to be nonrenewable. The world's reserves of coal were formed more than 200 million years ago and, once burned, are gone for good. Petroleum deposits can similarly be turned into smoke, and even if in some

The Doomsday Syndrome

parts of the world petroleum hydrocarbons are still being formed from decaying organic matter, consumption far outstrips the rate at which these materials are formed. So what will happen when all the reserves are exhausted?

Consumption of all kinds of fuel is bound to increase for a long time to come. For one thing, there are more people in need of warmth, transport and machinery. Then, for better or worse, economic development in advanced and developing countries usually implies that each person uses more energy each year. In the decade from 1959 to 1969, the amount of energy used by each person in the world increased by more than a third (35.6 percent), so that by the end of the decade energy to the equivalent of two tons of coal was used each year for each person then alive. With the growth of the world's population during the same period, the rate at which energy was consumed increased by just under two-thirds (63 percent) so that, in 1969, the amount of energy consumed in the whole world was the equivalent of a vast mountain of coal amounting to 6,500 million tons, roughly a cubic mile of coal.

Like any other indicator of economic advancement, the use of energy varies enormously from one country to another. In South America, for example, the energy used by each person in 1969 was less than 7 percent of that in North America. Africa used still less—for the continent as a whole in 1969, average consumption worked out at less than two-thirds of a ton for each person, but nearly two-thirds of all the fuel consumed was burned in South Africa. There is, however, evidence that the pace of growth of the fuel economy is greater in the developing regions than it is elsewhere, which is a sign that developing nations have embarked on the long road they will have to travel before reaching some kind of economic parity with the developed nations of the world. The arithmetic of this prospective economic competition is impressive—one-third of all the world's energy is at present consumed in North America, and if such a rate of energy consumption applied all over the world, six times as much fuel would have to be consumed each year. Instead of

The End of the Lode

one cubic mile of coal each year, the world's economy would require six cubic miles.

Where will all this energy come from? Estimating the amounts of coal, petroleum and other fuels in the surface of the earth is like estimating the frequency of undetected murders. It is, however, likely that among the fossil fuels, petroleum is most seriously threatened by the present growth of the demand for energy. The chances are that there are more, but not much more, than 300,000 million tons of petroleum still to be extracted from the ground, which would be enough to last for 135 years at the present rate of consumption, less than that if the advanced communities continue to increase their demand for petroleum and for an even shorter time if developing countries take a larger share of what is available.

It follows that at some stage in the next century, the petroleum business as it is at present known will come to an end. Either the price of petroleum products such as fuel oil and motor spirit will increase until it is cheaper to use alternatives, or the reserves will be exhausted. In the long view, however, this prospect should not keep people awake at night. For one thing, the petroleum reserves will not come to an abrupt end—instead, there will be a steady increase of price so that economically less valuable uses are eliminated first. Most probably, petroleum will remain the principal raw material for the plastics industry for centuries ahead, even if people have to keep their houses warm without the use of fuel oil. But there is also every reason why the exhaustion of petroleum reserves in the next 150 years should be matched by the exploitation of fresh sources of fuel.

The tar sands of Canada, already being exploited on a small scale, could yield the equivalent of only six years' energy consumption at the 1969 rate. But the likely reserves of natural gas would be able to supply the whole world at the same rate for more than 600 years, coal reserves would be good for 2,500 years and the vast oil shales which are to be found all over the world for no less than 40,000 years. Talk of an absolute shortage of fuel is in other words injustifiable. The important ques-

The Doomsday Syndrome

tions are to know just which kinds of fuel, at what prices, people will choose to use in the decades ahead.

All fears of a shortage of fuel should in any case have been dispelled by the coming of nuclear power, which has already broadened the range of choice. With present techniques, the equivalent of ten thousand tons of coal can be won from each ton of uranium; in the 1980s, the conversion rate will be something more like ten million tons of coal from each ton of uranium. Moreover, nuclear reactors will be able to use materials other than uranium, thorium perhaps. The development of nuclear energy in the past twenty years has increased tenfold the amount of energy that could economically be extracted from the earth's crust. The prospect, always unrealistically dramatic, of a crippling scarcity of energy has been exorcised by a single technological development.

This, however, is only a part of the story. It is now plain that ways will be found, before the end of the twentieth century, of converting hydrogen into heavier elements so as to release still larger quantities of energy. Each bucketful of water may yet be made to yield energy equivalent to one hundred tons of coal. By these standards, the hydrogen in the water of which the oceans are made may be thought of as equivalent to a coal seam covering the whole surface of the earth and extending downwards for a thousand miles. So why should anybody wring his hands about the prospect of increasing scarcity of one marginal source of energy, petroleum?

If the fuels from which energy can be extracted are for all practical purposes unlimited, it is nevertheless an important practical question to know which are the cheapest sources of energy, how quickly will they be consumed, how quickly will others replace them and how important an influence will the cost of energy be in regulating the pace of industrial activity. The 1950s and 1960s have provided several surprises.

In 1955, the British government was warned by the Ridley Commission that there would be a serious shortage of coal in the sixties and, given the then disinclination to spend foreign

The End of the Lode

exchange on imported petroleum, the government embarked on an ambitious program for the development of nuclear power stations. As events have shown, the decision was premature and in any case petroleum turned out to be cheaper than expected. The result was that by the early 1960s, a great deal of the slack created by the decline of the coal industry had been taken up not by nuclear power but by petroleum. In the 1960s, a further element of flexibility was introduced by the discovery of natural gas in the North Sea. Then came the discovery of petroleum deposits. The prospect of dire fuel shortage, urgent as it seemed in the 1950s, had been replaced within fifteen years by an almost embarrassing freedom of choice.

Freedom of choice entails cheapness, and one of the most remarkable characteristics of the world's fuel economy in the past two decades has been the way in which the costs of energy production have increased less quickly than other kinds of costs, especially the cost of labor. Part of the explanation is that the fuel industries have become progressively more efficient, so that fewer men are needed to extract the energy equivalent of a million tons. It has also been something of a surprise that newly discovered deposits of fossil fuels have been even larger than those already known—the petroleum beneath the North Slope of Alaska is the clearest illustration of this. If the earth must be likened to a spaceship, then it must be confessed that the occupants are remarkably ignorant of how it has to be supplied. But it is also important that the technical innovations of the past few years—not merely nuclear power stations but gas turbines, fuel cells and devices that convert heat into electricity without the intervention of moving parts—have given the fuel industries a much greater capacity to deliver energy to potential customers in precisely the forms in which it is needed.

The result is that in spite of the exploitation of energy reserves since the beginning of the Industrial Revolution, energy is now more plentiful and cheaper than it has ever been. Moreover, there is no reason why it should not continue to become more plentiful and even cheaper in every sense that matters.

The Doomsday Syndrome

The fact that developing countries will in the future make much greater demands on the world's fuel economy does not spell disaster. Long before there is any serious danger that fuel reserves will be exhausted, the consumption of energy will be limited by other considerations, possibly the need to restrict the dependence of advanced societies on energy consumption as modern industry becomes more sophisticated.

Fears of shortages of other minerals than the fossil fuels, and especially of the ores from which metals are extracted, have provoked all kinds of fears in the past few years. The Ehrlichs take a predictably gloomy view of the future. They hold that in the remainder of this century, developed countries

> *will not fare too badly since most of the UDCs [developing countries] will be unable to industrialize on any more than a modest scale. For approximately a century after that, mankind in general will do rather poorly, especially if any of several current trends continue. Beyond that time, the cost of energy required to extract whatever resources remain will tax far more than man's ingenuity.*

The trouble is that this prediction, like many others which are centered around emotive phrases such as "our plundered planet," is based on the assumption that the future will be like the present but more so. It makes no concession to the belief that with the passage of time, the human race will adapt to changes in the availability of raw materials much as it has done in the past two million years.

Of all the nonrenewable resources with which spaceship earth is said to be equipped, the most vulnerable are commonly supposed to be the metal ores. In the United States, fears of mineral shortages have been endemic since the late nineteenth century, chiefly because of the great pace at which new ore bodies were discovered and exploited in the western states. Indeed, the conservation movement in the United States at the

The End of the Lode

turn of the century was as much concerned with the conservation of mineral resources as with that of wild spaces. Since the Second World War, a great many studies have been carried out to determine the adequacy of minerals for the American economy—the Paley Commission in 1952 was one of the more conspicuous. The paradox is that there should be such alarm in the United States, which is still the envy of the rest of the world because of the mineral resources with which it is endowed.

The undercurrent of anxiety in the Paley Commission's report about the impending shortage of materials in the United States was echoed in 1960 by Mr. Vance Packard, who wrote in *The Waste Makers* that "more and more the United States is being forced to use thinner ores" and that "the United States dependency on foreign sources is bound to grow with each passing decade at a violently increasing rate if the population and the individual consuming habits of its citizens grow as briskly as marketers hope they will." But so what? Is it not an essential part of the structure of all mining industries that the richest deposits should be worked first? To behave otherwise would bring many mining companies to bankruptcy. And is it such a disaster that the United States should discover itself to be, like other countries, not entirely self-sufficient?

In the past few years, alarm about the future of natural resources has been sharpened, particularly in the United States, by what seems superficially to be an almost mathematical relationship between prosperity and the consumption of nonrenewable resources. With the passage of time and the growth of prosperity, the consumption of metals has grown enormously. In the United States, for example, the annual consumption of metal in the two decades after the Second World War increased by roughly 3 percent a year, more than twice as quickly as the size of the population. Will the same tendency continue indefinitely, so that the consumption of raw materials by the end of the century will have doubled in countries such as the United States and may have grown still more quickly elsewhere? The fallacy in this argument is that growing prosperity may well

The Doomsday Syndrome

bring with it profound changes in the pattern of use of these materials. Just as prosperity in countries now advanced has been accompanied by an actual decrease in the consumption of bread, so it is to be expected that affluence will make societies less dependent on metals such as steel.

Another fear, now widely expressed, is that the rapid use of raw materials by developed nations will rob countries of natural resources so that they will be unable to follow the path to prosperity which countries such as the United States have already trodden. As Mr. Dirck Van Sickle says,

> *industrialization will be impossible for under-developed nations, even if they overcome food and population problems, without metal. . . . It is criminal to continue life styles and consumption patterns which will not only leave future generations destitute but will create emergencies before the century ends.*

The false assumption here is that developing nations will follow an exactly similar path to prosperity to that which the advanced nations of the world have trodden. But in the world of the future, characterized by electronic computers and not the steam locomotives which gave the Industrial Revolution its special flavor, the use of raw materials will follow quite a different pattern from that with which the prophets are obsessed.

The most serious and persistent deficiency of the prophecies of scarcity is that they usually ignore the economic subtleties of the problems. And in spite of the pace with which resources are now being exploited, it is a telling paradox that the present seems to be a time when materials are becoming economically more plentiful, not more scarce. Techniques for exploration for and extraction of metals seem to have kept ahead of scarcity.

There is no doubt, of course, that many minerals are being consumed at a prodigious pace. In 1969, for example, aluminum smelters produced nine million tons of aluminum, about 40 percent of it in the United States and 12 percent in the Soviet Union. The production of aluminum in the world has in the

The End of the Lode

past few years doubled every nine years, but has grown even more rapidly in Western Europe and Japan. Most other metals are being extracted from their ores at a growing pace. The table shows the production of selected metals in 1969 and the percentage increase in the previous five years.

Table 3—Percentage increase of consumption of selected metals between 1964 and 1969.

	Production in 1969 (tons)	Percentage increase since 1964
Lead	3,200,000	24
Copper	6,000,000	25
Aluminum	9,030,000	54
Zinc	4,890,000	33
Tin	177,500	24
Magnesium	204,000	38

Will there be sufficient reserves of these materials to meet this continually growing demand? As with the fossil fuels, the question of absolute shortage is less interesting than the question of the prices at which the metals and other minerals necessary to sustain modern industry will be available.

The experience of the past few decades is encouraging, at least on a short-term view. Spaceship though it may be, the earth has vast resources still largely unexplored. Moreover, the techniques of exploration, mining and extraction have improved so quickly that the costs of producing industrial raw materials derived from minerals have been falling more or less uniformly over the years. Talk of how the earth is being "plundered" contrasts awkwardly with the way in which, for example, the uranium industry has developed in the past twenty years so that the metal is no longer rare and precious. In exactly the same way, cheap supplies of previously exotic metals such as silicon

The Doomsday Syndrome

and germanium have been organized so as to meet the needs of the electronics industry. Titanium, a curiosity in the 1940s, is now a familiar commodity.

Aluminum provides a striking illustration of how the technology of mining and metallurgy has for practical purposes increased the supply of the metal. Aluminum was first used on a large scale only in the early years of this century. To begin with, manufacture was impeded by the need for ore, called bauxite, which was chemically pure and, in particular, free from silica and iron. Over the years, techniques have been developed for purifying aluminum even in the presence of iron and silica, with the result that it is now possible to extract aluminum from ores that would have been quite useless in the 1930s. As long ago as the early 1960s, the monumental study by Landsberg, Fischman and Fisher, *Resources in America's Future,* estimated that proven world reserves of aluminum ore had doubled from 1,600 million tons to 3,600 million tons between 1950 and 1958, and that the chemical techniques available at the end of the 1950s made a further 5,000 million tons of aluminum ore accessible to the metallurgists. With the development of extraction plants capable of producing large quantities of aluminum metal at great speed, price has become much less dependent than it used to be on the quality of the ore. And now it is likely that the costs of extracting aluminum from ores of all kinds will be reduced by the development of a direct extraction process which avoids one of the expensive intermediate steps in the process. This is why it is no surprise that the price of aluminum metal has fallen gradually for the best part of two decades. Given inflation, this is tantamount to a substantial reduction of real cost, and there is no sign that this trend will be halted.

Another measure of the way in which the world seems to be living well within its physical limitations is provided by the striking changes in the past decade or so in the use of iron and steel, the traditional workhorses of heavy industry. World consumption of iron is growing less quickly than that of materials

The End of the Lode

such as copper and aluminum which are more directly of value in modern industries—electronics and aircraft manufacture, for example—but the production of pig iron in economically advanced countries is growing even less quickly than elsewhere. In the whole world, the production of pig iron increased by 31 percent between 1964 and 1969, but by only 12 percent in the United States. Since 1950, pig-iron production in the United States has fallen from being 47 percent of world production as a whole to 21 percent of the total.

Why should there be such a change of pattern? For several decades, there has been a steady decline of the importance of steel in the American economy. In the late 1920s, some 300 tons of steel were produced for every one million dollars of the gross national product. By 1969, there were fewer than 200 tons of steel for each one million dollars of the gross national product. Manufacturing processes increasingly depend on materials other than steel—either more exotic and expensive metals or chemicals such as plastics. Is it too fanciful to expect that in the development of an industrial economy, there will come a time when manufacturing industry is sated with the traditional productions of heavy industry—steel, cement and the like?

The present use of pig iron in the United States is also an illustration of flexibility in the use of natural resources. Each year, a large quantity of steel scrap accumulates in the United States, and indeed large quantities are exported for use elsewhere. Steelworks in advanced societies continue to manufacture and use pig iron in making steel only because this is economically advantageous. If there were to develop even a modest shortage of iron ore, it would be entirely possible for steelmakers to reduce drastically their consumption of iron ore, relying instead on the vast quantities of scrap which have accumulated.

Ringing the changes on pig iron and scrap iron in the steel industry is an illustration of how the substitution of one material for another may help to fend off threatened shortages of raw materials. Elsewhere in modern industry, more radical

The Doomsday Syndrome

substitutions of one material for another are commonplace. Aluminum, for example, can be used instead of copper in the electrical industry if copper is scarce (or too expensive) and none of those who bemoan the future scarcity of raw materials ever stops to complain that silver, in many ways the ideal conductor of electricity, has never been plentiful enough to make its full contribution to technology. Then magnesium can be substituted for, and is often preferable to, aluminum in the manufacture of aircraft parts. Synthetic abrasives, sometimes even diamonds, are used increasingly instead of the naturally occurring industrial diamonds won with great difficulty from the earth's crust.

The idea that some materials play such an important part in modern life that civilization would collapse without them is by all criteria an illusion. The most common short list includes naturally occurring substances as different as helium, copper and chromium. In reality, however, all these substances are but means to specific ends. Chromium is an element necessary for making stainless steel, but who would pretend that stainless steel is the only way of manufacturing such things as tableware or vats for the chemical industry? The past few years have shown vividly enough that other materials, synthetic chemicals, for example, can do the same jobs, possibly at greater cost and with less convenience. What this implies is that the objectives of modern industry can usually be attained in several ways by the use of alternative materials. Just as the nuclear-power industry will have to fall back on thorium as a fuel if it ever runs short of uranium, so manufacturers of concrete constructions will be forced to use other metals than steel as reinforcing bars if iron-ore supplies should run out.

The list of materials for which substitutes do not exist is exceedingly short. Indeed, in the last resort there is only the element helium, which has the special property of remaining liquid near the absolute zero of temperature and which is for that reason an essential ingredient in cooling scientific and industrial equipment to exceedingly low temperatures. As luck

The End of the Lode

will have it, it has now become apparent that helium will be produced as a by-product of controlled thermonuclear-power production when the small supplies now being collected from natural-gas wells are exhausted.

The tale of helium conservation is nevertheless important. In the early 1960s, the United States government took on itself responsibility for conserving helium, which is most easily won from the natural-gas wells of Texas. Under a scheme then introduced, natural-gas producers were required to separate helium from their product and to sell it to the strategic stockpile in the United States at a handsome price. But production turned out to be far in excess of demand, and the cost to the United States government of holding stocks of helium had become insupportable by 1970. The result is that the helium-conservation scheme has been wound up and it is now for natural-gas producers to make their own market for the material. The unwillingness of the United States government to continue stockpiling helium is, in the last resort, a measure of its unwillingness to deny present resources to American taxpayers now alive for the sake of posterity. The simplest justification is of course that nobody can tell what future generations will need. A more telling criticism of what appears to be fecklessness is that there are at present only the most rudimentary methods for striking a balance between long-term and short-term economic investments (see Chapter 9).

What of the complaint that the advanced nations of the world are robbing the developing nations of resources that they will in due course need themselves? This is a familiar problem, and governments such as the British have in the past been kicking themselves (or rather their predecessors) for having sold vast quantities of coal for export, with the result that there are only less easily mined deposits left to exploit. Yet this overlooks an important point. Countries with resources to sell must attempt to strike a balance between the advantages of immediate payment in cash and the more distant benefits of having cheap indigenous resources ready to hand. Calculations like

The Doomsday Syndrome

this are bound to be chancy, but developing countries with resources to sell should look at the world market price for their commodities with at least one eye on the future. To judge from the way in which in the late 1960s and early 1970s the oil-producing countries of the world have been able to extract a higher price for crude petroleum from purchasers abroad, this lesson has begun to sink in. It is in everybody's interests that it should do so quickly.

The Pollution Panic

4

Panic about pollution is the most conspicuous part of the environmental crisis and has its roots in the fear, entirely justifiable in the 1950s, that nuclear radioactivity from weapons tests might cause genetic and other damage throughout the world (see Chapter 1). If governments had then been more responsive to legitimate complaints, some of the more recent fears of environmental pollution might have been more level-headed.

In the event, radioactive fallout drew attention to several novel problems. The radioactive debris from nuclear explosions was carried over the surface of the whole earth and then slowly scattered down over several years, so that it was possible to fear that the whole environment had been poisoned. But radioactive materials damage living things surreptitiously. Strontium is indistinguishable from the calcium of human bones but, years later, it may cause cancer. Other radioactive materials cannot be detected except with special equipment, but they too, years later, may show up as inherited genetic defects or as thyroid cancer. Although it is now clear that radioactive fallout was indeed less dangerous than some people feared in the 1950s, there is still no justification for the protestations of governments then testing weapons that fallout then being released was entirely innocuous. But this sorry affair seems to have awakened people's sensibilities to the threat that the whole environment will be poisoned and that this may happen without warning, as apparently harmless chemicals insinuate themselves into food, drinking water or even the atmosphere. The environmentalists have learned efficiently how to play on these fears, but they have yet to demonstrate that people are about to wreck the environment on which they depend.

Alarm about nuclear installations of all kinds still persists. In 1971, for example, Drs. John W. Gofman and Arthur R.

The Doomsday Syndrome

Tamplin, employees of the Atomic Energy Commission in the United States until 1970, declared that:

> Radioactivity represents one of the worst, maybe the worst of all poisons. And it is manufactured in astronomical quantities as an inevitable by-product of nuclear electricity generation. One year of operation of a single, large nuclear power plant, generates as much of long-persisting radioactive poisons as one thousand Hiroshima-type atomic bombs. There is no way the electric power can be generated in nuclear plants without generating the radioactive poisons. Once any of these radioactive poisons are released to the environment, and this we believe is likely to occur, the pollution of our environment is irreversible. They will be with us for centuries. It is important that people learn how they are likely to be exposed to such poisons and how death-dealing injury is thereby produced in the individual and in all future generations.

The premise in this argument is true, at least so far as the generation of electricity by conventional nuclear plants—those burning uranium or thorium as fuel—is concerned. All existing nuclear power stations produce large quantities of radioactive isotopes. But there is no certainty in the argument that any of these "radioactive poisons" would permanently pollute the environment, for some of them are exceedingly short-lived. Worse still, the suggestion that pollution of this kind "is likely to occur" is strictly a subjective judgment. It implies that something will go wrong with the plans which nuclear engineers are making for the disposal of the waste products from nuclear plants. In that sense, the message which Drs. Gofman and Tamplin have by now carried throughout the United States, and which has contributed enormously to the difficulty of finding sites at which to build nuclear plants within the United States, is nothing but the message that they lack confidence in the engineers. Is that a sufficient basis for a crusade against nuclear electricity?

The Pollution Panic

The theme of secret and insidious poison runs through a great deal of contemporary discussion of the effects of chemicals on living things and particularly through Miss Rachel Carson's book *Silent Spring*. Writing of insecticides, but with a generality which has since been applied to other chemicals such as the cyclamates used as sweeteners in foodstuffs, Miss Carson said:

> Like the constant dripping of water that in turn wears away the hardest stone, this birth-to-death contact with dangerous chemicals may in the end prove disastrous. Each of these recurrent exposures, no matter how slight, contributes to the progressive build-up of chemicals in our bodies and so to cumulative poisoning. Probably no person is immune to contact with this spreading contamination unless he lives in the most isolated situation imaginable. Lulled by the soft sell and the hidden persuader, the average citizen is seldom aware of the deadly materials with which he is surrounding himself; indeed, he may not realize he is using them at all.

But are these chemicals as cumulative in their effects as Miss Carson says? It is a fact that left to himself a person will rid his body of any amount of DDT that may have accumulated in it. It would be wrong to think that none of the new chemicals is damaging, but a great deal of the anxiety which surrounds them springs from an entirely false analogy with radioactivity. In any case, it is natural that there should be most anxiety about the biological effects of insecticides in the United States, for more than half of all the insecticides used since the Second World War have been consumed there. Unlike fallout, which is literally world-wide, the newer chemicals in the environment are more easily dispersed.

But if the new chemicals in the environment are more easily recognizable, more locally concentrated and less insidious than Miss Carson's purple prose suggests, may it not nevertheless be the case that the ways in which people now interfere with the

The Doomsday Syndrome

environment might cause all kinds of irreversible damage? This is another now-common fear. In the past few years, there has been a great deal of speculation about world-wide calamity caused by simple chemicals such as carbon dioxide, the gas which people breathe out but which is also produced by the burning of fossil fuels, coal and petroleum. The trouble is that carbon dioxide is an efficient absorber of heat radiation, and in the ordinary course of events the small proportions of it in the atmosphere function as a kind of blanket, keeping heat on the surface of the earth. The gloomy speculation is that too much carbon dioxide might keep in too much heat, thus helping to melt the ice cap in Antarctica.

In his latest book, *The Closing Circle*, Dr. Barry Commoner says:

> *Thus, the higher the carbon dioxide concentration in the air, the larger the proportion of solar radiation that is retained by the earth as heat. This explains why on the early earth, when the carbon dioxide concentration was high, the average temperature of the earth approached the tropical. Then, as great masses of plants converted much of the carbon dioxide to vegetation—which became fossilized to coal, oil and gas—the earth became cooler. Now that we have been burning these fossil fuels and reconverting them to carbon dioxide, the carbon dioxide concentration of the atmosphere has been rising; what effect this may be having on the earth's temperature is now under intense scientific discussion.*

This argument, fortunately, is incomplete. In the world as it is at present, volcanoes share with power stations the distinction of being important sources of carbon dioxide for the atmosphere. And the seas are continually robbing the atmosphere of carbon dioxide. To know just how to strike a balance between these two effects is difficult, but the prophecy of calamity requires that all the uncertainties in the calculations should conspire to the most gloomy end. Especially because the tem-

The Pollution Panic

perature at the surface of the earth has if anything been declining in the past decade or so and not increasing as the pessimists say it should have been, it is surprising that these prophecies have carried weight not merely with impressionable people but even with President Nixon, who complained of the supposed threat of carbon dioxide in his State of the Union Message in 1970.

The threat of other kinds of environmental poisons was dramatized, in 1971, by the discovery of such large amounts of mercury in Pacific tuna fish that fishing was for a time restricted. These incidents have helped to create the impression that the oceans of the world are in some general sense polluted and that the pollution stems from industrial activity of a kind which is characteristic of the twentieth century. But it is hard, as will be seen, to take this gloomy speculation seriously. The seas as a whole contain 25–100 million tons of mercury, most of which has found its way there during the geological history of the earth by the breaking down of rocks and by the activities of volcanoes. The production of mercury in the world as a whole is at present no more than 10,000 tons a year, which means that even if all of it were immediately dumped into the oceans, it would take between 2,500 and 10,000 million years to double the concentration of mercury in the sea. It remains a puzzle why some tuna fish have much more mercury in their livers than others, but there is at least a possibility that the whole question of mercury pollution in sea animals has come about because there are now available such sensitive techniques for chemical analysis that the material can for the first time be detected in places where it has always been. And where other forms of oceanic pollution are concerned, it is salutary to remember that the great whales of the South Atlantic have been killed off by overfishing, not by pollution.

There remain, of course, all kinds of environmental problems which have arisen because of the introduction of new kinds of machines, among which the supersonic-transport aircraft is perhaps the most spectacular and the most controver-

The Doomsday Syndrome

sial, but which also include such now familiar devices as "ordinary" jet aircraft, road traffic and pneumatic drills. "Noise pollution" is a phrase in everyday use and it has become widely accepted, as Dr. Barry Commoner puts it, that "environmental degradation largely results from the introduction of new industrial and agricultural production technologies." In some minds, the argument can be carried further, and prosperity in general is increasingly held to be a source of inevitable environmental hazard. But who will say that pneumatic drills are a greater nuisance than the old steam hammers? Who will compare the nuisance from city traffic with that now banished from cities with any pretensions to good government—the city smogs such as those thought to have killed more than two thousand people in the Lancashire city of Salford in 1955? Who will say that the chemicals such as DDT which now find their way into rivers such as the Thames are worse than the huge quantities of untreated sewage which used to be discharged into them?

To the extent that communities still suffer from the side-effects of industrial activity and of communal living, it is within the scope of civic government to devise ways of regulating assaults on the environment so as to give ordinary people a socially acceptable blend of freedom and prosperity with good health and amenity. The truth is that technology and prosperity are not the inherent nuisances of which the environmentalists continually complain but, rather, the means by which a better environment could be created.

Pollution has a long history. Until the late eighteenth century, most cities lacked sewerage systems, so that the effluents which are now in some parts of the world dumped into rivers were disposed of by open drains running down the city streets. Noise has been a nuisance in cities since Roman times, for primitive industries were usually cottage industries. In medieval cities, whole narrow streets might be given over to blacksmiths' forges and an impression of how noisy they must have been can now be had in many of the old cities of the Mediterranean.

The Pollution Panic

With the coming of the Industrial Revolution, new insults to the environment were launched. Coal was burned in large quantities and crudely. Copper-smelting plants in the once lovely valleys of South Wales discharged to the atmosphere foul mixtures of gases, among which sulphuric acid was plentiful. By the end of the nineteenth century, in many parts of Western Europe and North America, whole landscapes had been transformed by pollution from the metallurgical industries. Rivers similarly became routes for the disposal of industrial effluent. Many parts of the industrialized world are still littered with spoil-heaps as monuments to that period when industrial activity was considered wholly virtuous and when pollution, as it would now be called, was synonymous with prosperity. The Lower Swansea Valley in South Wales remains, in spite of an ambitious attempt at rehabilitation, a monument to nineteenth-century pollution.

The nineteenth century also saw several bizarre examples of the injury of people by industrial pollutants. The use of a chemical containing mercury for dressing the beaver fur, then used for making fur hats, seems to have been responsible for the neurological disease called hatter's disease which, among other things, is commemorated by Alice's visit to the Mad Hatter's Tea Party. In Lancashire in the late nineteenth century, the use of phosphorus for vulcanizing rubber was directly responsible for cancer among rubber workers and for the particular deformity in which the chin bone is eaten away. From the 1870s on, growing concern for occupational health in industrialized countries had led to the increasingly tight control of nuisances like these, which is not to say that the industrial hazards of the nineteenth century have been entirely exorcised. In coal mining, for example, pneumoconiosis is still responsible for the deaths of 200 miners a year in Britain, and is thus more serious a cause of death among coal miners than the accidents underground in which people are killed by falling rock.

Municipal concern for the damage to health by industrial or other forms of pollution, in the course of the past century, led to several important and apparently effective systems of control.

The Doomsday Syndrome

In Britain, for example, the public water supply has been progressively improved in quality since the 1840s and the recognition that impure public water could spread typhoid through a community. The pollution of the environment by other kinds of infectious diseases has been steadily and successfully controlled by medical techniques. Diphtheria, for example, has been virtually eliminated in the advanced societies of the world and could be eradicated elsewhere comparatively easily. Tuberculosis, another form of pollution which happens to be transported by people, is similarly vulnerable to present medical techniques. Poliomyelitis is now eradicable.

In the past few decades, public authorities in Western Europe and the United States have been increasingly vigilant about clean air and clean water. In Britain, for example, simple legislation has made the air progressively free from smoke (which means particles of soot), sulphur dioxide and other menaces to public health. Where controls are effective, as on the River Trent, the quality of the river water has steadily improved. The central reaches of the River Thames are no longer devoid of oxygen in the summer.

Especially because pesticides now epitomize the supposed assault on the environment, it is significant that since the early part of the nineteenth century, all kinds of noxious chemicals have been used as insecticides. In the twentieth century, hydrogen cyanide, the most poisonous of gases, was widely used in fumigating against bedbugs and also for ridding ancient buildings of deathwatch beetles. Hydrogen cyanide was also used successfully against the cottony–cushion scale insect, a pest of citrus trees in California, until the hazards of the operation became insupportable and the insects became resistant even to this lethal gas.

Insecticides containing arsenic were introduced to agriculture during the nineteenth century, but few of them are now worth the risk. As with the persistent pesticides, these materials can also produce unexpected side effects—lead arsenate used against soil pests such as leatherjackets and wireworms may

The Pollution Panic

kill off earthworms as well. In 1939, nearly 30,000 tons of lead arsenate were manufactured for use as pesticides in the United States alone, but by the early 1960s only a fifth as much was used. Chemicals containing fluorine enjoyed a brief spell in fashion in the 1930s, but all of them are too dangerous to use in proximity with people, which is why the natural product called pyrethetrin, extracted from the pyrethrum flowers which grow in Kenya, was used before the Second World War in the control of human lice, the carriers of typhus.

The common failure of the environmentalists to recognize how much has been done in the past century to bring public nuisances under public control is damaging to their own cause, if only because they thereby overlook valuable precedents, legal and administrative. In the abatement of pollution, the serious problems are not technical but philosophical. How is it possible to strike an equitable balance between the interests of those who profit from pollution and those who gain nothing but may even lose? How is it possible to reconcile with old-fashioned notions of personal liberty industrial activities which create communal prosperity but which may bring damage to individuals as side effects? These problems are not in principle new. It is a great misfortune that so much of the present dispute about pollution is conducted as if they were.

Miss Rachel Carson's now classic assault on the use of pesticides in the United States has set the tone for much of the recent discussion of pollution and of environmental problems as a whole. Her book *Silent Spring* introduced and made respectable the most vivid form of the now common literary trick by means of which readers are given an awesome account of what might happen and are then advised that the full horror of this prospect can be avoided only if people and public institutions act more responsibly (see Chapter 1). The technique, of course, is that of the old preachers who would usher their listeners towards heaven with graphic accounts of what hell is like. Unhappily, by being too dramatic, Miss Carson's book has

The Doomsday Syndrome

probably done as much to confuse public discussion of government decisions as to promote the regulation of pesticides that circumstances unquestionably demand.

The chief targets of Miss Carson's attack were the pesticides of which DDT is the archetype, the "elixirs of death" as she called them. During the Second World War, it was quickly appreciated that DDT is a superior insecticide. A typhus plague in Naples in 1944 almost magically put to rout is one of the heroic tales. At the beginning, the essential qualities of DDT were that exceedingly small quantities of it would kill insects such as mosquitoes or house flies without harming people. After so much complaint about the hazards of DDT, it is often forgotten that it and its chemical relatives were first commended to the world at large because they were comparatively innocuous. In reality, DDT is no more poisonous to people than aspirin, but much more poisonous to most insects than, say, lead arsenate. DDT is, however, itself a stable chemical, not easily changed by the environment, which is why it seemed from the start to be a miraculous weapon against such things as the mosquitoes which carry malaria. Since the Second World War, the walls of houses in malarial regions have been sprayed with DDT in the assurance that the pesticide, insoluble in water as it is, would remain active for months on end, insinuating its way into the bloodstreams of insects that might happen to rest there before or after yet another blood meal. This persistence, of course, can also be a disadvantage.

The damage done by insect pests in the 1930s is also too easily forgotten, but even now, something like 10 percent of the crop of grain in the developing world is eaten by pests (rodents as well as insects). And in the 1930s, between two and five deaths in a hundred throughout the world must have been caused by insect-borne infections—malaria, yellow fever, plague and all the others.

In all the circumstances, it is no surprise that the new insecticides were first weclomed with enthusiasm and abandon. In countries such as Ceylon and Brazil, malaria was for prac-

The Pollution Panic

tical purposes quickly banished. Organizations such as the World Health Organization of the United Nations now recognize that there is more to the eradication of malaria than the eradication of mosquitoes, but nobody suggests that the use of DDT against mosquitoes carrying malaria parasites should be given up. The hazards of such a course are evident in the experience of Ceylon in the 1960s, when spraying with DDT was abandoned after the number of cases of malaria was reduced to seventeen in 1963. By 1967, the number of confirmed cases of malaria had grown to more than 3,000. In 1968, there were more than a million cases, with the result that spraying with DDT began again before the year was out.

With the chemistry of DDT as a guide, it was only natural that the 1940s and early 1950s should have seen an enthusiastic search for even more powerful insecticides. Closely related to DDT is the chemical called DDD. More distantly related is a class of insecticides, also called chlorinated hydrocarbons, including aldrin, dieldrin and heptachlor. These turned out to be not merely more effective than DDT but just as resistant to chemical decomposition—their particular interest in the history of the synthetic pesticides is that they are much more toxic to birds than DDT. The charitable view of the first excesses in the use of the synthetic pesticides is that both users and manufacturers were mesmerized by the apparent immunity of people.

The most valuable part of Miss Carson's book is her list of complaints about the profligate use of pesticides in agriculture. In the mid-fifties, attempts were made in Michigan to control the Japanese beetle by spraying from the air with aldrin, but these turned out to be more effective as ways of killing other forms of wildlife—birds and squirrels, for example. Another classic accident is that recorded at Clear Lake, California, ninety miles north of San Francisco, which in 1948 was sprayed with DDD (supposedly less toxic to fish than DDT) as part of a carefully calculated program under the supervision of the California Department of Public Health. The object was to get rid of the population of gnats which bred on the lake and discomfited visiting fishermen. After three successive applications of the insecticide, the gnats had certainly been decimated, but there were also a great many unexplained fatalities among the swanlike birds called the western grebe which breed on the lake, presumably for the sake of its fish.

This remains one of the best documented accounts of how comparatively small quantities of a persistent pesticide such as DDD can first of all be concentrated in the livers of fish and from there transferred to the birds which feed on them. The way in which the persistent pesticides can be passed along in this way from one link in a food chain to another, damaging in the process animals which may be especially susceptible, is one of the chief reasons for worrying about pesticides in the environment. People, after all, are at the end of a food chain—they eat other animals, and vegetables as well. As it happens, and for reasons which are straightforward in chemical terms, DDT and the other chlorinated hydrocarbons tend to concentrate in the liver and fat.

Upsetting some natural balance between species can be another of the subtle accompaniments of the use of pesticides. Here again, the classic tale of mishandling comes from California. The citrus scale insects that in the 1930s became resistant to hydrogen cyanide were eventually controlled by a species of imported ladybird, and kept in check, though not exterminated, for close on half a century. But the comparative freedom of the orchards from the scale insects was eventually upset when control with DDT was attempted in the years immediately after the war: the ladybirds turned out to be more susceptible than the scale insects, with the result that infestation became more serious than it had been. The ecological balance that kept the pests in check, artificial though its origin may have been, was upset by DDT.

These are horrendous tales, and the recitation of them by Miss Carson and her followers has helped to form the public view that the use of pesticides must be carefully controlled. In the past few years, governments everywhere have drafted tighter

The Pollution Panic

legislation for regulating the uses for particular pesticides and the manner in which they may be applied. In Britain, the discovery in the late 1950s that birds, especially wood pigeons, were being poisoned by seed dressed with aldrin, dieldrin or heptachlor has led to a general agreement that these pesticides should not be used indiscriminately although as yet there is no formal system for registration within some simple legal framework. In the United States, chemicals intended for use as pesticides must first of all be registered for the specific uses for which they are intended. Elsewhere, in the Netherlands and Sweden as in the United States, the use of pesticides is for practical purposes regulated at several levels—there are restrictions on the kinds of uses which can be made of these chemicals and also regulations which specify the degree to which foodstuffs may be contaminated. In several countries, it seems to be agreed that the next step should be legislation that requires those who plan the use of pesticides or those who actually take the spray guns in their hands to be properly trained in the necessary techniques.

In *Silent Spring,* as in other protests against DDT, the way in which insect populations often develop resistance to DDT has been singled out as if it were a reason for not using chemicals like this. "Nature fights back" is Miss Carson's chapter heading. The truth is that insects, like people, are resilient species. In hostile environments, the fittest are by definition those most able to survive, which means that those in a community which have immunity against obvious dangers will quickly put their genetic stamp on future generations. In people threatened by larger carnivores, for example, intelligence or a flair for climbing trees may be an advantage; among insects threatened with DDT, immunity is what matters. The fact that the insecticides such as DDT are unexpectedly effective is one of the reasons why immunity has appeared comparatively quickly within a decade or so. Writing of the largely successful wartime use of DDT against Italian mosquitoes, Miss Carson says in her book that "only a year later the first signs of trouble appeared . . . both

The Doomsday Syndrome

house-flies and mosquitoes of the genus *Culex* began to show resistance to the sprays." So what? is the only honest answer. If the doctrine of evolution and the science of ecology which is built on it mean anything at all, there are only two principal classes of insecticides—those which cause resistance in populations of the pests which are not entirely exterminated and those which are entirely ineffectual.

It follows, of course, that there are bound to be strict limits to what can be done with any one synthetic pesticide. Much of the heady postwar talk of the eradiction of malaria, for example, fanned along by specialist agencies of the United Nations, such as the World Health Organization and the Food and Agriculture Organization, was synonymous with the eradication of the mosquito *Anopheles gambia*. By now, however, it is plain that malaria will be eradicated not by the massive use of insecticides in a campaign against mosquitoes but by a combination of several applications of modern science, therapy and better sewerage systems included. So ecologists have a vital part to play, for only they can help to define safe ways to interfere with the natural world without inviting trouble. And ecology implies not that pesticides are too dangerous to use but that they must be used cleverly.

These are the chief reasons why the use of DDT and the insecticides related to it should have declined steadily since the early 1960s. Nearly two-thirds of the total tonnage of DDT and its close relatives has been manufactured in the United States. Since the end of the Second World War, rather more than two million tons of DDT have been manufactured in the United States and elsewhere. The production of the aldrin insecticides grew more quickly from a slower start, and reached a peak in 1966 with an output of 60,000 tons from American factories. Although production capacity has been growing outside the United States, restraint and the need to substitute newer pesticides against insects which have become resistant has helped along the decline. The newer materials, of which Miss Carson also complains, contain phosphorous and are much

The Pollution Panic

less persistent than the chlorinated hydrocarbons. In due course, many important insect pests will be resistant to them as well, and it will be a matter of great importance to know whether there will then be available still more effective means of killing insect pests.

The way in which Miss Carson drew attention to the misuses of DDT and the other persistent pesticides may have been a public service of a kind. The defect of *Silent Spring* is that it went much further and leveled complaints which were invalid at the time and which are, for that matter, still invalid. The danger now is that too zealous an attack on DDT and related chemicals may deprive the world of important benefits.

What is the case to answer? DDT and the related pesticides are persistent. They lodge in the soil and may remain unchanged for a decade or more. They accumulate in vegetables and cereals. They are washed by the rivers into lakes and into the sea, and may be incorporated into the tissues of plants or animals. In mammals, the pesticides are concentrated in fatty tissue—which is an effective device for keeping them out of the bloodstream and which may be a part of the reason why mammals are comparatively unharmed by them.

The sheer size of these residues is therefore unimportant. What matters is the extent to which the presence of the pesticides may be damaging. There is some evidence that fish can be and have been damaged. Fish-eating and carnivorous birds are also at risk. Brown pelicans in North America may, for example, have been damaged, and there is some doubt about the effects of DDT on the eagles of North America—but no doubt at all, unfortunately, that more of these majestic animals have been illicitly shot by farmers than have been killed by DDT. And there is no evidence that people have actually been harmed by persistent pesticides. One of the philosophical difficulties is to strike a balance between the interests of birds and those of people. The environmentalists have never been able to decide how many human lives should be put in hazard

The Doomsday Syndrome

for the sake of the maintenance of bird populations at the level determined by predators and the shortage of food.

Miss Carson's book is unhelpful because its passion too often obscures the truth. Even on simple matters of fact, *Silent Spring* is more definite than it should be. There is, for example, the simple question whether DDT stays permanently in a person's fat once it has lodged there. Physiologists would expect there to be a balance of some kind, perhaps a quite complicated balance, between the amount of DDT in the fat and the amount circulating in the blood. If the amounts of DDT in the blood are small, the fatty tissues will release some of their burden, and some of this will eventually be excreted. But if a person has only recently eaten a meal containing large amounts of DDT, some of this will be extracted from the blood and laid down in the fat. This is the kind of balance struck when radioactive strontium accumulates in people's bodies—there it is the skeleton and not the fat that serves to take foreign materials out of circulation.

Unhappily, *Silent Spring* is misleadingly stark. The book says at one point that "this pollution is for the most part irrecoverable—the chain of evil it initiates not only in the world that must support life but in living tissues is for the most part irreversible." Elsewhere Miss Carson says of the persistent insecticide chlordane that "like all other chlorinated hydrocarbons, its deposits build up in the body in cumulative fashion." These statements are, however, untrue. There is no reason to think that the balance struck between DDT in the blood and the fat is not reversible. Take a person away from DDT for a time, and he will get rid of some of what he has stored. The fact that the accumulation of these materials is not cumulative, as Miss Carson says, is important—whatever the dire consequences of DDT in the fat, the future is not necessarily imprisoned by the past.

In any case, the pesticide residues so far accumulated by people are extremely small. In the United States, human fat tends to contain between ten and twelve parts in a million of

The Pollution Panic

DDT, which is another way of saying that each pound of fat will contain one fifth of a thousandth of an ounce of DDT. The whole of the DDT in a man's body would at this rate yield less than a hundredth of an ounce of DDT, a tiny part of the dose needed to cause obvious poisoning. In countries other than the United States, where DDT and the other persistent pesticides have been used much less intensively, the amounts of DDT in the fat are correspondingly less. In Western Europe, for example, the average is about five parts per million and the fraction of the lethal dose locked up in a person's fat is also smaller.

Another complication in assessing the significance of these tiny doses of contamination is a confusion which has arisen between the insecticides such as DDT and other chlorinated hydrocarbons, not all of which are pesticides.

Many of the chemical measurements carried out before 1968 failed to distinguish between DDT and some chemicals called polychlorinated biphenyls, or PCBs for short. These have been widely used in industries such as the plastics industry since the early 1930s. Like DDT, they are chemically stable. If they can cause bodily harm to people and animals, however, there is no doubt that they are much less damaging than the pesticides. There is a high chance that some of the earlier measurements have exaggerated the amounts of DDT in such things as the livers of birds because of confusion between DDT and PCB, although there is no firm evidence that PCBs have yet been found in human tissues.

Another problem is that there seem to be large variations in the amount of DDT in fat from one person to another. Diet may be part of the explanation, which is probably the reason why Negroes in the southern United States have more DDT in their fat than Negroes from elsewhere, but individual variations of metabolism are no doubt involved as well. What this implies is that there is a need for a better understanding of the processes which determine the rate at which DDT and the other pesticides accumulate in a person's body.

The Doomsday Syndrome

But even if DDT residues cause no immediate damage, may they not have more subtle long-term effects? Or are the long-term effects of DDT negligible? Miss Carson seems to have been in very little doubt. Throughout *Silent Spring,* there are repeated suggestions that the "new synthetic insecticides may be capable of causing cancer." At one point, Miss Carson says that "they destroy the very enzymes whose function is to protect the body from harm, they block the oxidation processes from which the body receives its energy, they prevent the normal functioning of various organs and they may initiate in certain cells the slow and irreversible change that leads to malignancy."

How true is this? In the 1960s, it was clear that one of the effects of DDT circulating in the blood of an animal is to affect the natural chemicals or enzymes which play an essential part in nervous functions, which is why lethal doses of pesticides cause convulsions before they kill. It is also known that DDT and similar insecticides can affect the submicroscopic structures which normally regulate the energy of cells, using oxygen taken from the blood to convert the chemical energy of food into some other form. Liver cells are especially concerned in this process and the liver is also the organ chiefly responsible for eliminating unwanted material. Laboratory animals fed large quantities of insecticides develop enlarged livers, which shows how the efficiency of a liver cell can be impaired by the chlorinated hydrocarbons. There is, however, an immense gap between the amounts of material used in laboratory experiments like these and the doses of insecticides to which the liver of a human being is likely to be exposed.

It would be a great flight of fancy to relate the results of experiments to what might happen because of the small quantities of insecticide in people's fat. To be sure, Miss Carson introduces some circumstantial evidence:

> In connection with the nearly universal use of insecticides that are liver poisons, it is interesting to note the sharp rise in hepatitis that began during the 1950s and is continuing with

The Pollution Panic

a fluctuating climb. Cirrhosis also is said to be increasing. While it is admittedly difficult in dealing with human beings rather than laboratory animals to prove that cause A produces effect B, plain commonsense suggests that the relation between a soaring rate of liver disease and the prevalence of liver poisons in the environment is no coincidence.

This argument is entirely without foundation. The increased incidence of hepatitis in the United States in the fifties seems to have had an infective origin. The careful studies which have since been carried out in the United States and elsewhere have been unanimous in their finding that the residues of the organochlorine insecticides which accumulate in human tissues have so far had no detectable effect on the health of people. The special commission appointed in the United States under Professor Emil M. Mrak, which reported in December 1969, found no evidence that damage is actually done to people by the presence of pesticides in the environment. To be sure, some people, especially agricultural workers, are known to die of poisoning by large doses of these materials, but the commission said (page 319) that "apart from the occurrence of acute poisoning, the only long-term effect which can be unequivocally attributed to sustained exposure to organochlorine pesticides is the acquisition of a tissue residue. No causal association of these levels with disease has as yet been demonstrated." This conclusion was repeated in September 1971, when a special committee nominated by the U.S. National Academy of Sciences, to advise the Environmental Protection Agency, concluded that "the chronic toxicity studies on DDT have provided no indication that the insecticide is unsafe for humans when used in accordance with commonly recognized practice."

But may not the residues of DDT stored in people's fatty tissues cause cancer? In *Silent Spring*, Miss Carson describes "one of the most impressive theories of the origin of cancer cells," that is due to Professor Otto Warburg of West Germany. His view is that the origin of most cancer consists of an inter-

The Doomsday Syndrome

ference with the normal process of restoration or energy production in cells. The argument is that a cell in which the normal process of restoration has been interrupted may occasionally be able to compensate for this by relying on other methods of energy production which are those characteristic of cancer cells. Miss Carson says that "measured by the standards established by Warburg, most pesticides meet the criterion of the perfect carcinogen too well for comfort." Unhappily for Miss Carson, and for Professor Warburg, this view of the origin of cancer, speculative in the early 1960s, is now unfashionable as well.

More to the point, there is no experimental evidence that DDT and the related pesticides will cause cancer in laboratory animals. In 1969, the report of a complicated survey of the effects of feeding various chemicals, including DDT, to two different strains of mice, which had been commissioned by the National Cancer Institute in the United States and carried out by the Bionetics Laboratory, Inc., showed that there is a tendency for mice thus dealt with to develop the liver tumors called hapatomas. This result has since been confirmed by a series of experiments with laboratory mice sponsored by the International Agency for Research on Cancer. This research has shown that roughly half of a population of mice would develop hepatomas if they were fed for two years on a diet containing roughly a thousand times the concentration of DDT in the ordinary human diet. But there is no reason to think that the hepatomas would be followed by cancer even in the laboratory mice used in the experiments.

To be sure, in the United States, any material which causes cancer in laboratory animals is prohibited by act of Congress, however unrealistic the laboratory experiments may be, but there is no justification for the belief that DDT causes cancer, either in animals or in human beings. There is always a remote possibility, of course, that still higher doses of DDT, fed over longer periods of time, may cause malignancy, but it would in most circumstances be held to be irresponsible of Miss Carson to have so chilled her readers with hints of horrors which are as badly founded as this.

The Pollution Panic

What of the continued use of DDT and the other pesticides? So far as the health of people is concerned, there is clearly very little cause for anxiety. The DDT Advisory Committee in the United States has taken the view that it will be several years before the concentrations of pesticides in the soil decrease to a point at which the amounts of pesticides in food decrease significantly, but, by the same test, there is evidence that moderate use will bring about a marked increase in this concentration. Of course, it would be easier to be confident of these calculations if more were known about the way in which DDT and similar pesticides are carried from one place to another. The discovery that penguins and other birds in the Antarctic have extremely small concentrations of DDT in their fat—one hundredth or so of those found in sea birds near the coast of North America—has sometimes been taken as a sign that DDT is now spread through the whole environment, but the argument can, of course, be turned around to show how slow must be the processes by means of which pesticides are carried from the places where they are used in bulk, principally North America, to remote regions of the world. If after twenty years of intensive use, pesticides such as DDT have contaminated the environment in which Antarctic birds live to the extent of only 1 percent or so of that around the coasts of North America, they cannot be as mobile as popular legend suggests.

The hazards of calculating what happens to pesticides in the marine environment are well illustrated by a report of a committee under Dr. Edward D. Goldberg published by the United States National Academy of Sciences in July 1971. This declared: "The oceans are an ultimate accumulation site for the persistent chlorinated hydrocarbons. As much as 25 percent of the DDT compounds produced to date may have been transferred to the sea."

Unhappily, this assertion is based on an exceedingly shaky foundation and in particular on measurements of the amounts of DDT in rainwater made in Britain between August 1966 and July 1967. On the average, those rainwater samples contained eighty parts of DDT in every million million parts of water. Dr.

The Doomsday Syndrome

Goldberg's committee assumed that exactly the same concentrations of DDT would be found in all the rain falling on all the oceans of the world in any year—a total of 300 million million cubic meters of rain. Simple arithmetic then leads to the conclusion that 24,000 tons of DDT are carried by rainwater into the sea each year. The flaw in the argument is that the concentration of DDT in rainwater varies markedly from one place to another. Measurements in Florida, for example, have revealed such high concentrations that if they were used as the starting point for the same calculation, the conclusion would be that the total discharge to the oceans by this route exceeds the annual production—manifestly an absurd result. In any case, there is no reason to believe that the DDT in rainwater over oceans could be accurately represented by measurements made over the land, simply because of the way in which rainwater falling on the land must have scavenged pesticides from the atmosphere which would itself be contaminated with particles of soil and even insects. In short, the conclusion that a quarter of all the DDT which has ever been produced now resides in the oceans of the world is entirely meaningless.

The basis of this gloomy calculation was already invalidated by the report in August 1970 of the discovery that DDT and related pesticides are, in any case, unstable in seawater. A group of workers at the Gulf Breeze Laboratory of the U.S. Department of the Interior showed that DDT is quickly converted (in just under three weeks) into its degradation product DDE (which is no great surprise), but that DDE is then still further degraded, so that after a further twenty days, only 5 percent of it remained intact. For the pesticides as a whole, only 7 percent remained intact after forty days, which goes a long way to suggest that if pesticides eventually finish up in the oceans of the world, they will not remain there long without being turned into harmless chemicals.

The most striking features of these calculations is the extent to which they illustrate contemporary ignorance of what happens to pesticides in the environment. The Goldberg committee

The Pollution Panic

was entirely right, in its report in 1971, to plead for more systematic measurements of DDT in the ocean environment so as to provide a more secure basis for calculations of the kind which it attempted. That however is a long-term goal. For the present, there is no doubt that the effects of DDT and similar pesticides on living things are most significant in the regions surrounding places where DDT has been extensively used, North America in particular but also Western Europe, and it is clear that the living things which stand in greatest danger from the use of pesticides are certain animals living in the sea, sea birds which live on fish and predatory birds living off small land animals. In striking a balance between the advantages and the disadvantages of the continued use of pesticides, the well-being of these creatures is the only consideration of importance on the obverse side of the coin.

All these animals are at risk because they have a tendency to concentrate DDT gleaned from the food they eat. Sea birds are especially vulnerable because the fish on which they live contain large amounts of fat which, as with people, is a solvent for DDT.

What is the evidence? Laboratory experiments have shown that commercial species of shrimps and crabs can be killed if they are made to live in water containing less than one part in a thousand million parts of DDT, and some of the rivers flowing into the Gulf of Mexico from the United States are known to have been contaminated to such an extent. This is why it may be possible to link the decline of shrimp fishing in the Gulf of Mexico in recent years to DDT, although it is probable that more familiar forms of pollution have also played a part. Oysters might also be affected, although there seems to be no direct evidence that pesticides have had a noticeable influence on commercial oyster fisheries. There is more convincing evidence, still however circumstantial, that the dramatic decline of the sea-trout fishery in the Laguna Madre off the coast of Texas has been caused by pesticides—laboratory experiments have shown that the hatching of trout eggs containing several

The Doomsday Syndrome

parts per million of DDT may be unsuccessful—but this is a local phenomenon. Less heavily contaminated estuaries a hundred miles away support normal population of sea trout. The moral is that it is necessary to control the use of pesticides with such care that individual river estuaries or lagoons are not excessively contaminated.

With birds, the chief effect of DDT contamination is that eggs are laid with abnormally thin shells. One dramatic illustration of the damage that may be done was the virtual failure of the hatching season for brown pelicans off the coast of Southern California in 1969. And the chances are that by then, those particular breeding colonies were seriously at risk. The phenomenon of eggshell thinning has been observed with other species of predatory birds—cormorants and eagles, for example —but in no case has a breeding colony been as seriously affected as that of the California brown pelicans. It goes without saying that for most of the species which are laying thinner eggs, the effect of pesticides, whatever it may be, on the hatching of young birds will not usually be followed by a similar reduction of the numbers of those who survive to adulthood—the fewer young birds there are, the greater will be the proportion of those that survive to adulthood. And in any case, so far as can be told, the effects of pesticides on these vulnerable species are still for practical purposes localized in the regions where DDT has been used extensively. It follows that it is altogether too soon to think that the survival of some species may have been put in hazard, although there is no doubt that pesticides have increased the difficulty of survival for some of them.

So what balance is to be struck between the advantages and the disadvantages of pesticides? To the extent that the excessive use of these materials in North America and Sweden has damaged or has threatened to damage wildlife, which has commercial as well as aesthetic value, there is obviously a case for moderation. But even in North America, there is good reason to believe that the careful use of pesticides, properly monitored and controlled, can contribute in important ways to agricul-

The Pollution Panic

tural productivity without endangering important species of wild animals. Elsewhere in the world, where tractors and other aids to agricultural efficiency are underused, pesticides can contribute enormously to food production, and there is every reason to hope that more use will be made of DDT and its associated chemicals.

This case was put eloquently by Dr. Norman E. Borlaug, who received the Nobel Peace Prize in 1970 for his work on the development of the strains of wheat which have made the green revolution possible, when he gave evidence to a Congressional committee in the United States in October 1971. Environmentalists, he said,

> seek a simple solution to very complex problems. The pollution of the environment is the result of every human activity as well as the whims of nature. It is a tragic error to believe that agricultural chemicals are a prime factor in the deterioration of our environment. The indiscriminate cancellation, suspension or outright banning of such pesticides as DDT is a game of dominoes we will live to regret. . . . I have dedicated myself to find better methods of feeding the world's starving populations. Without DDT and other important agricultural chemicals, our goals are simply unattainable. Perhaps more than any other single factor in the world today, DDT has a unique contribution to make to the relief of human suffering.

The truth is of course that there can never be as simple and uncomplicated a policy towards DDT, other agricultural chemicals or any other chemicals which may have useful functions in the practical world as Miss Rachel Carson and the extreme environmentalists who have followed her proclaim. The threats of ecological calamity are hypothetical and in any case remote. The practical benefits are real and immediate. The choice to be made is not that between unrestricted exploitation of a new technological device and outright self-denial. Instead, means must be found of gaining benefits at a cost which is ac-

The Doomsday Syndrome

ceptable to all concerned. It will not be easy to find ways of balancing the advantages to farmers of unrestricted use of pesticides against the disadvantages to, say, fishermen of contaminating estuaries, and the problem of evaluating the health of animals such as bald eagles to the population of North America is one that has not yet been tackled. But to bury all these difficulties beneath a popular belief that DDT and other pesticides are inherently malevolent and potentially calamitous is not merely an assault on reason but an act of intellectual cowardice.

Among the causes of world-wide calamity that have been widely canvassed in the past few years, and one of the most awesome, is the notion that the climate of the earth as a whole may be changed, perhaps irreversibly, by human activity. One possibility is that dust from industrial activity may accumulate in the stratosphere and thus prevent significant amounts of solar energy from reaching the surface of the earth, with the result that the temperature is reduced. Another claim of circumstances would have the opposite effect—carbon dioxide from burning fuel may accumulate in the atmosphere so as to prevent the escape of heat radiation from the surface of the earth and thus increase the temperature—the greenhouse effect as it is called. Still other scenarios have been written; one of the most recent (and the most tenuous) is that supersonic-transport aircraft flying in the high atmosphere may release oxides of nitrogen which would in turn react with the ozone, which normally functions in the stratosphere as a shield for keeping ultraviolet light away from the surface of the earth. In this view, once fleets of supersonic transports are in service, more ultraviolet light will reach the surface of the earth and more people will get skin cancer as a result.

It is exceedingly difficult to make informed estimates of the likelihood of these developments. For one thing, the reaction of the upper atmosphere to sunlight and the presence of foreign materials is not understood. The influence of the upper atmos-

The Pollution Panic

phere on the climate on the surface of the earth is only improperly grasped. One obvious difficulty is that a proper understanding of what happens in the stratosphere has been possible only in the past few years with the development of instruments which can be carried aloft by rockets, balloons and high-flying aircraft. There are also great theoretical difficulties, typified by the quite remarkable ignorance of the reasons why Ice Ages come and go. In this sense, it is important to remember that the last great recession of the ice from middle latitudes was as recent as 10,000 years ago, that the climate at the present time is substantially no different from that likely to have been found on the surface of the earth during the three or four ice-free intervals which have occurred in the past million years and that the present time may indeed be simply an interval between two phases of glaciation. The climatic consequences of pollution, whatever they may be, should be judged against this perspective.

So far as the contamination of the upper atmosphere by dust particles is concerned, one difficulty is to compare the effects of artificial dust with the effect of dust from volcanic eruptions. In the past few years, dust collected from the stratosphere, six miles above the surface of the earth or more, has contained chemicals which can only result from atmospheric contamination at the surface of the earth. In other words, pollution has had some effect. But it is also known that the eruption of a single large volcano can instantaneously add much greater quantities of dust to the stratosphere. Such an explosion happened in 1887, and the great explosion of the Krakatoa volcano then left its mark on the succeeding decade in the form of a small reduction in the temperature of the surface of the earth. More recently, in 1963, the eruption of Mount Agung (on the island of Bali) is now known to have produced more dust in the upper atmosphere than had been there before. Moreover, the temperature of the upper atmosphere promptly increased by between six and eight degrees centigrade, showing that extra amounts of energy from the sun were being absorbed high in

The Doomsday Syndrome

the atmosphere and that as a consequence less energy was reaching the surface of the earth. The effects of the Mount Agung eruption were still apparent in the late 1960s, when temperatures in the upper atmosphere were still well above average, but so far it has not been possible to disentangle the effects of that eruption on the climate near the surface of the earth from other causes of climatic change.

In these circumstances, it is hard to know what importance to attach to the measurements which show that, since the 1930s, the amount of sunlight reaching the surface of the earth has decreased by about 4 percent. Has artificial contamination been more serious than volcanic dust? Have there in any case been fluctuations in the output of energy from the sun? And how is it possible to relate the reduced amount of solar energy, itself comparatively small as a proportion, to the likely course of climate change? Not nearly enough is known about the physical processes involved for meteorologists to be sure of the outcome. This is why there is a need for more vigorously directed programs of research on atmosphere dust. In the meantime, however, the fact that a single natural volcano can produce as much dust in the stratosphere as several years' industrial activity is a sign that the fear of calamity is misplaced.

Whether the accumulation of carbon dioxide in the high atmosphere is likely to have serious climate consequences is also an open question. There is no doubt that the proportions of carbon dioxide in the atmosphere have been increasing steadily in past decades. This may well be a result of the burning of fossil fuels. The notion that something like this might happen was first put forward at the turn of the nineteenth century, but fears that such changes could affect the climate have become impassioned only much more recently, partly because of recent success with techniques for sampling the stratosphere.

The average amount of carbon dioxide in the atmosphere amounts to something like three parts in 10,000, and the pro-

The Pollution Panic

portion is increasing by about one-fifth of a percent a year. There is also marked seasonal variation of the concentration of carbon dioxide in the lower atmosphere, which can be 2 percent more in the spring and early summer than in the autumn and early winter. The rate at which carbon dioxide is accumulating is comparable with, but less than, the rate at which carbon dioxide is produced by burning fuel. On the face of things, it looks as if roughly a half of the carbon dioxide produced in this way may stay in the atmosphere. The rest of it is absorbed in the oceans. The fact that this is so is an important sign that the accumulation of the gas need not be irreversible.

Even so, by the end of the century, this tendency could have brought about a quite substantial change in the concentration of carbon dioxide. According to one estimate, by the year 2000, the rate at which fossil fuel is burned will be three times that in 1970. Between 1970 and the year 2000, something like 831,000 million tons of carbon dioxide will have been released to the stratosphere from industrial establishments. If it is assumed that half of this extra amount stays in the atmosphere, then the proportions of carbon dioxide will have increased by nearly 15 percent. On this calculation, there will be an increase of the temperature on the surface of the earth by something like one-half of a degree centigrade. Given that the fluctuation of temperature from one year to another is usually no more than a tenth of a degree, this change could obviously be an important matter.

What is the chance that it will come about? The calculations so far carried out are necessarily concerned with the worst cases. In the first place, it is entirely possible that consumption of fossil fuel will not increase as quickly as the calculations suppose, chiefly because nuclear energy may play a rapidly growing part in the fuel economy of all countries from the 1980s on but also because the demand for energy may grow less quickly than has usually been supposed. There are also mechanisms which naturally scavenge carbon dioxide from the atmosphere.

In a world without industrial activity, carbon dioxide would

The Doomsday Syndrome

find its way into the atmosphere as a result of volcanic activity and the weathering of surface rocks, and would be removed from the atmosphere by the sea and by the growth of plants. If the concentration of the gas increases much above the present, it is likely that there will be an increased tendency for the gas to be dissolved in the sea where, eventually, it is converted either into the shells of sea animals which in turn become rocks such as chalk or directly into marine deposits on the bottom of the sea. But if there is more carbon dioxide in the atmosphere, larger amounts of it will become locked up in the tissues of living plants. It looks as if something like 70,000 million tons of carbon dioxide are consumed each year, between spring and autumn in the northern hemisphere, by the growth of the green vegetation. Especially if there were a tendency towards increased temperature, plant life would become sufficiently more luxuriant to help buffer the climate against the extra carbon dioxide. This could even help with the growth of plankton in the sea and thus with the production of food from the oceans.

None of this implies that there is nothing to worry about. At the same time, however, it is clear that the changes which have been observed are small and by no means irreversible. Moreover, natural phenomena such as volcanic eruptions show quite clearly that there are simple limits to the changes which these phenomena might work on the climate. And, if it turns out that the scale of industrial activity is so great that the accumulation of carbon dioxide threatens climatic change, the same ingenuity could be applied to regulate the concentration of the gas. To be sure, such an intervention would require expensive and historically important changes in industrial practice, but calamity is avoidable. This is why the most urgent need is not for public anxiety nor even for a change in industrial practice but, rather, vigilance and a better scientific understanding of what happens in the atmosphere.

The belief that supersonic aircraft might cause skin cancer is, by contrast, almost a classic case of how a remote and unlikely possibly can become an immediate threat. The possi-

The Pollution Panic

bility that supersonic aircraft might affect the climate of the world has been considered ever since the first supersonic aircraft ventured above 30,000 feet. The first fear, that supersonic aircraft might leave cirrus clouds behind them or even particles of soot, are now known to be improbable bogeymen. The notion that there might be more subtle effects to be considered was put forward in March 1971 by Dr. James D. McDonald of the University of Arizona at Tucson, who argued that the water vapor produced by the supersonic transports would react chemically with the ozone in the stratosphere so as to diminish the amount of ozone and thus to increase the amount of ultraviolet light filtering through to the surface of the earth. The result, he said, would be the equivalent of an extra dose of exposure to the potentially damaging ultraviolet rays from the sun which are already known to cause skin damage among sunbathers.

The uncertainties in this calculation are enormous. To begin with, Dr. McDonald had to assume that there would be a fleet of 500 supersonic-transport aircraft in service, each making four long journeys every day. He made assumptions about the efficiency with which the exhaust fumes would neutralize the natural ozone, assumptions about the rate at which ozone is naturally recreated by sunlight and assumptions about the extent to which reductions in the amount of ozone in the stratosphere would increase the amount of ultraviolet light filtering through. Finally, and without much evidence to help him, he made assumptions about the extent to which ultraviolet light will stimulate skin cancer. The outcome was supposed to be between 7,000 and 40,000 extra cases of skin cancer in the United States alone each year.

Dr. McDonald's argument was quickly destroyed on two grounds—water vapor turns out to be much less destructive of ozone than he had assumed and the link between ultraviolet light and cancer is much less strong than he supposed. As it turns out, much more water vapor is carried into the stratosphere by familiar meteorological processes than could ever be left there by supersonic aircraft. Another objection to this tor-

The Doomsday Syndrome

tuous theory, put forward at the public inquiry before the United States House of Representatives Committee on Appropriations in March 1971, was that the dire effects predicted could be avoided if only each person in the United States would wear a hat or carry a parasol one day during his or her lifetime.

This does not imply that there is nothing more to be said. In August 1971, Dr. Harold Johnston of the University of California at Berkeley argued that even if it is safe to ignore the effects of water vapor on the stratosphere, the gaseous oxides of nitrogen left behind by supersonic aircraft could affect the ozone layers. There is general agreement that not nearly enough is known of the complicated sequences of chemical events which first of all produce the layer of ozone and then determine the way in which foreign chemicals may interfere with it, and this possibility plainly calls for further investigation.

As luck will have it, the tools for further investigation of the upper atmosphere have in the past few years become available. Not merely are there high-atmosphere balloons and rockets to carry instruments above the ground, but there is also a sufficient understanding of the chemistry of the upper atmosphere for the processes which occur to be accurately described. In practical terms, what this implies is that if further investigation should show that supersonic aircraft could seriously affect the climate on the surface of the earth—an exceedingly improbable chain of events—it would be possible to get rid of the nuisance simply by restricting the operation of supersonic aircraft. After all, the ozone layer is contantly being reformed by solar radiation. For the time being, the reluctant airlines now being persuaded by their governments to equip themselves with supersonic transports would undoubtedly consider this curtailment of their freedom to be a much less serious economic risk than the others which they face. And, ironically, it is worth remembering that the sources of possible hazard which Dr. McDonald and Dr. Johnston have described would have been entirely unsuspected even a few years ago, without the understanding of the upper atmosphere that has been acquired by the scientific research.

The Pollution Panic

Against this background, it is surprising that the environmentalists seem not to admit that the influence of human activity on the stratosphere lies squarely within the control of human beings. Dr. Barry Commoner, in *The Closing Circle*, has a moderate statement of the case for worrying about the influence of supersonic transports on the stratosphere:

> *The continued existence of terrestrial life is dependent on the layer of ozone in the stratosphere—a protective device that itself is the product of life. Should the ozone in the stratosphere be reduced, terrestrial life would be seriously threatened by solar ultraviolet radiation. It is unfortunate that some human activities raise this threat. An example is the supersonic transport (the SST).*

What he neglects is that comparatively simple observation should be sufficient to show whether the threat is realistic, and comparatively straightforward regulation of the supersonic aircraft would then be sufficient to make the threat go away again.

In the long run, to be sure, the scale on which industry can be practiced on the surface of the earth will be limited by the amount of heat which is produced. In the past few decades, the consumption of energy has been growing rapidly in all countries of the world—electricity production, for example, appears to double every ten years or thereabouts in most industrial communities. But with energy consumption there is inevitably a waste of energy—automobile engines run hot, electricity generating plants give off nearly as much waste heat as the energy they produce in the form of electricity. The total amount of waste heat is expected to multiply at least five times between 1970 and 2000, and a century after that, if the pace of growth of energy consumption is somewhat maintained, will amount to 10 percent or so of the energy received from the sun. Long before then, it is clear, some densely industrialized areas will have created serious problems for themselves. Already large cities such as New York and London generate enough waste

The Doomsday Syndrome

heat to influence the local climate—the average temperature on Manhattan is two degrees centigrade higher than in the surrounding countryside. But there is no reason why these tendencies should imply calamity, regional or global, or even an intolerable restriction of industrial development. They will, however, create steady pressure to make more economical use of the energy resources of the earth.

What these arguments imply is that the ways in which the atmosphere of the earth might be affected in the foreseeable future by human activities of various kinds are not at present likely sources of disaster. Indeed, the prospect is still remote that industrial activities of any kind could compare in scale with the natural phenomena which have in the past million years or so produced a succession of Ice Ages. To be sure, the uncertainties which abound are a challenge to human understanding but they do not yet constitute a sign that the direction of industrial development should be changed.

Although the fear of world-wide catastrophe has given the past few years their characteristic flavor, the issues on which public attention has most immediately been concentrated are local and much more within the control of governments—in pollution, water pollution and mercury pollution, for example. To say this does not imply, as will be seen, that practical questions about the pollution of the environment have been answered rationally, but many of them provide useful precedents for a class of problems that will persist.

Excitement about mercury in the environment is one illustration of a problem which has sprung into people's minds not so much on the grounds of novelty but because the potential dangers have only recently been recognized. Mercury is rare in the rocks of the earth's crust, which may contain anything between ten pounds and ten tons of mercury in each million tons of rock. Because most chemicals containing mercury are unstable and because mercury itself can be vaporized comparatively easily, small traces of it are widely distributed.

The Pollution Panic

Indeed, the atmosphere contains quite large amounts of it—near most ore deposits, but especially near those which are mined for mercury, there may be as much as a pound of mercury vapor in a cubic mile of air. Elsewhere, and especially away from the land surfaces, the amount of mercury in the air may be less than a thousandth of this. A cubic meter of natural water may contain as much as a ten thousandth of a gram of mercury, and contaminated water supplies may have very much more.

The ubiquity of mercury has become conspicuous entirely because there are now methods of chemical analysis that can measure exceedingly small quantities. But it also known that quite small amounts of mercury can be damaging to people, especially where the mercury is in the form of one of the chemical compounds which are volatile—methyl mercury for example. As bad luck will have it, bacteria which turn chemicals containing mercury into one of the volatile forms occur in the flesh of decaying fish and fish, as it happens, seem to have a predilection for concentrating mercury in their flesh. As little as one milligram of mercury in the daily diet can cause serious damage to the nervous systems of people, which corresponds to no more than one ounce of mercury in the average lifetime. It is no wonder that the unfortunate people who in the nineteenth century worked with mercury compounds in making felt hats were frequently stricken with the nervous symptoms, chief among which is continual trembling, characteristic of the mad hatters.

So is it surprising that mercury contamination has caused all kinds of anxiety in the past years? Since the Second World War, there have been reported outbreaks of disease in the Middle East brought about because seed dressed with mercury compounds was fed either to people or to animals later eaten by people. In 1969, three children in a family in New Mexico were stricken with blindness and the other symptoms of mercury poisoning after their father had fed his pigs on sweepings from a granary floor and had fed the meat of one of the pigs to

The Doomsday Syndrome

his family. The best-known case of a serious accident with mercury is that which in the 1950s killed a total of forty-one people living around the Minamata River in Japan—the river was fed with the effluent from a chemical plant. In this case, the mercury found its way into people by means of fish.

If small quantities of mercury can be damaging, why is it that everybody is not at risk? This is the most moderate question to be asked. The first difficulty is to appreciate the vast difference between the small quantities of mercury which can do a person serious damage and the still smaller quantities to be found in the environment.

Since it became possible to estimate mercury with some accuracy, it has been possible to tell how much mercury there is likely to be in the average diet. In Britain in 1971, the average diet contained less than ten millionths of a gram of mercury, less than 1 percent of the amount likely to be damaging and less than a tenth of the safety limit usually applied. In Sweden, where is has been common for the past fifty years to protect seed corn against pests by dressing it with mercury compound, it is in retrospect clear that the environment has been steadily loaded with mercury. The most eloquent proof of this is that the concentration of mercury in the feathers of goshawks (some taken from museums) has multiplied tenfold between 1915 and 1965. Chemical analysis now shows that the diet of people in Scandinavia living principally on fish may contain nearly half of the amount of mercury regarded as safe and a twentieth of that known to cause serious damage. It is no wonder that the use of mercury in seed dressings has been stopped.

The chief lesson to be learned from this record of mercury contamination is that there is a need carefully to control the uses made of dangerous chemicals such as these but that, so far as can be told, no damage has been done by the small amounts of mercury likely to be present in the environment as a whole. But how is it possible to be sure? That is a natural question. The simplest answer is that the natural occurrence of mercury in the atmosphere and the oceans implies that people now and

The Pollution Panic

in the past have always been exposed to some of the material, which in turn suggests that sufficiently small quantities must be tolerable. Mercury contamination therefore becomes a specific problem in public or even occupational health.

Indeed, it is extraordinary how casual, until recently, have been the ways in which mercury has been used industrially, in the manufacture of chlorine, for example. It follows that authorities with responsibility for public health must be prepared to work with refinements in their methods of control which are almost without precedent. The new development is that they now have at their disposal the techniques with which this can be done safely. As a result, there is every prospect that the environment in which people work will in future be freer from mercury than in the past.

Unfortunately, these moderate lessons have not always been appreciated in the past few years. The wish to believe that the environment is insidiously contaminated seems to explain how, in the late 1950s, Dr. E. J. Sternglass of the University of Pittsburgh was able to win an audience for his claim that as a result of nuclear weapons tests in the United States, something like 400,000 children had died in infancy. Two years went by before the shakiness of Dr. Sternglass's statistics was recognized for what it was—an almost deliberate disavowal of the crucial difference which there may be between the small amounts of environmental poisons which are known to be damaging and the still smaller amounts of them known to be present in the environment.

In almost the same spirit, in 1970, Dr. John W. Gofman and Dr. Arthur R. Tamplin, at one stage employees of the United States Atomic Energy Commission, declared that small quantities of radioactivity released as radioactive iodine and radioactive caesium from civil nuclear power stations would be a hazard to public health. Nobody will dispute that radiation can be damaging and that even small quantities of it can cause some damage in a sufficiently large population, but the damage likely to be done by the quantities with which Drs. Gofman and

The Doomsday Syndrome

Tamplin were concerned is so insignificant compared with the damage done by natural causes that it is intrinsically undetectable.

In the United States in the past few years, there has been a pantomimic wave of overreaction to some of the supposed dangers of environmental contamination. Thus in 1969, the decision was suddenly taken by the then Secretary for Health, Education, and Welfare, Mr. Robert W. Finch, that the synthetic sweetening agents called cyclamates should be taken off the market as food additives on the strength of the first reports from the Bionetics Laboratory, Inc.—which at the same time had investigated the possibility that DDT might produce cancer (see page 132). Because of the statutory force of the Delaney Amendment, which stipulates that in the United States no food additive shall be used if it has been shown to cause cancer when fed either to human beings or to animals, the United States Administration had in principle no choice. But opinions were apparently so divided that the head of the Food and Drug Administration, Dr. Herbert J. Ley, quickly agreed that cyclamates might be used as sweetening agents so long as they were sold as "non-prescription drugs." Only with the departure of Dr. Ley from the Food and Drug Administration at the end of 1969 were cyclamates finally outlawed from American retail trade. A year later, Dr. Charles F. Edwards, the new administrator of the Food and Drug Administration, was hard pressed to explain to a Congressional committee whether or not cyclamates are capable of causing cancer. A good many of the foodstuffs still on the market are probably much more dangerous than the outlawed cyclamates.

Another case of overrapid reaction was the decision in the United States in 1970 to restrict the use of the herbicide called 2,4,5-T. The suspicion was that material could cause birth malformations. The restrictions were prompted by a series of experiments in which fertile hen's eggs were treated with the chemical and found to hatch deformed chicks. The herbicide in question was widely used as a defoliant in Vietnam in the early

The Pollution Panic

1960s, and there is, of course, every reason to fear that in that use, 2,4,5-T might seriously upset the balance of nature.

The experiments by means of which the Food and Drug Administration claimed to have demonstrated that 2,4,5-T is capable of producing birth malformations were, however, primitive to say the best of them. For one thing, there is only the most tenuous analogy between the way in which chemicals can damage hatching chicks and the way in which the same materials can produce malformed infants. But the quantities used in first experiments were also much larger than any to which the people are likely to have been exposed except in acute poisoning. Thus in spite of the pretentious arrangements made in October 1969 by no less an official than the President's Science Adviser, Dr. Lee DuBridge, to restrict the use of this herbicide, a Special Advisory Committee under Professor James G. Wilson informed the Environmental Protection Agency in August 1971 that the herbicide "represents no hazard to human reproduction." The most obvious results of shabby incidents like these is that they give science a bad name. They also make a laughing stock of public officials.

One of the most humiliating of all the recent occasions on which the United States Administration has been required to change its view is on detergents. By the late 1960s, the detergents most widely used in the past two decades were first of all held to be a public nuisance because of the persistent foam which they produced in rivers and sewage works, but afterwards they became a cause for complaint because of their content of phosphate, which is a plant nutrient and therefore one of the reasons why algae grow luxuriantly in polluted lakes. For several years, phosphates have been conspicuous among the targets of the environmentalists, and by mid-1970, several states in North America had already made plans to prohibit the sale of detergents containing phosphates.

The first setback was the discovery that nitrilotriacetic acid (NTA), welcomed as an acceptable substitute in the early months of 1970, was a hazard to human health—it was recog-

The Doomsday Syndrome

nized as such before the year was out. Worse was to follow, for by September 1971 it was plain that the other components in the substitute detergents were themselves either toxic or damaging. The chances now are that there will be a rapid but humiliating return to the detergents which seemed to have brought tranquillity forever to domestic housekeeping in the 1960s.

Contamination may in some situations be such a direct hazard to health or prosperity that it must be prevented at all costs; discharging mercury into rivers and other restricted bodies of water should, for example, be prevented by law. Elsewhere, and for all the excitement there has been and which persists about pollution, the fact remains that the essence of the problems with which public administration is concerned is how much money taxpayers are willing to spend for how much improvement in the environment. One of the reasons why the United States appears to be at the center of the environmental whirlpool is that, in the past, American taxpayers have been singularly unwilling to devote resources to the improvement of the environment, and American politicians have been singularly cowardly in demonstrating that what is called the quality of life is something that must be paid for. There are those who say that the necessary connection between benefit and the cost of it will only be established, in the United States, when taxpayers and their elected representatives have adopted as a crusade and not as a policy in public administration the steady improvement of the quality of the environment. The danger, of course, is that in the process, many of the decisions that are made will turn out to be misguided.

Water pollution and the sad case of Lake Erie is the best starting point. By now, the lake commands as much attention as a supernatural phenomenon. The common complaint is that Lake Erie is dead, but that is a long way from the truth—although there has been a steady decline since the 1930s of the annual catch of fish such as cisco, blue pike and walleye, more common fish such as yellow perch, smelt and carp have

The Pollution Panic

grown in numbers to such an extent that several thousands of tons are taken from the lake each year. What has been happening in Lake Erie, the shallowest of the five Great Lakes, is an acceleration of the natural process of aging by means of which any fresh-water lake can be expected to go through a sequence of well-defined stages until it finishes up as a swamp. The impression is sometimes given that artificial interference has somehow tilted a delicate natural balance in the lake so as to turn fresh water into polluted water, but the truth is quite the opposite. Indeed, it is a great surprise that such a comparatively modest body of water as Lake Erie should be able still to accommodate the sewage from a population of close on thirteen million, much of it without treatment of any kind, and still maintain some semblance of an open lake.

Lake Erie is a communal dumping ground for the cities of Detroit, Cleveland and Toledo. In 1968, when the state of affairs was investigated by the United States Department of the Interior, the total amount of organic waste reaching the lake each year would have required something like 200,000 tons of oxygen if it were to be converted into harmless inorganic materials. As elsewhere in the world, in rivers such as the Thames, for example, the consequence of such a chemical assault on a body of fresh water is that oxygen disappears from large parts of the water mass when the demand for it is greatest, chiefly in the summer.

In Lake Erie, the bottom water is often entirely devoid of oxygen over two-thirds of the lake during the summer season. But the chief cause of oxygen scarcity is not the organic waste, chiefly untreated sewage, fed into the lake, but the large masses of algae which grow and then decay. Where do the algae come from? They need phosphates and nitrates if they are to grow, and in 1968 it seems that something like sixty tons of phosphorus in the form of phosphate was being dumped each day into the lake, most of it in sewage (in which connection treated sewage may be as harmful as untreated sewage). Because of this steady supply of nutrients, Lake Erie is not a funnel

The Doomsday Syndrome

through which waste of all kinds can be channeled towards the sea but, rather, a trap for materials such as phosphates, which accumulate from year, making the problem worse.

What is to be done? Hand-wringing is of very little value. The most immediate need is that the discharge of untreated sewage and other materials which consume oxygen from the lake water should be reduced. At the same time, something will have to be done either to reduce the amount of phosphate fed into the lake or to ensure that it is carried more quickly into Lake Ontario and then to the sea. None of these tasks is impossible—indeed, all of them are well within the scope of contemporary technology. The question to be decided is how much the federal and state governments are prepared to pay for a lake which supports a greater diversity of fish and which does not smell foul in the summer months. In 1968, the Department of the Interior in the United States estimated that the total cost of providing the necessary sewage treatment plant would amount to more than $1,000 million, and that a further $300 million would be needed to cleanse the industrial effluent. So far, nothing like this sum of money has been spent on Lake Erie, which presumably is a sign of the insouciance with which taxpayers approach the problem of cleansing it.

If it should be thought that Lake Erie is alone among conspicuous mementoes of pollution, it is worth recalling that most countries have their own black spots. In Britain, for example, the Thames has been a scandal for well over two centuries. In the 1870s, it was customary for the House of Commons to be protected from the stench from the river by hanging wet sackcloth over the river terrace. As recently as 1960 it was discovered that a small tributary of the Thames, the River Wandle, was more heavily polluted before it entered the main stream than was permissible for the effluent from industrial factories. In recent years, the condition of the river has been measured by the distance over which it is almost devoid of oxygen in the late summer. By means of stricter controls of effluents discharged into the Thames, this distance has shrunk dramatically from

The Pollution Panic

more than twenty miles to much less than ten miles. Elsewhere, the River Trent has until recently been heavily polluted to such an extent that no fish survive. The Rhine has been called an international sewer, but only with some hyperbole—unlike the Thames in its tidal reaches, the Rhine can still support fish. The Baltic Sea, in its way very much like Lake Erie, is being assaulted with too great a load of sewage. In the Soviet Union, Lake Baikal has become an anxiety for very similar reasons.

The only satisfactory basis on which problems like these can be tackled is economic. In the United States, the setting up of the Council on Environmental Quality in 1969 and the Environmental Protection Agency a year later has put flesh on the bones of this principle. By the end of 1970, something like 70 percent of the American population was linked to a sewerage system of some kind—which is another way of saying that the waste from three people in ten was disposed of by more primitive means. One of the technical problems to be dealt with in the United States is that the sewerage system in most cities is designed to handle both domestic waste and run-off from the streets, which means that arrangements have to be made to bypass sewage treatment plants after heavy rainfall.

No less than $48,000 million is reckoned to be necessary if this defect in the present system is to be remedied. Further sums would be needed to bring the present sewage treatment plants up to standard. If all improvements were implemented, the cost each year would be between twenty dollars and twenty-two dollars a person, close on two-thirds of United States expenditure on education. It is, of course, a great puzzle that the population of the United States, which made its way in the world in the 1920s on the strength of its reputation in domestic plumbing, should still be content with such a rudimentary method of disposing of municipal waste. The high estimate of the cost of modernizing the existing system is of course in part a reflection of the way in which the American population is widely dispersed. Elsewhere, the cost would be lower. It remains an awkward truth that any community now seeking to provide

The Doomsday Syndrome

itself with clean water must find ways of screwing up its courage to pay the cost.

Air pollution is an exactly similar case. Populations must again balance benefit against cost, with the complication that air pollution is known to be damaging to the health and survival of people. A comparison of the death rates in American cities in 1960 has shown that a 10 percent decrease in pollution by particles in the air will reduce the death rate as a whole by more than one half of a percent. Decreasing the amount of sulphur in the air has a similar effect. On this view, a 50 percent reduction of air pollution would increase the life expectancy at birth in the United States by between three and five years. Unsure though the calculations may be, there is no doubt that air pollution does considerable damage, and that considerable costs are incurred as a result. It follows that in deciding how much to pay for cleaner air, communities can hope that their purchase is itself an economic benefit.

So how much is it worth paying for cleaner air? The first thing to be said is that the amounts of the gases put out by industrial machinery but especially motor vehicles are really very large. In 1965, for example, automobiles in the United States produced 66 million tons of carbon monoxide and 16 million tons of unburned hydrocarbons of various kinds. In the same year, power stations in the United States produced 13 million tons of sulphur dioxide, more than half of all the sulphur dioxide released into the American atmosphere in 1965. High chimneys make it possible to disperse the smoke and other exhaust gases from industrial plants, so that their consequences are minimized and, at worst, visited on other people.

Motor car exhausts, especially in cities, are harder to deal with, which is why in the United States there has been an increasingly severe limit on the amounts of polluting materials which motor cars may discharge. Thus in 1968, the first year when regulations were introduced, the amount of unburned hydrocarbon in the exhaust from a new car was intended not to exceed 275 parts in a million, the equivalent of 4.6 grams for every mile of travel. By 1975, this standard will have been re-

The Pollution Panic

duced to 0.5 grams a mile. In the same period of five years, the permitted amounts of carbon monoxide in the exhaust from a motor car will have been reduced from 47 grams a mile to 11 grams a mile. The state of California has played a leading part in restricting the quantities of these effluents in the exhaust fumes from motor cars, but there are now serious doubts whether the standards laid down for 1975 are attainable. The chances are that the motor manufacturers will have to be given extra time in which to meet the targets laid down for them. In any case, it now seems likely that something like an extra $250, rather more than 10 percent, will be added to the cost of each new car.

Nobody complains that governments in controlling air pollution must balance benefit against increased cost, chiefly for consumers and taxpayers. In the United States, the program now under way is exceedingly ambitious, and entails by 1975 a reduction of something like 86 percent in smoke emission, 69 percent in sulphur dioxide emission, and 94 percent in the discharge of carbon monoxide to the atmosphere. This is a more spectacular decrease than that by means of which the United Kingdom has cleansed the air of smoke from burning coal—a procedure which has done nothing to control motor car exhausts and sulphur dioxide from industrial combustion but which has at least got rid of London smogs.

In the United States, the full implementation of this air quality control will add 0.1 percent to what otherwise would be the level of prices, which implies an annual cost of $300 million. The objections, which deserve a better hearing than they have had so far, are that in striking a balance between the cost of cleaner air and the potential benefits, little has been done to exploit on behalf of the community such natural resources as the capacity of the atmosphere to get rid of air pollution. Should rural motor cars be restricted with all the severity which is applied to city vehicles? Are taxpayers benefiting to the same extent from the sums now being spent on air pollution from vehicles and from power stations?

The overriding difficulty in this kind of analysis is not so

The Doomsday Syndrome

much that the calculations are necessarily uncertain but that there is no easy way of putting a value on the interest of the community at large. This problem crops up everywhere. In the use of pesticides, for example, farmers have an interest in using larger amounts of DDT on their crops than are in the public interest, but there is also a case for saying that the community as a whole should not dispense entirely with DDT. The interest of the community is different from that of the farmer but not necessarily at odds with it. Here as in the regulation of water and air pollution, public administrations must seek somehow to define in economic terms what constitutes the public good.

Nobody will now maintain that the interests of the community at large are served best when individuals are free to do what they think fit, even if this should entail intolerable air pollution. The error in much of the present wish of the environmentalists that pollution would go away is that the communal interest is the sum of the interests of the same individuals. At this level, however, the problems created by novel forms of pollution are in principle identical with those occasioned in the past by other sources of social nuisance—the conflict of interest between Victorian mill owners eager for the last iota of profit and their workers, hopeful of a life free from occupational disease. Environmental pollution is not so much a threat to the global environment, and the existence of the human race, as a demonstration of the need for the vigorous application of social instruments, laws and taxes, which are as old as society itself.

Ecology Is a State of Mind

□

The once humdrum word ecology has, in the past few years, become a rallying cry for the environmentalists. There are journals with titles such as *Ecology* and *The Ecologist*, dealing with all kinds of issues from the control of exhausts from motor cars to the design of buildings and even cities. In 1971, there was something of a scandal in the United States when a handsomely packaged washing powder called Ecolo-G, which had been marketed with great flair and with the claim that by lacking phosphorus it would help to cut down water pollution, turned out to be not merely a pollutant of a different kind but also ineffectual as a washing powder. These, of course, are occasions when even the environmentalists regret some of the uses to which this respectable label is put, although they have only themselves to blame. There is now a tendency to describe anybody who shakes his fist at innovation—a new airport or a harbor extension, for example—as an ecologist. One professional ecologist told a Congressional committee in 1970 that "ecology is no longer a scientific discipline—it's an attitude of mind."

What is ecology and why is it relevant? The first thing to say is that ecology helped to make natural history scientifically respectable. It goes beyond the mere cataloguing or description of animal and plant species to the understanding of how these manage to coexist.

Of temperate woodland, for example, the ecologists will be the first to point out that animals such as rabbits survive only if there is enough food for them to graze on and, because the poor things need to keep eating all through the year, a variety of vegetation as well. Ideally there should be young tree shoots to feed off in the spring, grasses and, to the chagrin of farmers, ripe grain at the end of the growing season. But rabbits them-

The Doomsday Syndrome

selves are also food for other creatures, foxes, perhaps, or birds of prey such as falcons and eagles. Not all rabbits, of course, die in the jaws of a predator—many escape that fate so as to die of starvation, disease or even old age—yet without the existence of rabbits and similar mammals there would be nothing for the larger carnivores to eat, and they too would disappear. Thus it is that an enforced scarcity of some plant food that may be an essential part of the diet of rabbits can also cause the death by starvation of foxes, carnivores to the last gasp. There is no dispute that the study of this interdependence, hardly more than half a century old, is one of the most important parts of contemporary biology.

The essence of ecology is that different kinds of living things are interdependent. Populations of animals or plants, which happen in some places to coexist, can usually be assumed to have struck a balance of conflicting interests in their mixed community. But are not people animals? Does it not follow that the survival of the human race depends on the maintenance of a natural balance between human beings and the animal and plant species which inhabit the common environment? And must not all living species somehow strike a collective balance with the physical environment—the oceans and the atmosphere?

These are the questions on which the environmentalists tend to hang their proclamation that the human race is endangered by the threat of what is called ecological catastrophe. What they assert is that pollution, the consumption of natural resources and the destruction of species other than human beings is in danger of upsetting the natural balance and thus of bringing the human race itself to an end. As the Ehrlichs say, "Spaceship Earth is now filled to capacity or beyond and is running out of food. And yet the people traveling first class are, without thinking, demolishing the ship's already overstrained life-support systems. The food-producing mechanism is being sabotaged. The devices that maintain the atmosphere are being turned off. The temperature-control system is being altered at random. Thermonuclear bombs, poison gases, and super-germs have been

Ecology Is a State of Mind

manufactured and stockpiled by people in the few first-class compartments for possible future use against other first-class passengers in their competitive struggles for dwindling resources —or perhaps even against the expectant but weaker masses of humanity in steerage. But, unaware that there is no one at the controls of their ship, many of the passengers ignore the chaos or view it with cheerful optimism, convinced that everything will turn out all right."

The question that must be asked of those who preach this kind of ecological disaster is whether the assessment of the facts is accurate. Nobody will pretend that ecological catastrophe cannot be engineered by a sufficiently violent attack on the natural environment. The practical issue, however, is whether present tendencies will bring about such a gloomy end. The specters which the environmentalists have raised so far are not sufficient to suggest that the end of the human race is close at hand.

It is surprising that Darwin, who laid the foundations of ecology, made only incidental contributions to the subject, although he did invent the phrase "the web of life." One obvious difficulty in the attempt to assess the implications of ecology for human survival is to reconcile the two apparently conflicting notions—the concept of evolution in Darwin's sense and the concept of natural balance between species in coexistence. Evolution means change but ecology means equilibrium. For all his many faults, Herbert Spencer, Darwin's uninvited and unwelcomed interpreter, was one of the first to show (without using the words) how the ecological pressures on a community which create the appearance of a balance between competing organisms at any time can also be the driving forces which keep evolution in being. The equilibrium between species, the balance of nature as it is called, is bound to be a dynamic equilibrium. The populations of rabbits and of foxes in a wood may have struck some kind of equilibrium. But their numbers will fluctuate from one year to another as the climate changes or as one species or the other is assaulted by disease, myxomatosis

The Doomsday Syndrome

for example, and in the long run there is even a chance that one species or the other might be eliminated without harm—if foxes could learn to live off game birds, they could do without the rabbits.

Spencer also anticipated some present preoccupations with his declaration that ecology applies not merely to species such as rabbits and foxes but to people as well. In the optimistic second half of the nineteenth century, it was of course natural that he should have taken the view that the human race, like all other species, would inevitably discover an equilibrium with its environment. This sanguine view does not, of course, exclude the possibility that equilibrium for the human race might mean extinction, and that is the side of the coin which many people now seem most eager to display. Instead of the Victorian concept that the web of life is a robust construction within which most species can find a place, it is now customary to emphasize the fragility of the system. Thus in 1970, Dr. Leo Marx was saying that "the philosophical root of ecology is the secular idea that man (including his works, the man-made environment) is wholly and ineluctably embedded in the tissue of natural process. The interconnections are delicate, infinitely complex, never to be severed. If this organic (or holistic) view of nature has not been popular, it is partly because it calls into question many presuppositions of our culture."

There is no doubt that the interconnectedness of living processes has become a powerful practical tool in agriculture and the management of natural resources. Ecologists have done much to show that apparently simple attempts to exploit the natural environment for human ends may be fraught with unexpected complications. In retrospect, for example, it is plain that the way in which the British government invested £35 million in a gigantic scheme to develop parts of Tanganyika for the growth of groundnuts was doomed from the start because it ignored the need of the plants for regular and plentiful rainfall and the opportunities which the new crops would provide for the insect pests and diseases of East Africa. The failure of

Ecology Is a State of Mind

Mr. N. Khrushchev's attempts in the late 1950s to grow wheat on the virgin lands of the Soviet Union is another example of this kind. The lessons to be learned are not that big changes are never possible, but simply that those who wish to change the environment in which they live should begin by understanding it.

The recent past is full of vivid, if less grandiose, illustrations of this principle. Rat-catchers, for example, are frequently frustrated to find that the more successful they are in clearing sewers of adult rats, the more quickly young rats grow to take the places of those killed off. The reason is that in many sewers, the population of rats is limited almost entirely by the food supply. The more rats killed off by poison, the fewer die of starvation and its consequences. To recognize this does not mean that there is no way of getting rid of rats, but merely that efficient rat-catchers should first of all understand the communities which they attack.

Ecology also has an important bearing on ordinary everyday agriculture. As Mr. L. C. Carpenter, vice-president of the Midcontinent Farmers Association in the United States, told Mr. Edmund Muskie's Senate Subcommittee on Air and Water Pollution in April 1971:

> *The American farmer was an ecologist long before the term became fashionable. . . . But the farmer is a practicing ecologist, as distinguished from the growing crop of speechmakers who pontificate from atop their own little towers of theory and opinion. . . . He learns his ecology at first hand, living with and earning a living from the natural interaction of the elements.*

Mr. Carpenter might have added that farmers seem to have learned their ecology the hardest way of all, by learning from one failure how to avoid another. The prairies of the southwestern United States are now much less productive than they used to be because they were grazed too intensively. The duststorms of the 1930s are scandals without precedent. By good

The Doomsday Syndrome

fortune, however, there seems to have been a deliberate attempt to anticipate the ecological consequences of the recent intensification of livestock farming, especially in the United States, but it will be easier to be sure when more time has elapsed.

Although ecology may have its roots in natural history, its methods are frequently similar to those of the exact, or the nearly exact, sciences. Because the pressures on a community of animals or plants can accumulate from one generation to another, apparently unimportant changes in the environment can have far-reaching consequences for living species. This is why ecologists have been forced to develop techniques for computing the consequences of small differences in the environment within which a community of animals or plants must live and this, in turn, is why ecology has now become one of the few parts of biology which is more than fortuitously numerate.

The fact that the web of life is complicated also means that nobody will expect to be able to construct simple theories to describe how it functions. If small changes in the environment may sometimes be followed by a complicated chain of consequences, ecology cannot be asked to produce exact predictions of what will happen. And there are so many different possibilities to be kept in mind that predicting what will happen to some small part of the web of life is a little like predicting what will happen to a national economy if there should be a change in the rate of income tax. Indeed, the models which economists are now fond of constructing to predict, for example, the effect of a change in the rate of corporation tax on the rate of industrial investment are in principle exactly the same as the models which the ecologists might be trying to construct so as to predict, say, the consequences of a plague of myxomatosis among rabbits on the welfare of the foxes which rely on rabbits for at least part of their diet.

This is why ecology is conceptually a little like that technique in the exact sciences called systems analysis. There is a great deal to be learned by somehow arranging that computers can simulate electronically what happens in real life. For all the confidence with which ecologists now move from one public

Ecology Is a State of Mind

forum to another, it remains a stark and shameful truth that they are far less well equipped to attain the goals which they have set for themselves than professional scientists should be. Inside too many ecologists are natural historians trying to burst out.

To the extent that ecology often consists of a demonstration that it is usually harder to make changes in the environment than simple expectations would suggest, there are simple rules of thumb to be learned from the physical sciences and even from sociology. Quite often, in the operation of a complicated system, changes are at least in part self-defeating.

It might, for example, be thought sensible to increase the maximum speed of a bicycle by fitting it with larger wheels. Theoretically, such a device should function reasonably well, but in practice the effort needed to make a bicycle accelerate to the increased speed would be so considerable that for much of its time the machine would be traveling less quickly than if the wheels were smaller. In other words, the time taken to cover a specific distance would not be nearly as great as the theoretical savings might have been, and there may even be circumstances in which bigger wheels would make for a slower journey. It is also relevant that chemists have for more than a century lived with a rule of thumb called Le Chatelier's Principle—if some change is made in one of the changeable characteristics of a chemical system whose several parts are more or less in some kind of stable relationship with each other, the side effects of the change will tend to cancel out the change intended. More dramatic illustrations of the same tendency are to be found in, for example, the provision of new roads so as to get rid of traffic congestion. By now it is a commonplace that any new road will generate traffic so that only a part of its benefit will result in faster travel. The rest will consist of more travel for vehicles that would otherwise have gone by some still slower route or even not have made the journey at all. But in none of these situations are the changes entirely canceled out by the side effects.

What does the new exact ecology say about the interaction

The Doomsday Syndrome

between the human population and the environment in which it lives and which it seeks to manipulate? This is where the arguments begin, for there is a regrettable tendency among ecologists to use the complexities of their subject to complicate answers to this question. In *The Closing Circle,* for example, Dr. Commoner goes so far as to formulate what he calls the four laws of ecology, the first of which is that "Everything Is Connected To Everything Else." On the face of things, this implies that even the most apparently innocuous changes which may be brought about by human beings are a potential threat to their survival.

Complicated though the web of life may be, it is not as complicated as that. If, for example, the remaining blue whales in the South Atlantic were exterminated, the survival of human beings would not be endangered. If the few remaining herds of Père David's deer were to disappear, survival for the human race would not be jeopardized. Since the disappearance of the ice 10,000 years ago, hundreds of animal species have disappeared from the now-temperate regions, and it is still not known whether the mammoths were killed off by human beings or by other causes, possibly climatic. There is no reason to think that the human race as at present organized is less well equipped to survive equally large changes in the composition of the natural environment. On the contrary, it is now better placed than ever to obtain food and other raw materials from a diversity of sources. To say this does not of course imply that people should not lift a finger to preserve species threatened with extinction—there are good reasons for doing so—but there is nothing in ecology to suggest that the survival of the human race is inextricably bound up with, say, the survival of the blue whale.

The striving after complexity by ecologists, although sometimes appropriate, is frequently a departure from good scientific practice. Dr. Commoner, elsewhere in *The Closing Circle,* excuses the inability of ecologists to analyze all the complexities of the web of life by saying:

[168]

Ecology Is a State of Mind

Few of us in the scientific community are well prepared to deal with this degree of complexity. We have been trained by modern science to think about events that are vastly more simple—how one particle bounces off another, or how molecule A reacts with molecule B. Confronted by a situation as complex as the environment and its vast array of living inhabitants, we are likely—some more than others—to attempt to reduce it in our minds to a set of separate, simple events, in the hope that their sum will somehow picture the whole. The existence of the environmental crisis warns us that this is an illusory hope. For some time now, biologists have studied isolated animals and plants, and biochemists have studied molecules isolated in test tubes, accumulating the vast, detailed literature of modern biological science. Yet these separate data have yielded no sums that explain the ecology of a lake, for instance, and its vulnerability.

The implication that the study of isolated animals or plants is ecologically irrelevant is unwarrantable. Is there any reason why the methods of science which have in the past been used to analyze and to account for the behavior of complicated systems such as galaxies containing thousands of millions of stars, chemical molecules made up of thousands of separate particles and materials such as liquids, with their complicated and intricate set of internal interrelations, should not be applied in biology as well? Indeed, the cleverness of modern science consists largely in the case with which complicated systems can be described in simple terms or by simple models. Its flair consists in knowing when simple models are a good guide to understanding and when they are insufficient. If ecologists insist that the complicated problems are the only ones worth solving, they will deny themselves a great deal of the power of the scientific approach. Dr. Commoner's first law of ecology seems to be a good prescription for just that.

The Doomsday Syndrome

Dr. Commoner's third law of ecology gives greater offense. Its simple statement is "Nature Knows Best." The argument is that the natural world is such an intricate assemblage of animal species and natural phenomena that "any major man-made change in a natural system is likely to be detrimental to that system." It is hard to know how far the principle is meant to be carried. Was the invention of clothing by primitive people in some sense detrimental? If it had not been for clothing, it would have been impossible for human beings to colonize the whole of the surface of the earth, with the result that their influence would now be much less marked and some people may think that that would have been an advantage, but it might also have turned out to be the case that if primitive people, 500,000 years ago, had been confined in a narrow ecological niche, they might have been snuffed out by some accident. And is the principle intended to imply that "the man-made change in a natural system" which consisted of, first, the discovery of bacteria and then of means of preventing infectious disease are to be counted as "detrimental to the system"? And if so, what part of the system is detrimentally affected? The bacteria, of course, are confined within a narrower sphere of influence, the people are more free. But there is no reason to think that the survival of living things as a whole or of people in particular is jeopardized by the development of antibiotics and the other defenses against infection.

In short, there is a serious danger that what Dr. Commoner calls the third law of ecology is either an epigrammatic way of saying that those who would exploit the natural environment had better do so perceptively (*vide* the groundnuts scheme) or something close to a nonsense.

Dr. Commoner's particular conclusion from his third law of ecology is that

> given these considerations, it would be prudent, I believe, to regard every man-made organic chemical not found in nature which has a strong action on any one organism as

Ecology Is a State of Mind

> *potentially dangerous to other forms of life.
> Operationally, this view means that all man-
> made organic compounds that are at all active
> biologically ought to be treated as we do drugs,
> or rather as we should treat them—prudently,
> cautiously. Such caution or prudence is, of
> course, impossible when billions of pounds of
> the substance are produced and broadly dis-
> seminated into the ecosystem where it can
> reach and affect numerous organisms not
> under our observation. Yet this is precisely
> what we have done with detergents, insecti-
> cides, and herbicides. The often catastrophic
> results lend considerable force to the view that
> "Nature knows best."*

Does this train of argument really require the backing of such a solemn formulation? Is it not prudent that any techno-logical innovation, not merely those which consist of organic chemicals but also agricultural techniques such as ploughing (which can cause soil erosion) or land clearance (which reduces woodland cover) should be carefully planned in such a way that the consequences can be guessed at if not anticipated exactly? Among the ways in which the human race has influenced the natural environment in the past 500,000 years, the organic chemicals of the past few decades hardly deserve to be singled out for such special attention. And in any case, if the question with which Dr. Commoner is concerned is the survival of the human race, is not the overriding question whether innovation will be detrimental to human beings, not to the ecological system as a whole? Unhappily, in the popular clamor now called ecology, it is often hard to tell just where the participants stand. Are they for people or for foxes?

The belief that human beings are on the edge of disaster for ecological reasons is typified by Dr. Commoner's declaration at the Thirteenth National Conference of the United States National Commission for UNESCO in 1969. He then said:

The Doomsday Syndrome

The ecological facts of life are grim. The survival of all living things—including man—depends on the integrity of the complex web of biological processes which comprise the earth's ecosystem. However, what man is now doing on the earth violates this fundamental requisite of human existence. For modern technologies act on the ecosystem which supports us in ways that threaten its stability; with tragic perversity we have linked much of our productive economy to precisely those features of technology which are ecologically destructive.

What does Dr. Commoner imply? In what ways have human beings put the future of the human race in jeopardy by indifference to the principles of ecology? The environmentalists make a number of specific complaints. The first of them, and perhaps the simplest, is that by changing the environment, and in particular by adding pollutants to the atmosphere and the sea as well as chemical materials to the food chain on which human beings depend, people have so drastically changed the circumstances usually considered to be fit for life that they have endangered their own future. Dr. Commoner says that one of the characteristics of the past few decades is that "technology has had effects on the ecosystem which approach the magnitude of the natural processes themselves." He goes on to explain that the use of bacteria to convert sewage into inorganic and theoretically disposable waste product is often, in part, frustrated by the way in which the materials concerned, chiefly phosphorus, become nutrients for the growth of algae in the rivers and lakes into which they are discharged. He explains that the more intensive use of the Middle West of the United States for raising cattle, with the replacement of free grazing on the prairies by the more deliberate use of land for raising cattle feed, has first of all made it necessary to supply the land with artificial nitrogenous fertilizer but also to find some way of disposing harmlessly of the nitrogenous excreta of the ani-

Ecology Is a State of Mind

mals. But then there are problems with detergents which are not easily degraded by natural processes but which help the growth of algae, the use of insecticides which have often been applied in such a way as to kill off not principally the most obviously damaging pests but, rather, the predator insects which can usually be relied upon to provide a natural check on the size of a population of pests.

A slightly different point, but with the same flavor, is that made by the Ehrlichs: "World agriculture today is an ecological disaster area. We carefully breed out of plants their natural chemical defenses. The poisons usually don't taste good to us, although some of our spices, which we use in small quantities, are produced by plants to serve as insecticides. We plant our crops in tight, simple monocultures, inviting pest outbreaks, to which we then respond with synthetic pesticides, often killing a higher proportion of some nontarget insect populations than we kill of the target population of pests. There are a few hopeful signs that ecologically sound agricultural practices may eventually be adopted, but so far the general trend has been in the opposite direction."

The fears of the ecologists go further than this. In a remarkable declaration to a symposium at the Brookhaven National Laboratory in 1969, Dr. Garrett Hardin parried the ecological doctrine that attempts to change the ecosystem yield not merely direct effects but side effects with a number of paradoxes. Of the green revolution in India, for example, he said that "in the long term, we can't conquer famine with food. . . . The natural reproduction rate is directly proportional to the supply of food, within realistic limits." He also argued that Indian agriculturalists would be unable to prevent the specialized strains of wheat now available to them from succumbing to the specialized plant diseases.

> *We mean well in India, but we are making her situation worse. When the present round of well-intended efforts comes to an end, what will we find? That we have bought a few*

The Doomsday Syndrome

*years' moratorium with our improved varieties
of grains, thus raising the suffering population
of India to a higher level and increasing the
magnitude of the ultimate catastrophe. The
improved grains have unfortunately given another excuse to those who would criminally
deny the truth that we cannot solve population
problems by technological means.*

How realistic are these fears? Although by now there is a
long list of occasions on which attempts to modify or to exploit
the natural environment have failed through ignorance of ecology, these particular offenses against the natural environment
do not threaten the survival of the human race. Even if the
pollution of Lake Erie should continue unabated (and there are
good reasons why it should be stopped), that need not imply
that ecological catastrophe will follow or even that the survival
of the human race will thereby be jeopardized. What the third
law of ecology implies is that the thirteen million people living
around the lake would be cleverer, and would be able to live
more economically as well, if they would change their ways, but
that is just a different conclusion. And if the new cereals are
more vulnerable to plant diseases than the less intensively bred
varieties previously in use, the moral is, for the time being at
least, not that the survival of the human race is threatened but
that the plant breeders must be on their toes.

The pollution of fresh-water lakes and estuaries is also high
on the list of supposed causes of ecological catastrophe. The
first thing to say is that extravagant insults to the natural environment such as that which has characterized the pollution of
Lake Erie in the past half century are so gross that the remedy
is to be found in elementary public administration, not ecology.
To be sure, there are more subtle problems that would repay
careful study. Are the vast quantities of algae which form in the
lake in late summer really controlled by phosphate or is some
other nutrient more important? Off the Atlantic Coast of the
United States, it is already clear that nitrates are more important, but traces of metals may be even more critical. What bene-

Ecology Is a State of Mind

fit would there be in dredging the lake bottom for the sediments rich in phosphates and nutrients which at present serve as reservoirs of nutrients for the growth of algae, but which might be used as fertilizers? Are there ways in which the lake waters could be made to empty themselves more quickly over Niagara, preferably without reducing the height of the falls? What are the chances of restocking Lake Erie with fish more valuable than those now harvested there, to the tune of 25,000 tons a year? It is by now apparent that the digging of the Welland Canal a century ago to bypass Niagara has put an end to some of the most valuable fish in Lakes Huron and Michigan by providing a passage for the sea lampreys, a kind of fish leech, and there can be no assurance that similar influences may not be responsible for the changed character of the fish in Lake Erie (where sea lampreys have nonetheless failed to find a footing). While steps are being taken to prevent the wanton pollution of the lake, the Lake Erie ecologists should occupy themselves with pertinent questions like these, for there is no cause to abandon hope.

The avoidance of trouble such as that which has beset Lake Erie is splendidly illustrated by the record of the San Francisco Bay in the past twenty years. In many ways, this body of water connected with the sea by the narrow Golden Gate is more vulnerable than Lake Erie. The water is shallow—two-thirds of the bay (nearly 700 square miles) is less than eighteen feet deep. The surrounding population is large and growing quickly. The region contains one large naval port and several commercial harbors, and there are industrial plants of various kinds as well. Yet the quality of water in San Francisco Bay has so improved in the past twenty years that shrimp are returning, and the fishing has improved. There are only a few signs of oxygen deficiency in the summer months, chiefly around the mouths of tributaries carrying effluents, and occasional crops of algae are to be seen in the same places.

Much of the credit for these improvements is attributable to the steps which municipal authorities have taken to prevent the discharge of raw sewage into the bay. Yet the defense of San

The Doomsday Syndrome

Francisco Bay has become so sensitive that at the public hearing held in San Francisco in August 1969 by the United States House of Representatives Committee on Government Operations, there were powerful pleas that river discharges into the bay should not be diverted for irrigation elsewhere in California for fear that the natural turbidity of the bay should be reduced. This, the argument goes, would mean that sunlight would be able to penetrate farther down beneath the surface of the water, thus helping with the growth of algae, while there would be fewer solid particles on which phosphates and other materials would be absorbed.

In the event, the conservationists were rewarded not with a guarantee that the rivers would flow as they used to but with strict prohibitions on further encroachment by land reclamation, the most immediate threat to the integrity of the bay. One of the ironies of this situation is that the sediments carried into the bay amount each year to an average of about a sixth of an inch for the whole surface of the bay, which means that many parts of it will in any case have disappeared naturally within a century.

The case of San Francisco Bay is a good illustration of the conflict of interests which must attend the management of the natural environment. In 1969, the demand for extra land within the bay came chiefly from airport and harbor authorities, but there is also a continuing demand from industrial interests for small parcels of land within the bay or on the marshes which surround it (many of which are in any case used for manufacturing salt by solar evaporation).

What measure can there be of the conflicting interests? The potential value of the bay's surface can be guessed at by supposing that roughly a half of the bay could be filled without much cost, and that the land thus obtained would be sold for a profit of roughly $1,000 an acre. In other words, the potential economic value of the bay's surface is roughly $200 million. The view implicit in the decision not to sanction further land reclamation is that the availability of this capital resource

Ecology Is a State of Mind

would not be sufficient compensation for the losses that would be entailed.

What are the interests on the other side? At the public inquiry in 1969, much was made of the possibility that a shellfish industry could be restarted, bringing an annual income of something like 10 million a year. It is also beyond dispute that the bay and the rivers which feed into it provide spawning grounds for salmon which are afterwards distributed over much of the Pacific Coast of the United States. There is some uncertainty about the climatic effect of such a large body of water so near a large city, but there are some who hold that the presence of the bay contributes in important ways to the climate of California. These, however, are comparatively small and intangible benefits.

The real reason why San Francisco Bay is for the time being at least to be preserved is that the people who live nearby like it the way it is. Whether their decision would be the same if the economic value of the reclaimed land were, say, a hundred times the present value and if there were ways of making sure that the economic benefit became a communal benefit is another question. The fact that it has not been discussed does however, suggest that, as well as the construction of a physical model to follow and sometimes to predict the consequences of changing such things as the flow of water into the bay, there is also a case for constructing an economic model to tell just how this natural resource should be used most effectively. The conservationists need not be afraid, for in present form there is little doubt that the prudent course is to keep the bay much as it is.

In a rational world, the balance between conservation and exploitation would be struck in the opposite direction in the strange case of the Alaskan pipeline. Since the early 1960s, it has been clear that the North Slope of Alaska was bound to be one of the world's most prolific oilfields. Since 1968, oil companies have been exploring territory leased to them for substantial sums of money by the government of the United States,

The Doomsday Syndrome

the title owner of offshore mineral rights. Since early in 1969, a consortium of oil companies has been anxious to start work on a pipeline to carry petroleum to the southern coast of Alaska, crossing on the way several hundred miles of what is literally the frozen north—terrain which is technically called tundra and which appears to be solid only because the surface layers down to the bedrock are saturated with water which has frozen and which melts only exceptionally. Vegetation is sparse and highly specialized to the region. The principal animal is the caribou, and one of the fears occasioned by the pipeline project is that its migration from east to west might be impeded by a long strip of ground somehow freed from ice.

Since early in 1969, successive Secretaries of the Interior in the United States have been haunted by the Alaska pipeline. The first proposal to bury it would have entailed a progressive melting of the frozen ground in the neighborhood, sometimes to a depth of 100 feet or more, with the attendant danger of vast flows of mud from one place to another. But even variations of the construction scheme in which the pipeline would have been carried above ground for much of its length have led to fears of permanent damage to the tundra, for even building roads across this frozen ground can by itself permanently scar the land.

How then should the issue be decided? The view that permanent damage to the permafrost is intolerable and should not be allowed, which has so far held up the construction of the pipeline, contains the belief that much of Alaska must perpetually remain untouched and unexploited. As things are, however, not enough is known of the necessarily delicate balance of climate in the far north to be sure that the tundra will remain in perpetuity even if its pristine condition is preserved. After all, the whole natural phenomenon is a legacy from the Ice Age, and it is known that several parts of the world are still recovering from the trauma of being buried in ice. May not the permafrost of Alaska be less permanent than it sometimes seems? In the circumstances, might it not be the best strategy

Ecology Is a State of Mind

for all concerned, exploiters, the exploited and the United States government, to devise a route from north to south in Alaska—not necessarily the shortest route—which could be used for extracting oil in the years immediately ahead and which in the future would become a channel within which to confine future exploration of Alaska?

Compared with these vast projects, most of the public issues in which considerations of ecology arise are comparatively minor affairs. In the late 1950s, when the first nuclear power stations were being built in Britain, there were detailed attempts to predict how living things would be affected by the large amounts of cooling water which the power stations would discharge. The second nuclear power station to be built, at Bradwell on the River Blackwater in Essex, was held to be capable of affecting the oyster fisheries lower down the estuary and its construction was opposed on precisely those grounds. In the event, the oysters in the river appear to have been unaffected by the power station, the warm water from which seems also to have been ineffectual in protecting the Blackwater oysters from the severe winter of 1962–1963.

Conflicts like these, between public authorities and private developers on the one hand, and local communities on the other, are unavoidable in the modern world, and indeed there is a need for allowing them to be more explicit. In reality, however, ecology as such is usually less relevant than other considerations—the amenities that would be destroyed by the proposed development or even simply the inclinations and prejudices of the local community.

Thus the decision not to extend the runways at New York International Airport into Jamaica Bay turned principally on a calculation of how much extra noise would be visited on the local people. Although the committee of the National Academy of Sciences which in 1970 put forward this recommendation had much to say about the ecology of the impoverished communities of plants and animals that seem somehow to have survived the horrors of Jamaica Bay, and although the com-

The Doomsday Syndrome

mittee advocated the construction of artificial beaches in the neighborhood—a proposal which the New York administration is unlikely to take seriously—even ecologists would have been unwilling to go to the stake for the sake of the marginal forms of life which the fetid water supports. In other words, the case of Jamaica Bay is not so much a study in the conflict between exploitation and preservation of the natural environment but a vivid illustration of a failure of city planning. Why build a large international airport and then allow people to live so close to it that it cannot be developed?

There is therefore no basis for Dr. Commoner's declaration that "modern technologies act on the ecosystem which supports us in ways that threaten its stability" in the long record of cases in which those who wish to change the environment are legitimately in conflict with those who wish to keep it as it is. The problem is how to strike a balance between a variety of interests and, as always, the economics of communal choice play a decisive part. Much the same can be said, as it happens, of the other potential sources of ecological catastrophe over which heads have been shaken in the past few years.

The fears of Dr. Ehrlich and Dr. Hardin that specialized forms of agricultural plants may invite calamity because they are potentially more susceptible to plant diseases can be entertained only if they are isolated from wider considerations. In North America in the past few decades, there have been several occasions on which crops of wheat have been attacked by rust and crops of maize have been attacked by corn blight. The plant diseases have been able to make headway only because the plants which they attacked were genetically uniform. If one corn plant was vulnerable to a fungus of some particular strain, the chances were high that neighboring plants would be similarly affected. Thus the ecologists are right to say that genetically more diverse crops are bound to be less susceptible to plant diseases. The penalty, of course, is that a mixture of genetic types is bound to be less productive.

In other words, to grow the same amount of wheat or corn

Ecology Is a State of Mind

in which disease resistance stems from genetic diversity requires more land and greater harvesting costs. Especially in North America, where the acreage under the plough is declining steadily as the years go by, it would be feasible to turn back the clock and abandon the specialized strains of cereals. The argument for not doing so is that costs of production would then be substantially increased. In any case, damaging though plant diseases can be to harvests, there is no more reason to fear that they need go uncontrolled than there is to fear that infectious diseases that sweep the human population like medieval plagues will again be a hazard to human survival. The question therefore is not whether highly selected strains entail a greater risk of plant disease but how best to balance the cost of occasional infestation against the extra cost of producing less intensively selected crops.

For all these reasons, there is little evidence at present of discernible threats to the survival of the human race in the lessons to be learned from ecology. The questions with which ecology is intimately bound up are much more practical and bear directly on knowing how the human race should arrange most efficiently to manage the natural environment. Knowing when to leave well enough alone is an important part of this, but inaction is much less often the correct solution than it is supposed to be. And one of the most immediate dangers, the long record of ecological mishap notwithstanding, is that too slavish a concern for what is thought to be ecology will inhibit people from taking prudent steps to safeguard the future of the human race.

What does ecology have to say about the policy which human beings should follow in the conservation of other species? The question is important for several practical reasons but also because it should help in deciding what should be the relationship between the human race and the natural environment in its entirety.

For Britain, Africa has been a principal battleground for

The Doomsday Syndrome

conservationists, almost as if collective guilt about the way in which Africans were treated when the British Empire was strong might be assuaged by a proper concern, at this late stage, for the animals which are uniquely to be found there. In the past few years, a great many organizations, the World Wildlife Fund chief among them, have done valiant work in showing just how precarious is the plight of some of the great mammals of Africa. Some species, antelopes especially, have diminished markedly in number. Others—elephants, for example—have become a public nuisance because they are apparently unwilling to stay within the territories allotted to them by the local governments. One of the most important lessons so far apparent is that conservation is in no way synonymous with attempts to save the lives of individual animals. Rather, the objective is to ensure that wild populations protected from hunters and other predators do not grow so quickly that they run into the old Malthusian trouble of being too many for the food supply.

In Britain, to be sure, where the primeval fauna has long since disappeared, conservation usually entails that groups of volunteer bird watchers band together to make sure that some isolated osprey nest is not raided by egg collectors, but this is not a problem for ecologists but for men with strong arms. And there is no way of making sure that the small mammals— weasels and badgers, for example—are preserved from the damage which can be done to them not so much by predators or poachers but by motor cars on country roads. To be sure, there are some parts of Britain where animals can be too numerous—red deer have become a nuisance in Scotland, much to the surprise of the Forestry Commission whose land they inhabit. It remains, however, something of a puzzle that until a few years ago the same Forestry Commission was so alarmed by the appearance of gray squirrels in its forests that it used to pay a bounty for the tails which huntsmen were able to deliver.

In the United States, conservation began at home at the end

Ecology Is a State of Mind

of the nineteenth century and was fanned by the enthusiasm for the American way of life which President Theodore Roosevelt generated during his first term of office. At that time it was clear that even the rich and varied wildlife of North America would not long survive the hunters who killed off the great herds of bison in the prairies (partly in an attempt to starve out the Indians) and who also eradicated the huge flocks of passenger pigeons in the closing decades of the nineteenth century. In the past few decades organizations, such as the Audubon Society and the Sierra Club, have done wonders to persuade the United States Administration to go beyond the setting up of the great national parks in the early decades of this century and there now appears to be good reason to hope for the establishment of a substantial acreage of more or less primeval wilderness. No part of Wetsern Europe is as well provided.

In the past few years, conservationists have managed somehow to preserve animals that seemed well on the way to extinction. Père David's deer now seems to be safe, as are the primitive Caucasian horses that have managed to survive in Eastern Europe. A substantial herd of bison has been kept alive in North America. Urgent, but still somewhat ineffectual, attempts are being made to preserve the communities of manatees which live off the coasts of Guyana, especially now that it seems possible that these placid and defenseless animals might help with the clearing of water hyacinths—a great waterweed—from canals and waterways in the tropics. Although it remains a haunting truth that a long list of animal species is threatened with extinction, the successes of the past few years suggest that preserving threatened species more or less in their natural surroundings should not be entirely impossible.

But why should governments and their taxpayers take all this trouble to preserve communities of wild animals and plants from harm? The case for conservation is powerful but often muddied by too much sentiment. It goes without saying that there are many circumstances in which conservation may bring immediate benefits. In the past few years, it has seemed

The Doomsday Syndrome

that many of the commercial fisheries of the northern hemisphere are being fished too intensively (see Chapter 3), and this is a field in which ecologists have an important contribution to make to the future of an important source of food for human beings.

The survival of as great a diversity of animal and plant life as possible is also important for the proper understanding of living things. Nobody at this stage can be sure that the way in which desert animals or plants adapt to their surroundings has no lessons for the ways in which domesticated animals or cultivated plants should be managed in modern agriculture.

Techniques of animal and plant breeding now available will make it possible to graft on to the commercial animals and plants characteristics which have enabled wild species of all kinds to survive in circumstances in which commercial animals and plants do not thrive well. One of the acknowledged goals of many animal breeders is to develop a domestic animal for central Africa that will somehow combine the productivity of temperate cattle with the resistance to tsetse fly disease, trypanosomiasis, to which many wild animals in Africa are immune.

These arguments by themselves are enough to justify vigorous and imaginative programs for the conservation of animals and plants. Money spent on work like this is every bit as important as the capital expenditure which most governments seem now prepared to make in the capital equipment of modern science—rockets and particle accelerators, for example.

Yet some species, it must be acknowledged, are economically neutral. Usually these have in common with human beings the characteristic of being at the top of some food chain—they consume food derived from simpler species but they are not themselves important means of sustenance for other species. The whales of the southern oceans are one vivid illustration, but even so it is a scandal that the International Whaling Commission, which is ostensibly responsible for conserving the stocks of whales, should so have mismanaged its affairs since the 1930s that many species are on the way to extinction.

Ecology Is a State of Mind

Blue whales have been killed off. After intensive fishing in the late 1930s, when tens of thousands of them were killed each year, there seems to have been a modest recovery of the stocks of blue whales after the Second World War, but by the mid-sixties they had disappeared. Fin whales, to which the whaling boats have more recently turned their attention, killing some 30,000 a year throughout the 1950s and 1960s, are now in danger of extinction. The smaller animals, sei whales and sperm whales, are the next in line. Theoretically, the International Whaling Commission seeks to limit the numbers of whales that its member nations will kill in each year, but for one thing there is no means of policing this agreement, and in any case the limits are habitually set well above those which are likely to ensure that stocks survive.

For this reason, it was brave, if by itself useless, of the United States to have declared in 1971 that American vessels would no longer be allowed to hunt for whales—only if there is an international agreement on a moratorium will such restraint help to ensure that some whales survive. And without some agreement of this kind, the best hope for the survival of at least some species of whales is that their increasing scarcity will so increase the cost of hunting them that the chase will become uneconomic. The failure to conserve stocks of whales in the past several years has in other words meant the end of one kind of fishing industry and, at the same time, the disappearance of at least some species of animals which are unique.

On the other side of the coin are the species which seem universally to be recognized as pests. Nobody has a fond word to say for rats, for example. Even though their activities as scavengers may have the virtue of removing some items of waste organic matter—food, for example—that would otherwise become situations in which bacteria might multiply, their vast consumption of agricultural produce, the damage they do to woodwork and even the fact that one species of rat is probably the only way in which bubonic plague could sweep across the earth again means that rats have few defenders. Mosquitoes, tsetse flies and locusts are some of the other creatures for which

The Doomsday Syndrome

there is hardly a good word to be said. Although the prospects of eliminating these species altogether are probably remote, the ideal place for them is in a zoo. And although it is now customary in the United States to lament the destruction of the passenger pigeons, the arrival of one of these great flocks must have been so much like a plague of locusts that it is unthinkable that the birds would be tolerated now.

Although in the past few years there has been an entirely welcome tendency (at least among conservationists) to regard conservation as an instrument in the harmonious exploitation of the natural environment by people, it must be acknowledged that they have not always been sufficiently hard-headed in doing this. In the late 1960s, for example, a great many British botanists were up in arms because of a proposal to build a reservoir at a place that would flood isolated communities of alpine flowers probably established in this remote corner of Northumberland before the melting of the last Ice Age. As it happens, identical but much larger communities of alpine flowers still flourish in Switzerland. There may have been valid reasons why the building of the reservoir should have been turned down because it interfered with recreation, and there is evidently some interest in the question of whether the alpine flowers in Cow Green are relevant in any important way to the disappearance of the British ice cap, but there is no danger that the flooding of the valley will prevent people from understanding how communities of alpine flowers survive. The important issue is not the preservation of Cow Green but an assurance that a representative and large community of these plants is preserved in circumstances much more like those to which it is accustomed. The Swiss Alps are the obvious place for such a reservation.

Another difficulty is that conservation is increasingly bound up with what might be called the leisure industry. In the United States, for example, there has been some concern in the past few years about agricultural encroachment on the glacial ponds in the northern states such as Wisconsin. The issue is important

Ecology Is a State of Mind

because the ponds provide summer quarters for much of the waterfowl population of North America. Now that the ecological importance of these ponds is recognized, it seems to have been agreed that most of them should be preserved, but it does not follow that the populations of waterfowl will flourish, for hunting is increasingly popular in the United States. There is no way of knowing how many birds are killed each year by hunters in the United States, but the annual sale of gun licenses exceeds a million. There are even reports that some waterfowl are dying from lead poisoning acquired by swallowing lead shot picked up from the water courses in the northern states. In the circumstances, ought not ecologists and conservationists devote at least some of their energy to the task of estimating how much easier it would be to conserve the essential stocks of wild animals if hunting were prohibited?

In the long run, the overriding question is to know what limits ecology imposes on the freedom of the human race to exploit the natural environment. The old-fashioned concept of "mastery over nature" may be an anachronism, but people are not nearly as much at the mercy of the environment as Dr. Rene Dubos suggested when he wrote, "Any attempt to shape the world and modify human personality in order to create a self-chosen pattern of life involves many unknown consequences. Human destiny is bound to remain a gamble, because at some unpredictable time and in some unforseeable manner nature will strike back."

Just where should modern society draw the line that separates safe exploitation from potential danger? The first thing to be said is that ecologists could do much more to help. Quite properly, for example, there has been a growing recognition that the area of shallow sea and brackish water in which fish and marine animals spend a large part of their life cycle has been diminishing. Land has been reclaimed or turned into marsh. Rivers have been kept in narrow channels, thus making estuaries smaller. And near harbors, natural silting has been

The Doomsday Syndrome

prevented by dredging. So why not arrange that suitable parts of the coastline should be made into estuarine breeding grounds? In short, why not artificially create the environment in which young fish might breed? That is one task for ecologists.

The pressure of the growing population on the limited amount of ocean beach also raises the question why steps are not taken to create beaches on which people can sunbathe and from which they can swim. To be sure, the feasibility of projects like these will depend entirely on the cost, but there are several places in the world where shoaling is already a serious problem and where imaginative construction might cheaply provide more bathing space. In much the same spirit, there is no reason to gainsay attempts to drain polluted lakes, to increase the productivity of some parts of the ocean either by artificial fertilizers or by the diversion of ocean currents and—less easily—to hope to affect the climate in some localities by planting trees in strategic places (as has been tried in Israel and the Soviet Union without much success).

Schemes like these are merely the modern equivalents of the ways in which, for the past two million years, people and their primitive ancestors have set out to change the surface of the land. By their capacity to attempt such changes, people have been from the start distinct from other species. To be sure, beavers in their time must have done a great deal to change the appearance of the land in North America, but that was instinctive and repetitious behavior. It is also true, of course, that in the past a great many human interventions in the environment have backfired. The early attempts to clear primeval forests by the use of fire must often have been counterproductive. Yet there is no reason to complain at the way in which dams such as the Aswan Dam are known to fill with silt and eventually become unproductive of electricity—this, after all, is what used to happen to beaver dams on a much smaller scale. And who in the United Arab Republic will scoff at the prospect of a plentiful supply of electricity for the next half century and then, when Lake Nasser is full of silt, a huge fertile plain on which crops will grow?

Ecology Is a State of Mind

But is there not a danger that in seeking to manipulate the natural environment, human beings will become so isolated from other components of the web of life that they will be vulnerable to some hidden danger? This is the fear underlying a good deal of the speculation about ecological catastrophe. And it is true, of course, that a good part of the machinery of modern society, at least in industrialized communities, is intended to isolate people from ecological pressures. Steps are taken to ensure whenever possible that children do not die in infancy. Much of modern medicine is intended to isolate people from death in early life, which means that the processes of natural selection in the old Darwinian sense are muted. Does this in particular imply that the human race is accumulating a genetic inheritance that will eventually bring about catastrophe? The dinosaurs, after all, have gone for good.

To turn back the clock and to connect the human race more intimately with ecological pressures would be possible only by creating a situation in which infant mortality was more frequent and in which natural diseases of the kind which afflict animals in the wild were also rife among people. The reasons why human populations have chosen to escape from circumstances like these are not merely that individuals prefer to live as long as possible, but also that the economic burden of illness in a humane society is something to be avoided on strictly economic grounds. Human populations, in other words, cannot return to the primitive condition in which their future development in all senses, social and genetic, is determined by the pressures from the natural environment and the influences of other species, most of them competitive.

From this point of view, statements such as that of Dr. Leo Marx (see page 164) that the human race is "ineluctably" a part of the "tissue of natural process" are, at best, exaggerations. The truth is that the qualities which allowed the early ancestors of modern man to be successful—the capacity both to climb and to walk, the capacity to use tools and the capacity to learn—have made it possible and also inevitable that people should become, to some extent, detached from the ordinary

The Doomsday Syndrome

pressures of ecology. If this is the mark of Cain, it is not something that many people complain about.

What then will replace for human beings the ecological pressures to which other species are exposed? Stark eugenics is neither necessary nor yet desirable. For the time being at least, there is no evidence that the human race has failed to profit from its relative detachment from the rest of the natural world. To the extent that the ecologists deny this proposition, and even pretend that human beings and, say, rabbits occupy equivalent positions in the natural scheme of things, they are false prophets. Their most pervasive influence could yet be that they will undermine the capacity of people to do for the human race what natural selection and ecological pressures do for other species and, in particular, deliberately to take steps to ensure survival.

Man-made Men

□

Ever since Aldous Huxley described his vision of what the future might be like in *Brave New World,* biological research has seemed a kind of Pandora's box. This may be inevitable. Research which is directly concerned with the processes of life, survival and death is bound to stir up all kinds of emotional reactions, not merely among bystanders but among the researchers as well. It was much in this spirit, for example, that the Victorians were intrigued by the development of automatons. Is it really possible to substitute machinery for living things? But this preoccupation is the public reflection of what used to be a serious, and often bitter, dispute among professional scientists on the question whether living things are inherently distinct from inanimate things. The first chemical synthesis (by Wöhler in the 1820s) of urea, previously thought to be essentially lifelike in character, did not put an end to the doctrines of the vitalists that there is indeed an essentially distinctive quality in living things.

Only in the past few years, and in particular since the early 1950s, has it become clear that living things are indeed simply assemblages of chemical molecules, which differ from the chemical molecules found in inanimate materials merely by their complexity. And if the chemical components of living things are inherently complicated, so too are the ways in which these chemicals are put together to form cells and the other components of living tissues. So, does it follow that life itself has become something which can be accounted for in terms of ordinary chemistry and physics? This question is at least partly responsible for the fear of the implications of biological research which has characterized the past few years. The fear is, as will be seen, unnecessary, but it is ironical that it should have come to a head when biological research and its applications in medicine have helped enormously to liberate people from the most inhumane of all terrors—avoidable death.

The most persistent, awesome speculation about biological research is that it may help in due course to modify the nature of human beings. It is, therefore, important to acknowledge that this train of thought has often been optimistic. The distinguished geneticist, the late H. J. Muller, was, for example, a believer, as recently as 1967, in the possibility of developing a genetic material which would in some sense spell perfection for human inheritance. M. Jean Rostand, in *Can Man Be Modified?* similarly took the view that such modifications of human inheritance as there might be would tend to be beneficial in character.

Only in the past few years have these speculations taken a more gloomy turn. The very term genetic engineering, now widely used to describe the modification of inheritance in people and other organisms, is in itself a sign that the prospect is distasteful. Sometimes it is held that genetic engineering will be used for purposes which are frankly sinister. Sometimes it is held that even attempts to use genetic engineering to improve the human condition as, for example, by the removal of hereditary diseases, are likely to have unforeseen and unwelcome consequences.

Transplant surgery has become another focus for discontent, in part at least because some of the first attempts to transplant kidneys and hearts from one body (living or dead) to another (still alive) were mishandled. But the public unconscious seems also to have taken fright at some of the ethical problems raised by the whole question of transplant surgery. There are questions of when a person should be considered dead, and whether it is permissible to subject a patient who is already sick to a surgical operation which entails a high degree of risk so as to treat a condition which, left to itself, would bring death by natural causes much less traumatically. Then there are questions of which patients should receive transplants when the supply of organs is less than the demand.

Artificial fertilization is still more provocative. This, of

Man-made Men

course, is the acting out of Aldous Huxley's test-tube baby factory. Several laboratories are engaged on work like this, and the consciences of all kinds of people, professional scientists and others, are engaged. The most obvious line of development is artificial fertilization, followed by artificial nurture for the embryo that results. A variant on this theme is the development of identical individuals from single cells of living tissue—still very much a piece of science fiction, where human beings or even domestic animals are concerned. Evidently many people's imaginations have run cold at the prospect that this technique of cloning, which works well enough for carrots, should be used to produce either a clone of Albert Einstein or—some think this more probable—a clone of worker people, the human analogues of the biological slaves in insect communities.

A particularly horrid, but unreal, vein of speculation has been stimulated by a line of research opened up at the University of Oxford in which cells from quite different species have been fused together and have remained alive. Hybrid cells have been made from human beings and mice, and the shadow of Dr. Frankenstein has trotted through the pages of popular newspapers and magazines. Mules and hinnies are unnatural enough, and there has been a tendency to brood on the problems of quite dissimilar species such as mice and men. Will the technique of fusing cells together serve as a method of making living creatures to some predetermined specification? By comparison with the shadows cast by this development, the consequences of techniques for helping to decide whether the results of a routine fertilization of a human egg will be a boy or a girl are to be regarded as a comparatively benign development. Luckily, as will be seen, all these are unrealistic fears.

So too are those which spring from the research which in the past few years has begun to throw light on the way in which the nervous system functions. Will a detailed understanding of the chemicals which help to transmit messages from one nerve cell to another, or which sometimes inhibit the transfer, lead to the development of drugs which can alter behavior or mood in

The Doomsday Syndrome

predetermined ways? Will it be possible, by injecting a chemical or implanting an electrode, for some people to control the ways in which others behave? These are only some of the suggestions which have been made in recent years to impart a sinister character to biological research. These are also profoundly mistaken.

Two general principles must therefore be spelled out. First, the many lines of research which customarily evoke this list of horrors are among the marvels of modern science. If there is any truth in the proposition that intellectual understanding is spiritually beneficial, these developments cannot be scorned. But they are also squarely in the mainstream of the tradition that medicine, and the biological research from which it springs, should be curative and humane. One of the most powerful incentives in the recruitment of people to these professions is the belief, sometimes cruelly disappointed, that the practice of medicine is a social virtue. How is it possible that such a body of do-gooders should turn out to be as malevolent as their critics pretend?

The most obvious thing to say about genetic engineering and the fears which it occasions is that there is no difference in principle between the attempt to remedy the deficiencies with which a person is born and the practice of medicine in its most mundane forms. Both are attempts to avoid remediable handicap and untimely death. In this spirit, nobody complains that a person born with some crippling disability, *spina bifida* for example, should be helped as far as possible to lead a normal life. If the genetic engineers are now able to remove the symptoms of inherited hemophilia, will they be justly pilloried?

In reality, there have already been several attempts to make up for impoverished genetic inheritance. Insulin obtained from pigs, cows and horses is, for example, used for treating people suffering from diabetes. The human pancreas does not function properly, so the product of an animal's pancreas is used instead. But it is beyond dispute that inheritance plays an im-

Man-made Men

portant part in the determination of diabetes, even though there is still some argument about the extent to which it is brought on by such things as overeating. In short, insulin is a way of making good an inherited deficiency. Why is not insulin therapy called genetic engineering, and pilloried in public discussions about the future of biology?

Genetic engineering in the modern sense is also indistinguishable from much of what plant breeders and animal breeders have done to provide modern agriculture with productive strains. The consequences have been far-reaching. The Phoenicians may have been successful colonists because they carried improved strains of wheat with them. Now, new strains of wheat are the foundations for the green revolution. Cattle in Western Europe and North America are engineered animals, made the way they are by rigorous artificial selection and breeding. Horses are genetically also the products of human ingenuity but, for some reason, horse breeders are not called genetic engineers and abused for reasons which have nothing to do with the supposed subversion of genetic inheritance.

The more urgent fears of what will happen when it is possible to transform the inherited characteristics of individuals have sprung from the discoveries of modern biochemistry which, in the past twenty years, have been called molecular biology. The material which carries genetic information from one generation to the next, the substance of which chromosomes are chiefly made, is a chemical with the code name DNA. Each molecule of this material is constructed as a long chain of smaller chemical units. In most organisms each unit in the chain is one of four comparatively simple chemicals, and the way in which the changes are rung on these four components determines the inherited characteristics of the individual in which that molecule is embodied. One of the simplest of all recipes for genetic engineering is to change the chemical composition of these DNA molecules, or even to replace whole sections expressing one set of characteristics by some other.

A technique like this would have several important applica-

The Doomsday Syndrome

tions. People suffering from inherited deficiency diseases such as hemophilia or diabetes, for example, differ from normal people in the chemical constitution of a particular part of their DNA molecules. Replacing the defective piece of DNA by the piece that would be normally found there would make good the inherited deficiency. But yet another possibility is that it might be possible to improve naturally inherited characteristics —to push up the IQ a few points, for example.

The chief difficulty in all this is that direct chemical manipulation of the genetic material is almost inconceivable. The genetic engineers will have to be more devious than that. Any chemical treatment that may affect one of the four units of which DNA molecules are constructed, without affecting the other three, would inevitably affect the chain at several places along its length, so that one sought-after change (or mutation) would be accompanied by several uncovenanted changes. But there is also a high chance that direct chemical manipulation of the DNA would frequently go awry, so that planned changes would be accompanied by unplanned and unpredictable changes, many of them undesirable. It is not irrelevant that some theories of the causation of cancer start with the assumption that the root cause is a change in the composition of a DNA molecule. In short, there is virtually no prospect that the most obvious technique of genetic engineering will ever be workable.

If chemistry will never be the basis for genetic engineering, what else may be accomplished? Something can be learned from the techniques which have been used to mold the genetic characteristics of simpler organisms than human beings or mammals. Many of these are already of great commercial importance. Thus, in the manufacture of antibiotics, by the cultivation of the cells of certain molds, it often turns out that unnatural strains of the mold are much more productive than those which occur naturally. These abnormal strains are often isolated by subjecting wild cells to some chemical treatment or even to nuclear radiation. In the process, many of the original cells are killed off. The desirable abnormalities among the

Man-made Men

remainder are singled out by encouraging them to grow at the expense of their less desirable, but possibly more normal, relatives. Unnatural selection is the watchword, as with race horses. The result is a whole strain of bacteria, the equivalent of a race in the human population, which is superbly efficient at some biochemical task.

In the past few years techniques like this have been widely used. One obvious possibility is to use artificially selected strains of bacteria, and other microorganisms such as molds, for producing complicated chemicals such as Vitamin B_{12}. There is clearly a future for genetic engineering as an exceedingly sophisticated branch of chemical engineering. In the quite near future it should be possible to manufacture, by the proper exploitation of suitable strains of bacteria, a great variety of complicated biological chemicals of value in medicine or industry—enzymes for use in the treatment of leukemia, for example.

Artificial selection is, however, necessarily somewhat hit or miss, which is why, in the past few years, there has been great interest in techniques for transferring pieces of genetic material from one organism to another. Bacteria can now be dealt with in this way with great confidence. The viruses which plague bacteria are known to be able to transfer pieces of DNA molecules from one bacterial cell to another. In other words, they are able to infect one bacterium with genetic characteristics which belong by rights to some other. Other agents are also able to transfer genetic characteristics between bacteria. One annoying illustration is the way in which bacteria, which have become resistant to some antibiotic, can transfer the genetic capacity for resistance to some other strain.

By exploiting the ease with which pieces of genetic material can be moved from one bacterium to another, the genetic engineers are able deliberately to make up for a deficiency with which a bacterium may be genetically endowed. The same techniques have recently been used to provide a single bacterium with several copies of the same piece of genetic material,

The Doomsday Syndrome

thereby arranging that the abnormal cells manufacture abnormally large quantities of chosen chemical materials. In short, techniques of bacterial genetics already well understood make possible not merely the deliberate selection of genetic attributes but the preparation of strains of bacteria which are unusually efficient at performing specified chemical tasks.

What are the chances that these techniques will be applied to higher organisms than bacteria, perhaps to people? To begin with, there are obvious differences which are bound to restrict genetic engineering. Although bacterial viruses may transfer genetic characteristics from one bacterial cell to another, this seems not to happen with people. When was a human inherited deficiency removed by an infection with a virus carrying genetic material from elsewhere? Obviously the genetic material of human cells is less malleable than that of bacteria, although it will at some stage no doubt be relevant that the predisposition to cancer in some kinds of human cells seems to be linked with the presence of genetic material carried by a virus.

In the circumstances it is a little startling that there have recently been reports of the incorporation of the genetic characteristic of one of the familiar bacterial virus (called by the code name lambda) into the genetic apparatus of human cells growing in the laboratory. In October 1971 a group of scientists from the National Institutes of Health and of Mental Health in Bethesda, Maryland, reported a remarkable experiment with cells taken from a patient suffering from galactosemia, an inherited disease in which a particular biological chemical, an enzyme, is deficient. It happens that the bacterial virus called lambda is able to manufacture this chemical, and on the face of things it seems that virus can also infect the human galactosemia cells and that, when it has done so, the inherited deficiency is made good.

The authors of these experiments realize the potential importance of their work. At the same time, however, it is far from clear that the result cannot be explained in some other way. But there is at least a chance that some forms of genetic material

Man-made Men

can be transferred from bacteria to people by means of viruses.

Another possibility is that whole pieces of chromosomes carrying particular genetic characteristics might be transferred from one strain to another, or from one species to another. Transfers of genetic material like this have been widely exploited in plant breeding, and especially in the development of new kinds of wheat. In most circumstances, the set of chromosomes which gives a species its distinctive characteristics cannot be much changed without making the species sterile or even nonviable, but it does seem that in some kinds of plants, the constitution of the chromosomes is much less stringently determined. It remains to be seen whether the genetic constitution of animals can be similarly malleable, and that could be one of the results of the experiments in which the cells of different species such as mouse and man are being fused together.

What does all this imply for the application of new techniques in genetic engineering to human beings, and to mammals with similar genetic complexity? The obvious situations in which the genetic constitution of a person needs to be changed are those in which he has inherited a genetic disease. By now, there is a long list of such diseases. Thus hemophilia, one of the best known, stems from the absence in the bloodstream of the biological chemical which is naturally responsible for blood clotting. Diabetes is probably another, where insulin deficiency is characteristic. There is also a wide range of diseases inherited genetically which cause mental deficiency of severe kinds—phenylketonuria is one of the best known of these diseases. Because of their specific character, and because the chemical explanation of these deficiency diseases is or soon will be understood, it is feasible to think of making good the defect.

Theoretically, there are several ways in which this might be done. One possibility is that a virus might be developed to carry the missing genetic material. Such a virus might, for example, infect some of the cells in a hemophiliac with the genetic capacity to make the blood clotting factor. In suitable circumstances the result would be a kind of artificial organ (the infected cells)

The Doomsday Syndrome

for manufacturing blood clotting factor. As yet, however, there is no knowing whether suitable viruses will be found, or that it will be possible to use them efficiently for infecting body cells with missing genetic material. Until questions like that are settled the application of genetic engineering to people is entirely problematical.

It goes without saying that if these methods brought success, few people would complain. It would be preferable to treat inherited deficiency diseases once and for all with a benign infection than to make those who suffer from them dependent for life on chemicals externally supplied. And even then, the solutions would be only partial solutions. Such a technique might cure a person of the symptoms of inherited disease, but would not prevent him from passing on the disease to future generations. To do that would require not merely genetic engineering of a kind which seems perhaps distantly within the bounds of possibility but also the techniques of artificial fertilization which are themselves remote and dubious possibilities.

More positive steps to change the nature of human inheritance are bound, in the nature of things, to be more difficult, chiefly because so little is known of the way in which most features of the human inheritance are determined. Physique, for example, is almost certainly the product of several disparate pieces of genetic material, as can be told from the way in which the sons and daughters of athletes are not necessarily good at athletics themselves. And much though a person may covet the longevity with which some families appear to be endowed, it is extremely difficult to see how such intangible components of physical inheritance can be related to the transfer from one generation to the next of genetic chemicals. In short, for the time being and for the foreseeable future, the would-be genetic engineer will be little more than a kind of motor mechanic who is able to replace parts which are deficient but who is entirely incompetent to design and to put together the bits and pieces from which his machinery is made.

Tinkering with more subtle attributes of human inheritance,

Man-made Men

such as the genetic part of intelligence, is equally beyond present and foreseeable capacity. To the extent that human intelligence is genetically determined, it is clear that several chromosomes must play a part in ways that are not at present understood. Quite possibly what matters is the way in which chromosomes decide the pattern in which nerve cells are laid down during the development of the brain in the months before birth. But the same process may also be influenced by external factors, the mother's diet, for example. At present, nobody can tell. It follows that any attempt to modify such an inherited characteristic, even malevolently, would require so much more profound an understanding of the nature of intelligence than is at present available, let alone of the degree to which it is inherited, that genetic engineering is an inappropriate fantasy. If the objective were the improvement of the general level of intelligence, the improvement of teaching methods in the light of a comprehensive theory of the psychology of learning has much more to offer than genetic engineering. Similarly, the corruption of intelligence, if that were desired, would probably be most simply accomplished by the techniques for the deliberate impoverishment of the human spirit which are all too widely understood and practiced.

This is why the most practical way of using such understanding of human genetics as has accumulated is in a more vigorous and more intelligent attempt to prevent the birth of children with unfortunate genetic characteristics. Already it is common practice among physicians to warn parents against conception when the chances are high that children will carry some inherited defect. For the time being this positive approach to what used to be called eugenics is as much as could be looked for.

As understanding of the inheritance of the deficiency diseases grows, so too will the opportunities for genetic counseling. Because it is hard to expect that intending parents should permanently forgo children in circumstances like these, there is a strong case for asking that genetic counseling should be rein-

The Doomsday Syndrome

forced by a more ready availability of artificial insemination for people. There is also a strong case for a more systematic attempt to tell soon after conception whether a growing embryo carries some obvious genetic defect, the extra chromosome characteristic of some forms of mongolism for example. This could now be made a straightforward part of medical eugenics. And such techniques will be far preferable, for a long time to come, to the necessarily uncertain and intricate procedures of what is called genetic engineering.

But what of the prospects for determining the sex of children in advance? This has been a cherished goal of animal breeders for a great many years. Theoretically, it should be possible to separate the sperms which lead to male children from those which, after fertilizing an egg, produce females, for the male chromosome is smaller than the female chromosome. The economic importance of a successful technique for doing this would of course be immense—the breeding potential of dairy cattle, for example, would be, for practical purposes, enormously increased if steps could be taken to ensure that males were hardly ever born.

Where people are concerned, there would be some advantages if it were possible for couples, who by chance had produced a long succession of either boys or girls, to ensure against the repetition of the same sex. No doubt, if a technique for sex determination were easily available, there would also be a tendency for couples deliberately to choose some pattern of sexes among their children, although there is nothing to suggest that the result would be a radical change in the present ratio of boys to girls in the population as a whole. But the only practical method of determining sex at present is to let conception go ahead, to extract some cells from the uterus at an early stage and then to carry out an abortion if the embryo is discovered to be of the unwanted sex. In due course, it might be feasible to think of using artificial fertilizers as a more convenient, more rapid and safer alternative. But here again, the methods now available are so distasteful that they are unlikely

Man-made Men

to be used. As yet, there is no sign of a simpler technique, although it is only fair to say that in this field, research could yield quick success.

What does all this imply the future of genetic engineering? First of all, there is a good prospect that genetic manipulation of bacteria and other microorganisms will make it possible to improve the efficiency of the biological chemical industry. Important work has been done already, and there is much more to be done. Second, there are obvious and plentiful plants of various kinds. The difficulty, as the development of the new strains of wheat has shown, is that several growing seasons must go by before the intermediate results of these experiments can be assessed, so that engineering new kinds of plants is bound to be a slow process, productive though it promises to be. Third, there is a chance—as things stand, it is no more than that—that one of the several techniques which are known to be effective in transferring genetic material from one bacterium to another may be used to remedy inherited deficiency diseases in people and other mammals. Whether it will ever be possible more positively to manipulate the human genetic inheritance is at present entirely uncertain. That question can only be answered when the formidable task of unraveling some of the complications of human genetics has been accomplished. But it follows from all this that the best use that can be made of recent developments in molecular biology is that genetic counseling might be made more efficient and more imaginative.

That is a far cry from the horrors of genetic engineering now frequently depicted.

Organ transplantation is another source of public anxiety about the direction of modern biology, but the reasons are hard to define. After all, it has been accepted medical practice for more than three centuries that people unfortunate enough to be born with defective vision should be provided with spectacles. Nobody complains about false teeth, and for a long time it has

The Doomsday Syndrome

been standard practice to treat people with cataracts by fitting them with a cornea from the eye of some person quite often long since dead. Skin grafting is also an acceptable part of medical practice, pieces of plastic are increasingly used for repairing bones, blood vessels and other structures in the human body, and people with heart block are now fitted with electrical machines which can keep the heart beating. Blood transfusions for Rhesus babies are also standard therapy. When these devices are considered to be desirable instruments of therapy why should the transplanting of organs so often offend susceptibilities?

To begin with, it is fair to say that the techniques of organ transplantation have a small but important part to play in medical practice. Since the first transplants, in the late 1950s, kidney transplantation has become a routine method of treating kidney failure. The treatment is preferable to the use of a kidney machine to extract waste materials from the bloodstream, as least when the patient is likely to be able to withstand the operation and when suitable kidneys are accessible. Although the kidney transplant operation can be hazardous, the most serious danger is that the transplanted kidney will fail to function after an interval of anything between a few days and a few years. But even where medical practice is advanced, as in Britain and the United States, for example, large numbers of people die each year from kidney failure without treatment by either method. Machines or kidneys are not sufficiently available.

Transplanting other organs than the human kidney is a much less certain process. Liver transplants have been undertaken at a few hospitals, but the operation is intricate and has only occasionally been successful. Attempts to transplant the pancreas from one person to another have only recently been attempted, but could yet be a way of treating diabetes. Bone-marrow transplants have been attempted in cases of acute leukemia, so far without much success. And exactly the same must be said of the most spectacular of all transplantation

Man-made Men

experiments—the attempts since the mid-1960s to transplant hearts from one person to another. As events have shown, heart transplants are often catastrophically unsuccessful. When the transplanted hearts function at all, their life in the body of their recipients tends to be short, and even unpleasant.

Why has organ transplantation been so controversial? Surgeons themselves have done the most mischief. Since the earliest kidney transplants the overriding difficulty has been to make sure that the natural defenses of the body of a recipient will not reject a transplanted organ, as it will normally reject foreign living things, bacteria for example. Over the years the development of biological materials which can suppress this immune reaction has helped to smooth the way for organ transplantation but, in the early days, success seemed to require that the donor of an organ, a kidney say, should be a close relative of the recipient. These are circumstances in which the sense of drama inseparable from major surgical operations is heightened by the poignant question whether the sacrifice of a kidney by a relative will turn out to have been in vain. In the early operations a great many hospitals, and their surgeons, gave the cause of transplantation a bad name by giving publicity to these harrowing situations.

Although organs for transplantation no longer have to come from a close relative, or from a person still alive, the problem of supply remains a source of great anxiety. The most obvious danger is that medical men seeking organs to transplant into patients sorely in need of them will consciously or unconsciously muddy their criteria of how to distinguish life from death. In the first few attempts at transplanting hearts the donor was often artificially supported for the last few hours of his life, usually with mechanical respirator. The most obvious source of anxiety was that overanxious surgeons might switch off the respirator and promptly sign a death certificate when it suited them and not the potential donor.

The publicity surrounding heart transplants, and the way in which the medical people concerned have often been seen to

The Doomsday Syndrome

welcome publicity, is another reason why, quite understandably, heart transplantation lies under a cloud of public disapproval. Is there something about heart surgery that makes its practitioners more than usually flamboyant? Are they perhaps responding to the popular conviction that, of all the organs in the body, the heart is most like the source of life? Whatever the explanation, there is no ready excuse for the way in which some heart transplanters, but Dr. Christian Barnard in particular, have publicized their activities.

The hazard of too much publicity is that it confuses the already complicated question of what should be the relationship between medical innovators and the patients who are necessarily their experimental subjects. In the first place, it is bound to offensive if new techniques and operations are introduced with people as experimental subjects if there has not been in advance a careful program of research with animals. Unhappily, many of the teams of surgeons who followed the fashion for heart transplantation in 1969 and 1970 were ill-prepared in this respect. But it is also important that those who take part as subjects in medical innovations should have some reasonable hope that success will bring some kind of benefit. All too often, in the past few years, heart transplantation has been offered as a cure and not as an attempted cure.

It will be a great misfortune if these failings should impede the development of techniques which have an important part to play in the prevention of untimely death. In the circumstances it is heartening that there is emerging quickly an ethical and administrative framework within which transplant operations can be carried out. In many countries, for example, it has been agreed that the medical team wishing to use an organ for transplantation should not include the doctor responsible for deciding whether the potential donor is to be counted dead. In this and other ways, even the novel and taxing problems of organ transplantation seem to have been accommodated in the framework of medical practice. To be sure, governments have usually done much less than they could have done to help make

Man-made Men

potential donors known. And it remains a somewhat shameful truth that public authorities have not yet applied themselves to the economic questions of what place transplantation should occupy in medical practice. How much is it worth paying for an expensive operation, not universally available, to prolong an individual life for a few years?

That luckily is a question that needs to be asked of all new medical techniques. The fact that it cannot yet be answered for organ transplantation is a proof that this technique is still experimental.

Of all the sources of horrific speculation about biological research, the work being done in several research laboratories to follow the course of human fertilization by laboratory experiments has pride of place. People ask whether Aldous Huxley was not a prophet, and whether the test-tube baby is only a few years off. And stimulated by what is being done to understand how living things began, it is natural to ask whether entirely synthetic forms of life may one day be produced.

In many ways, artificial fertilization is as old as the hills. With trout, for example, it has been for a long time standard practice among breeders to milk female fish of their eggs and to arrange for these to be fertilized artificially, but fish differ markedly from mammals in that fertilization takes place outside the body. The same is true of amphibian fertilization, which is why there are no outcries at the artificial manipulation of frogs' eggs. In animal husbandry it is also now routine practice that male sperm should be stored and used in artificial insemination, although it remains something of a paradox that organizations such as the Milk Marketing Board in Britain, and the Agricultural Research Services in the United States, should encourage the artificial insemination of cattle and sheep while corresponding organizations responsible for the control of pedigree status in horses, dogs, cats and other domesticated animals should have set their faces against the practice.

Artificial fertilization in the strict sense requires that the

The Doomsday Syndrome

egg and the sperm should be manipulated outside the body. The first success in doing this for mammals seems to have been that of Mr. L. E. A. Rowson who, at Cambridge in the late 1940s, succeeded in fertilizing sheep eggs outside the body, transferring them to the uterus and letting them develop normally there. Since then it has taken more than two decades to provide unambiguous evidence that it is possible artificially to fertilize human eggs. With domesticated animals confirmation is of course relatively easy to come by, for there is no objection to the use of the mother as a recipient for what may be a growing embryo. With people there are clearly serious ethical problems to be solved before such a direct test would be acceptable. In the experiments so far carried out with human eggs, success has been signaled chiefly by the way in which fertile eggs were stimulated to divide. By the late 1960s, several laboratories in the United States and Britain were seriously engaged in research on the artificial fertilization of human eggs, as well as those from other kinds of mammals. The experience which has accumulated is a telling proof that the artificial replication of the entire development of a human embryo is bound to be exceedingly difficult.

The first difficulty is to obtain a human egg at precisely that point in its cycle of development when it is almost literally ripe. By 1968 enough was known of the way in which human eggs develop, under the influence of the sex hormones called gonadotrophins, for Dr. R. G. Edwards and his colleagues, working at Cambridge, to be able to obtain suitable human eggs from women's ovaries by means of a simple, but not trivial, operation. In real life, in the normal passage between the ovary and the uterus, the eggs of all mammals undergo a process of maturation which requires the presence of a fluid well supplied with essential hormones. Finding a laboratory substitute for the natural material was an important impediment to development. A further difficulty, not yet fully understood, is that sperms will not freely fertilize mature eggs unless they too have undergone a process of maturation, which has implied a further search for

Man-made Men

just the right medium in which to keep the eggs to be fertilized.

By 1968 Dr. Edwards and his colleagues were able to describe the fertilization of eggs in test tubes in such a way that the cell consisting of the fusion of egg and sperm went through three successive processes of cell division, leaving a tiny mass of eight cells, a primitive embryo. By 1971 it was possible to grow the fertilized eggs to what is called the blastocyst stage, in which as many as a hundred different cells could be identified in a hollow shell, apparently entirely like the embryonic structures that occur naturally. A similar blastocyst of a hundred cells or so was grown at about the same time by Dr. L. B. Shettles, working in New York.

What happens next? There seems to be no possibility of prolonging life in the embryo without returning it to a uterus. Dr. Edwards and his colleagues plan to use their technique for treating certain kinds of infertility in women, principally when the Fallopian tubes which normally channel eggs from the ovary to the uterus are for some reason blocked. In such a procedure, it would be necessary to ensure that the uterus was in a fit state to receive the fertilized egg, which implies a suitable treatment with hormones in advance. The procedure is simple enough in rabbits, sheep and other mammals, and there is no reason to expect that it will fail with women.

Replicating the human uterus would be a much more daunting task. In the first place there are mechanical difficulties, and it is not yet clear how much of the development of a mammalian embryo depends on the transfer of nutrients along the umbilical cord and how much comes through the fluid in which it is immersed. Then there are chemical problems—not nearly enough is known about the way in which the chemical composition of maternal blood varies with the development of the embryo, or whether these variations are important. But it is beyond dispute that, in the present state of knowledge and for a long time to come, it will always be easier to work with a properly self-regulating animal than with a purely artificial system. In short, artificial fertilization, with sperms and eggs selected deliberately

The Doomsday Syndrome

from human donors, may be a practical possibility, but there is very little chance that the artificial uterus will be anything more than a tool in academic research.

This conclusion is entirely in accord with a familiar consideration in biology—that there are many circumstances in which it is more economical to use a living system to carry out some complicated chemical function than to attempt to replicate this in the laboratory. If it is not merely more convenient but cheaper to breed microorganisms which produce particular antibiotics than to fall back on chemical synthesis, are not the chances high that the animal body will always be a simpler way of telling what ingredients are needed for the development of an embryo than any sequence of chemical recipes that may emerge from continued research? In other words, convenience and economy conspire with ordinary susceptibility to suggest that the artificial uterus is a valueless concept, let alone one that is probably unattainable.

What are the objectives of research in artificial fertilization? The best of it—some has been second-rate—should provide a rounded understanding of the natural process. The practical benefits could be important. For animals of all kinds a better understanding of the process of fertilization should help in important ways in regulating fertility. People may wish to have fewer children. Farmers may seek to make their herds more productive. But, with people, as with other animals, it is improbable that strictly artificial fertilization will ever be cheaper or more convenient than natural fertilization, but the understanding which this research could provide may be of great economic value. Only in exceptional circumstances will test-tube fertilization be more than a laboratory tool.

Laboratory fertilization and early development is, however, relevant to the understanding of congenital diseases, especially those which spring from defects in early development. One important outstanding body of ignorance is the process in which embryos with congenital malformations are rejected during uterine development. Why should this be? And what are the implications for medicine?

Man-made Men

In some circumstances there may also be benefits in storing germ tissue. In agriculture, it is already common practice to store the sperms of bulls in frozen form. More recently, Dr. D. G. Whittingham of the University of Cambridge has been able artificially to fertilize mouse eggs and to store them at the temperature of liquid air. He considers that the same technique could be used for other species. It could be used to keep indefinitely, and in a convenient fashion, particular strains of animals, chiefly those used in laboratories, and with large domestic animals it could become a convenient method of disseminating desirable stock. Already the techniques of artificial fertilization and implantation have been used in ways like this —one of the most striking experiments of this kind was the transfer of a fertilized sheep egg from Britain to South Africa in the uterus of a rabbit.

Of all the reasons for supporting research in artificial fertilization, the strongest is that it will help in understanding a crucial process in human physiology. To that extent, artificial fertilization remains an academic subject. The potential benefits in agriculture and in medical practice are likely to be indirect, at least for several years to come. And the test-tube baby, in the strict sense, is, for the time being at least, entirely beyond reach—there is no prospect of the development of an artificial uterus and if there were the hazards in the shape of genetic malformation would probably be entirely insupportable. In the circumstances it is hard to think that the new techniques will ever be widely applied among people. It follows that the issues of principle with which the researchers have been challenged are those that belong to the ethics of laboratory research, not to ethics of medical practice. The complaint that experiments which create living blastocysts and then, at the end of the experiment, destroy them, are a kind of infanticide, one of the points made by Professor James Watson of Harvard University in 1971, is for the time being a debating point. It will be a different matter, and a more difficult one, to know what principle should regulate the implantation of blastocysts in the uterus except when the intention is to treat infertility.

The Doomsday Syndrome

Fears of the technique called cloning occupy a special place in the literature of doomsday, chiefly because successful cloning would make it possible to produce large numbers of identical individuals starting with a single cell taken from an intact organism. Cloning already occupies an important place in agriculture. There have also been a few experiments in which the technique has been used to produce nearly identical copies of a frog. Although nobody has yet been able to apply the technique to mammals of any kind, speculation runs rife about the problems that would arise if that were possible. Would there be attempts to populate the world with identical copies of intellectual giants, Albert Einsteins for example? Or would the racecourses of the world be filled with identical copies of race horses with a proven reputation? These are evidently different questions which touch many important institutions in society. Luckily, they are also hypothetical, and are likely to remain so for decades to come.

Cloning is, for practical purposes, at present confined to some species of plants. The first successful experiments were carried out in the late 1950s, when Dr. F. C. Steward and his colleagues at Cornell University showed that cells taken from the tip of a growing carrot would, first of all, multiply, and then produce shoots which, in due course, became the roots and leaves of intact plantlets if they were suspended in coconut milk. This remarkable method of reproduction is possible because each cell contains enough genetic material to specify all the parts of the intact organism although, in normal circumstances, in cells from the tip of a growing carrot or any other part of it, the genetic material not relevant to its special function is masked off. The coconut milk in these experiments functions as a source of plant hormones of a kind which are normally produced in growing plants, and which can now be manufactured in large quantities.

Evidently this technique has important scientific value, for it provides a way of following the details of plant development. It is also a powerful demonstration that the genetic material

Man-made Men

tucked away in every living cell remains intact, even though much of it may be at any time inactive, and can in suitable circumstances be brought fully into play. But, where plants are concerned, the technique has obvious practical importance as well. For one thing, it is a convenient way of propagating plant material. For another, it is a convenient way of mixing together genetic material from different plants so as to produce hybrids that could never have been made by orthodox plant breeding.

Plants, however, are a far cry from mammals, which is no doubt why the fact that cloning is by now a standard technique for plant material causes little general alarm. What has awakened anxiety is the experiment in 1967 in which Dr. J. B. Gurdon of the University of Oxford transferred the nucleus of a cell from the intestine of a frog to an unfertilized egg from the same creature. Just as the genetic material of carrot cells is stimulated by coconut milk to produce a whole new carrot plant, so the transplanted nucleus seems to have been stimulated by the cytoplasm of the unfertilized egg to set about producing several intact frogs. In due course the technique was used to produce several identical creatures from the same transplanted nucleus. All of them were, of course, identical with the frog from which the nucleus was taken.

If cloning works for frogs, why not for people? This is the question now being asked. Part of the answer turns on the difference between the eggs of frogs and those of women, and indeed most other species of mammals. A frog's egg is comparatively large—visible to the naked eye. The nucleus can be identified easily and can be removed mechanically without damaging the egg. Mammalian cells are quite different. They are smaller and more susceptible to damage from outside. The result is that attempts to repeat Dr. Gurdon's experiment with a mammalian species have so far been unsuccessful. At least a part of the reason is that the genetic material in mammalian cells is masked off in a more complicated fashion than with frogs. For the time being, therefore, those wishing to investigate what happens with the cloning of mammalian cells are being

The Doomsday Syndrome

forced to wait until the techniques of artificial fertilization have improved to such a point that they can be a source of genetic material for cloning.

It is clear already from the experiments with frogs that there will be powerful reasons why cloning will not be applied to human beings. Even with the easily manipulated frog's eggs, a great many of the offspring were seriously malformed. The risk of malformation will be much greater if the technique is ever applied to the more sensitive mammalian eggs. It will not even be known how serious is the risk until there has been a more successful attempt than any so far to see what happens to the progeny from cloned mammalian cells. And it goes without saying that cloning on any substantial scale would require first of all a technique for transferring a young embryo to the uterus of a woman and then a plentiful supply of women ready to collaborate. This, then, is another situation in which a remote, and as yet untested, possibility has been elevated, in public discussion, into a prospect which is altogether too real.

In this and in other questions—transplantation, for example —it will, in any case, be clear that the mere feasibility of some manipulation of inheritance need not prevent society from deciding how best to use—or not to use—the technique. If cloning for mammals ever became a practical possibility, the breeders of farm animals would no doubt be encouraged to make what use they could of it. In the same way the pedigree associations, which regulate the breeding of horses, dogs and other economically irrelevant animals, would be as successful in resisting cloning as they have been in keeping artificial insemination at bay. Where people are concerned, the high risk of genetic errors would be a powerful deterrent, the disposal of erroneous replicas of some chosen individual would probably be illegal and, in any case, no government can be so sure of the qualities that make for a productive and harmonious population that it would take the risk of replicating one type before all others. Genetic diversity in a community is an asset not likely to be discarded.

These, in any case, are nightmare speculations. The truth is

Man-made Men

that cloning for mammals may never be possible, and is certainly a long way off. It is as unhelpful at this stage to ask what steps society should take to adapt itself to the remote threat of cloning as it would be to insist on knowing precisely what steps would have to be taken if the earth collided with a comet.

Exactly the same is true of the suggestions, now frequently to be heard, that developments in the understanding of how the brain and the nervous system function will make it possible for large numbers of people to be, in some sense or another, controlled by others. Here again, the scientific problem of understanding is much greater than legend supposes. To be sure, there may be scope for the development of psychotropic drugs for use in medical treatment, but it is hard to see how the malevolent dictatorship, usually supposed to be behind these attemps to control the behavior of large numbers of people, would be able to exploit such blunderbuss devices. And would it not in any case be simpler and safer for the malevolent to exploit the techniques already available for conditioning people to respond in predictable ways in known circumstances?

Speculation about the social consequences of the possibility of synthesizing living matter is irresponsibly premature for the same reasons. It is true, of course, that a great deal is known about the way that living things began. Synthesizing simple biological chemicals in conditions which are chemically similar to those on the primeval earth 3,000 million years ago is a familiar activity in several laboratories. Valuable work is also being done to understand how the apparatus for the sustenance of life, and particularly the functioning of genetic material such as DNA, has evolved. Especially now that it has been possible to synthesize in the laboratory pieces of the genetic molecules with predetermined chemical properties, is it not only a matter of time before living things themselves are made synthetically? That is how the gloomy preoccupations go. The truth is that here again there is a great gulf between the kinds of experiments which can be done in the laboratory, with simple materials that serve as models for the real thing, and the vast

The Doomsday Syndrome

complexity of the corresponding materials and processes in real life. The relationship between the laboratory models and true living creatures is rather like that between the abacus which can be used to demonstrate some principles of computing and the large electronic computers now in service.

This relationship goes a long way to explain the difficulty which many biologists have found in accepting the notion that the new molecular biology is in some sense a basis for explaining the workings of all living things. Dr. Barry Commoner says, for example, that "one of the conceits pressed upon us by the illusory successes of molecular biology is the idea that life is, after all, nothing but a mixture of chemical reactions." Apart from a technical argument about the quality of the proof that DNA is indeed the crucial molecule of living matter, his position is that with living things, the whole is "greater than the sum of its parts."

If this is to be understood as a declaration that there is some quality in living things which is inexplicable in the kind of language now being elaborated in molecular biology, it is the old vitalism and there is no support for it. If, on the other hand, the statement means that the sheer complexity of living things is so much greater than that of the models with which the molecular biologists are necessarily concerned, it is at once an entirely plausible declaration that the essential quality of living things is their self-regulating complexity and an assurance that nothing in the recent doings of molecular biologists is likely to make it feasible, let alone worthwhile, to think of making living things artificially.

Prosperity Is Possible

---■

The most paradoxical feature of the present discontent is the common disenchantment with science and all its works, especially technology. Dr. Barry Commoner says that "the age of innocent faith in science and technology may be over." Professor Rene Dubos is more explicit: " . . . the technological and other practical applications of science have been oversold. In fact, the production of goods and the development of what is now called technological 'fixes' may not be the most valuable contribution that scientists can make to society." These statements and the point of view that they represent have by now given a characteristic flavor to the present crisis of confidence in the future. In reality, however, they can only be half-truths. Was "innocent" faith in science and technology ever justifiable?

Whatever the origin of the complaints, they are a recent phenomenon. Immediately after the Second World War, governments and their electors looked to science and technology for all kinds of benefits and especially the solution of economic problems. This confidence was in part based on the success with which it was possible to manufacture nuclear weapons more or less to order in the four years between 1941 and 1945. If science and technology could accomplish such wonders during wartime, why should they not also make people healthy, prosperous and even wise? But since the beginning of the 1960s, the opposing view—that science and technology are suspect and even inherently malevolent—has been gaining ground, at least in advanced societies.

One common cause for discontent is that the side effects of technological development are often unpredicted and are sometimes even unpredictable. After all, the argument goes, what did the pesticide technologists know, in the years immediately

The Doomsday Syndrome

after the Second World War, about the persistence of DDT and its effects on birds and fish? What could have been done to avoid the thalidomide disaster? What have aeronautical engineers ever done to make noise pollution go away? Why did not the automobile engineers anticipate the consequences of carbon monoxide in the atmosphere? The suspicion is that each success conceals catastrophe of some kind. As Dr. Commoner puts it: "Technology has not only built the magnificent material base of modern society, but also confronts us with threats to survival which cannot be corrected unless we solve very grave economical, social and political problems." But what reason can there ever have been for supposing that technical innovations would always be unmixed blessings?

A more general version of the same complaint is that technology is a means of sustaining economic growth and that economic growth is in itself undesirable. For growth also has unpleasant side effects—it enables more people to buy motor cars, for example. To the extent that economic growth implies the production of more goods for people to use or to consume, it also implies the more rapid extraction of minerals, the more severe pollution of rivers (which take the discharges from the steelworks and the power stations which drive them) and increased demand for services such as air transport or sunbathing space on the beaches of the world. Paraphrasing an argument originally due to Dr. G. Hardin, W. W. Murdoch says, "there is no evidence that we can increase production, resource utilisation on food production and so on without putting ever greater stress on the environment and causing more environmental degradation, even though it is true that some local pollution problems in the past have been worse than some pollution problems now."

Dr. Commoner says, in *The Closing Circle*, that "pollution tends to become intensified by the displacement of older production technologies by new, ecologically faulty, but more profitable technologies. Thus, in these cases, pollution is an unintended concomitant of the natural drive of the economic system to introduce new technologies that increase productivity."

Prosperity Is Possible

The general argument is that both technical innovation and economic growth diminish people's enjoyment of the fruits of technology. As the Ehrlichs say, "While the American GNP has been growing, the quality of life in the United States has been deteriorating. The GNP roughly doubled in the decade 1960–1969. Can anyone claim that the average individual's life has greatly improved in the same period?" The short if impolite answer is that the Ehrlichs should enquire of those in the United States who, by the end of the 1960s, had found it possible to send their children to universities and to acquire for themselves the habit of foreign travel. And in any case, as—fair play—Dr. Commoner recognizes, new technologies are not always more serious sources of pollution than those which they replace. Steam locomotives, for example, have almost disappeared from advanced societies, and not because of their offensiveness to the environment but because they are less efficient than diesel or electric locomotives. In due course, motor cars will disappear from city streets as more efficient and less noisome means of communal transport are developed. And who complains of pollution from the electronics industry and its products—the most rapidly growing sector of all advanced economies?

A striking feature of the complaints about economic growth is that they often single out for scorn the harmless economic statistic called the Gross National Product. Dr. Rene Dubos, for example, says that "contemporary utopians . . . are primarily interested in using science to manipulate external nature and man's nature. They postulate societies in which the Gross National Product will continuously increase." The Ehrlichs fear not merely the notion that growth of the GNP is desirable but the mistaken corollary that a growing population means a growing GNP.

It is true—so much is self-evident—that there are serious limitations on the use of the GNP as a measure of social well being or even of economic advancement. Certainly it cannot be used to compare social welfare of very different countries. Dr. Kenneth Boulding of the University of Colorado is one of the most amusing and vigorous critics of the use of the GNP in the

The Doomsday Syndrome

international comparison of economic advancement. "The GNP is like the Red Queen," he says. "It runs as fast as it can to stay where it is."

The mistake here is the supposition that the GNP, which is simply the arithmetical sum for a particular country of what people, public authorities and the central government spend on goods, services and investment, can ever have been intended as a measure of human happiness. In principle, at least, affluence can take several forms. Communities are free to decide to spend more or less of their resources on health care, education, housing, travel, nourishment and the gadgets of modern life—motor cars, for example. And the idea that it should be possible to compare the prosperity of people in the United States and India by quoting the GNP per head of population is entirely farcical—to the extent that much of the food in less developed countries is produced by subsistence farmers and eaten by their families, its cost never appears in the accounts of the GNP.

One of the most recent manifestations of the environmental movement is the use of the GNP as an Aunt Sally. After a perfectly valid assertion that the GNP is not "a comprehensive measure of the quality of life," the Ehrlichs go on to say: "But even economists can change. . . . Economists of the next generation may be weaned away from their concentration on perpetual growth and high production-consumption. . . ."

There are two things to be said. First, the classical economics of the West, from John Stuart Mill and Alfred Marshall to Keynes, have continually wrestled with the problem of how to build into their conceptual framework the economic value of such intangible qualities as leisure, and it is uncharitable of the environmentalists to overlook those important contributions to modern thought. Keynes, who invented the concept, would never have misused the GNP as the Ehrlichs say it is misused.

Second, there is no reason why the economic cost of controlling pollution and other public nuisances should not be accommodated within the system of classical economics. The issue here, as Dr. Commoner quite rightly says, is that "the costs of

Prosperity Is Possible

environmental degradation are chiefly borne not by the producer but by society as a whole, in the form of 'externalities.' " That, at least, is what happens if society at large imposes no restraints on what producers do. But what if there are effective regulations for the abatement of pollution? Or if the producer is required to pay for the damage he does by the payment of a levy, thus "internalizing the externalities" as the jargon has it? Then, of course, his costs are increased, as are the prices of his products. Undoubtedly devices like this would impose significant economic penalties on producers as a whole, and the community in which they worked would find itself affording less of their products—it would sense itself to be relatively impoverished. In compensation, however, there would be an abatement of some public nuisance, in every sense a communal purchase. This is exactly what happens when a community decides that a municipal airport must be sited where it will cause only a tolerable amount of noise—the amenity is paid for by the extra cost of getting travelers to their aircraft.

Although the environmental movement has recently stimulated a resurgence of interest in what is called the economics of the common good, there is nothing in these arguments that suggests, as Dr. Commoner says, that:

> the environmental crisis not only reveals serious incompatibilities between the private enterprise system and the ecological base on which it depends, but may also help to explain why—as the crisis silently matured within the fabric of the ecosystem—these inherent faults in the economic system were covered over and could be tolerated. In this sense, the emergence of a full-blown crisis in the ecosystem can be regarded, as well, as the signal of an emerging crisis in the economic system.

That is a little like a motorist complaining that he must change his vehicle because there is a corner in the road ahead, when the remedy is simply to turn the steering wheel.

But is not technology a kind of industrial cancer, autono-

The Doomsday Syndrome

mous and uncontrollable? That is another common complaint of those associated with the environmental movement. Dr. J. K. Galbraith, for example, in *The New Industrial Estate*, talks about "the imperatives of technology" and complains that the course of events within a nation is now determined by what he calls the technostructure, the framework within which corporations seek to exploit technology. To some extent, these views spring from the frustration of private citizens who find themselves unable to stop technological development first set in train by governmental money. The continuing battle between the private citizen and the huge corporation is further fuel for the flames. It remains a sobering fact that the United States Congress put an end to the supersonic transport aircraft project in 1971 after a calculation that if the project were not stopped then, it might not be politically possible to make the right decision at a more appropriate time.

Another complaint is that technology is dehumanizing. As Dr. Jacques Ellul, one of the prophets of the present mood, has said: "The machine has created an inhuman atmosphere. The machine, so characteristic of the nineteenth century, made an abrupt entrance into a society which, from the political, institutional and human points of view, was not made to receive it; and man has had to put up with it as best he can." Other writers take the same line. Mr. Lewis Mumford, for example, says: "The machine is anti-social. It tends by reason of its progressive character to the most acute forms of human exploitation." Although a great deal of the anger with which these statements are suffused is historical, dating from the awesome legends of the nineteenth century, satanic mills and all, from the introduction of conveyer-belt assembly lines (as in Chaplin's *Modern Times*) and from the more present fear that some of the unpleasant features of those industrial innovations will be repeated now that electronic computers are working everywhere, the fact that they are so widely expressed is a sign that people also fear that the new machinery may change important patterns in society.

For the sake of completeness, this list of discontents should

Prosperity Is Possible

also include the other more literal interpretation of Dr. Dubos' lament that technology has been oversold. Increasingly, there are accumulating illustrations of how some innovations has failed to live up to its prospectus. Electronic computers are a continuing disappointment to those who have bought them. In Britain, hovercraft ships have failed to live up to expectation. Projects for developing aircraft are a constant source of disappointment. For every environmentalist who says that the promise of technology should be ignored, there is a disappointed customer who is angry over a promise that seems to have been broken.

In reality, questions of the benefits to be expected from science and technology, since they are bound to be in part estimates of what will happen in the future, entail subjective judgments. In other words, there is room for legitimate disagreement about the value of this or that innovation. For that reason, however, there is a danger that the exaggerations of the present complaints against technology may themselves be damaging—they may create circumstances in which technology is undervalued to the disadvantage of everybody.

This is why it is important that there should be a more sensitive understanding of the complicated relationship between science and technology, and of the processes by means of which one or the other can yield beneficial results. There also needs to be a fuller understanding of the relationship between technological innovations and economic growth. How, in particular, should societies determine their priorities in technology? What machinery do they need for forming public policies for the support of innovation? And is there not in any case a sense in which the particular kinds of economic growth which technology can support, like the understanding of the natural world which science can provide, are humane influences and not the opposite?

The link between science and technology is comparatively new. Until the beginning of the First World War, indeed, there were very few occasions on which a strictly scientific discovery led

The Doomsday Syndrome

immediately to a practical application. The outstanding case is that of Faraday, who discovered the essential principles of electromagnetism in the 1830s, more than half a century before the first electricity generating station built on those principles came into service. Such a delay would now be unthinkable.

In the nineteenth century, however, science and technology were poles apart. The technical innovations on which the Industrial Revolution was based were devised empirically, by engineers who were often ignorant of and almost always indifferent to scientific principles. Even the great enterprises which became the automobile industry in North America were, at the beginning, put together in an informal way. Only in the chemical industry, growing rapidly in Germany and the United States in the last two decades of the nineteenth century, were scientific principles exploited deliberately for the useful innovations they might yield.

The First World War was a powerful incentive both for the intervention of governments and for the marriage of science and technology. So much was evident in the programs for developing new types of military aircraft then begun. In retrospect, it is surprising that governments such as those of the United States and Britain did comparatively little, between the First and Second World Wars, to keep alive the relationship between the slowly growing community of civilian scientists and the military services, by then provided with science and technology of their own. The coming of the Second World War, however, left nobody in doubt that the deliberate exploitation of scientific principles was an essential way of producing necessary weapons. In most industrialized nations, the pattern of the relationship between government, civil science and military technology that was then established has persisted ever since.

For better or worse, the Second World War has given modern technology its characteristic stamp. Nuclear weapons were the starting point. How to turn a scientific possibility into a technological reality? To begin with, there was no assurance

Prosperity Is Possible

that the weapons could actually be manufactured. Success came as it had been predicted. Since then there have been other successes, some just as spectacular—the journey to the moon, for example. The trick is to carry through a technological development whose feasibility can only be estimated at the beginning.

By now, it is clear that the essential skill of technology as distinct from science is to pick out from among a whole range of possibilities, mostly desirable, those which are also feasible. For all its uncertainties, science is a more well-determined discipline than technology. The most obvious technological failures are those that come about because designers have been over-ambitious, but it is equally bad practice (and usually uneconomic as well) for the design of a technological innovation to be made in such a conservative way that there is plenty of room for error.

Much of the suspicion about technology and its motivation springs from misunderstanding of the difference between bright ideas and feasible projects. Not to be in conflict with scientific principles is a poor way of distinguishing between the two, which is why Leonardo's notebooks are not contributions to technology but to the literature of fantasy. Many of the fears of what science and technology will accomplish in the near future stem from the belief that what is possible will be done.

In reality, there is a world of difference between the degree of confidence an aircraft designer, for example, would have in a project to build an aircraft traveling at twice the speed of sound and one traveling five times as fast, hypersonically as it is said. The first design although entirely unproven, will be informed by experience gathered with other types of aircraft, many of them in service. The other project, on the other hand, would be a leap into the dark. One of the most fruitful sources of error in the assessment of the potentiality of technology is the unreasonable anticipation of the future. When, for example, Dr. Dubos says that "before long the discoveries of the behavioral and social sciences will make possible the manipulation of

The Doomsday Syndrome

individual human beings and entire populations," he overlooks the disciplined and detailed studies that would have to be carried out before technologists would accept that that possibility is feasible—and before sponsors would provide the necessary funds.

In what ways does science contribute to technology? There is no simple generalization. Some important techniques have sprung directly from the research laboratories—lasers, for example, or the techniques of holography. On other occasions, the chief role of science has been to provide the background of understanding necessary to mount vast enterprises in technology. This is the spirit, for example, in which governments after the Second World War sponsored the basic research in the nuclear science necessary to sustain the civil and military applications of nuclear fission.

Governments, which of necessity must provide the financial support for scientific research, are constantly exercised to know how best to strike a balance between basic research of this kind and the more abstract lines of research which have no immediate usefulness, and usually find it necessary to influence the way in which the balance is struck by maintaining laboratories of their own for some basic research. Governments and the scientific community itself are also continually trying to discover the most efficient ways of choosing lines of fundamental research which are likely to be productive, but this is a much more difficult exercise in clairvoyance. Who is to say whether astronomy is likely in the long run to be more productive of innovation than the physics of fundamental particles?

The pace at which the innovation industry has grown is as striking as the way in which its character has changed. In Western Europe and North America, research and development is now a large fraction of all economic activity. By the mid-1960s, in the United States and Britain, close on 3 percent of the GNP was being spent each year on scientific research, partly in academic establishments and partly in government or commercial laboratories, and on technological developments of various kinds, mostly paid for with government funds.

Prosperity Is Possible

The character of science and technology in the years since the Second World War has also been transformed by the forging of links with the academic community. Here again, the origin of change was the dependence of military research on the talents that could be recruited from the universities in the years before and during the Second World War. In Western Europe and North America, at least, there has since grown up an intimate relationship between the academic institutions and applied research of all kinds, industrial as well as that supported by governments, civil as well as military. Indeed, Dr. Daniel Bell suggests that the university may have replaced the business community as the chief source of social innovation, but that is to neglect what the universities contributed in the 1930s—and J. M. Keynes was, after all, an academic—and also to assume that the influence of universities in the 1960s will persist. Already there are signs that the universities are in retreat, and there is a possibility that the environmentalists may hasten the process, at least where science and technology are concerned.

What has technology accomplished in the past few decades, and what is the promise for the years ahead? One of the strangest features of the present time is the way in which innovations are taken for granted. In the 1920s, the first radio sets were a source of great public excitement. Now, however, even more spectacular innovations, the prospect of civil thermonuclear energy, for example, create much less of a stir. Has the pace of change become so rapid that change itself is unremarkable? People expect that aircraft will continually be made to fly faster, that medical practice will be steadily improved as the tools with which doctors work are made more powerful and that, in spite of gloomy preoccupations with the prospect of starvation, plant breeders will repeatedly bring forward the new strains of wheat and rice necessary to improve agricultural productivity and to keep one step ahead of new plant diseases. But is it seemly that the benefits of technology should be regarded as inevitable and that the public interest should be encouraged to

The Doomsday Syndrome

center only on the side effects? It may be proper to seek to regulate the effluents from motor cars, but is it seemly in the process to take so much for granted their usefulness?

Medical research and its applications is a long saga of beneficial achievement which must properly be counted a part of technology. And although economists sometimes set out to value such things as the increased expectation of life, no elaborate calculus is needed to persuade the 1,000 million or so people now alive who would have died without the postwar improvements in medical technology that these have been a benefit. In the same way, the reduction of mortality among children, mainspring though it may have been for the rapid growth of population, is not merely a statistical matter for the parents concerned.

One of the most cheerful aspects of these developments is that the people whose load of misery is lightened are predominantly poor people. But modern medicine has enormously reduced the risk that children will be orphaned. The list of avoidable diseases is growing steadily—intensive care of a largely orthodox character is helping, for example, to reduce the death rate from heart failure among young adults. The prospects are bright that cancer in some of its forms will soon be added to the list. All this no doubt has contributed to the economic productivity of nations in which medical practice is efficient, for early deaths or disabilities are economic penalties, but who will say that these same developments have not improved the quality of life?

If the earth is a spaceship, then the improvements of its natural resources is an essential piece of interplanetary housekeeping (see Chapter 3). It is easy, so far after the event, to forget that aluminum became a component of engineering practice only at the turn of the century. Since then, the materials industry has been able to reduce the real cost of manufacturing not merely aluminum but most other familiar metals. At the same time, new materials have been invented and are now being manufactured. The plastics industry, which did not

Prosperity Is Possible

exist in the early 1930s, produced 25 million tons of materials in 1969. World production is at present doubling every six years, a striking proof of its utility for the world at large.

The introduction of these new materials is neither a random process nor a dictate of the "technological imperative," whatever that may be, but the result of a succession of economic opportunities. Dr. Commoner affects surprise, in *The Closing Circle*, that newer technologies are more profitable than those which they replace, but is that not a simple demonstration, in terms of the economic system as it exists, that the new products are economically beneficial, and regarded as such by those who buy them?

At the other end of the scale, comparatively rare materials are being put to use for the first time. The modern electronics industry would not exist if it were not for the comparatively small quantities of germanium and silicon now being manufactured. But who will deny that telecommunications are a social boon? Even transistor radios are not an unmitigated curse.

The contributions of technology to transport appear to offend those who are alarmed about the pollution of the atmosphere caused by motor cars and the noise which aircraft can produce. It is, therefore, important that modern transport has been liberalizing. The Victorian discovery of the bicycle is now commemorated in the richest of all Edwardian literature— horses, as it even then appeared, were as much encumbrances as means of getting about. Now, nearly a century later, it is customary to complain at the congestion and the pollution caused by motor cars, yet they have helped to diminish the depopulation of the country, they have helped the mobility of populations within whole continents and they are still an indispensable economic resource. Those who complain that motor cars are an abomination in all circumstances should occasionally reflect that they may in this way have hit on an effective way of driving a wedge between advanced nations and those still hoping to enjoy the benefits of convenient transport.

The Doomsday Syndrome

In the United States, the production of motor cars reached its peak in 1965, but elsewhere in the world they are still quite properly regarded as liberating and, ultimately, liberalizing agents. So too are aircraft. In the world as a whole, the volume of air transport (measured as the number of passengers carried and the distance which they travel) seems to have been doubling in five years or less for more than a decade. Who will protest because people can now visit the Antipodes and get back again in days, not months?

The hallmark of the new technology is the contribution of telecommunications not merely to the GNP of countries such as the United States but to the ease with which people can actually communicate with each other. One indicator of this trend is that the number of telephones in the world multiplied by three in the fifteen years to 1969, a remarkable pace of growth when the pace of growth in many countries is markedly held back by high capital cost. And if it should be thought that the telephone is merely an instrument of business and privilege, a poignant measure of the value of access to a telephone is provided by the way in which telephone traffic within New York City increased much more quickly than anybody had thought possible once the city authorities had agreed that poor people in New York could claim welfare assistance for their telephone bills.

Computers go hand in hand with telecommunications. In a mere quarter of a century, the computer manufacturing industry has become one of the largest in the world. The machines themselves have become quicker and able to handle larger amounts of information as they have shrunk physically in size. From the beginning in the mid-1940s, the new computers have made their way in the world because they are able to do simple arithmetic more quickly than people or old-fashioned arithmetical machinery. Those who bought the first machines hoped to get their money back by paying out less in wages to the armies of clerks who kept business and commerce alive in the 1930s, but it may be more important that even the first genera-

Prosperity Is Possible

tion of computers has made it possible to tackle jobs which could not be tackled at all by human beings. One result is that the working of businesses and governments is better understood than ever.

Even the earliest computers were capable of such complicated tasks that the slur that "computers are merely calculating morons" has seemed to be a comfortable anodyne for their users. The speed of computing machinery has steadily increased in the past two decades, but the changes which there have been in the way that computers can be used are probably even more significant. First, since the early 1960s, it has been possible for dozens of users to be linked to the same computing machine, and to make use of it simultaneously. The result is a degree of informality in the use of computers that is a vivid contrast with earlier experience. The computer terminal in every office is not far off. At the same time, it has become easier for people to give instructions to computers, so that those who can communicate with them are no longer high priests of the new technology. But it is now also clear that computing machinery can be used in ways that are much less cut and dried than used to be the case. People are still in charge, but a good deal of what used to pass for thinking—brooding over statistics, for example—can already be delegated to computers.

All this implies that computers will contribute to the further liberation of people from the drudgery of repetitive jobs. And who will say that clerking is less tedious than a repetitive job on an assembly line? Computers may not produce the leisure they were once expected to provide, and they may turn out to be less money-saving than some purchasers had hoped, but there is no doubt that by the 1980s, they will be as important in the economy of every advanced society as was steel production in the late nineteenth century.

Although the economic consequences of these and other developments in high technology are already considerable, it is a profound but common mistake to think that high technology is the whole of technology. Most of the benefits of technical

The Doomsday Syndrome

innovation turn up as devices for cheapening or improving the performance of familiar things. Even the maligned motor car is each year safer. Bridges are more slender yet longer. Food is each year more varied, at least in advanced societies—the technology of the deep freeze may be comparable in importance with that of the computer. Cheaper water pumps will do more for the people of developing nations in the next few years than all the majesty of electronic computers.

The confusion between high technology and the rest has an important bearing on the now popular discontent with technology as a whole. Inevitably, the innovations which excite visions of the future seem irrelevant to most people's lives. Not many people wish to go to the Antipodes in a few hours. Such developments may leave a mark on future decades, but the useful arts of humdrum technology are an immediate benefit. One of the practical questions in the management of innovation is to strike a proper balance between investment in the future and the present.

Whatever errors and excesses there may have been in the application of high technology in the past few decades, there is no room for dispute that ordinary humdrum technology has helped to bring about a profound change in the character of life in advanced societies. To a great many people, especially those directly affected, this change appears to be the same as an improvement in the quality of life. Why is it that the environmentalists wring their hands over what they consider to be assaults on the environment without at the same time acknowledging that industrialization in advanced societies has brought with it more leisure, more prosperity and more freedom as well as a greater chance of living to a decent age than used to be attainable?

By now the change in the character of advanced societies stimulated by technical innovation has led to a host of sociological descriptions. Thus Dr. Daniel Bell has argued that the point which arrived in the mid-1950s in the United States, when the number of manual workers was for the first time less

Prosperity Is Possible

than half the total labor force, represented a watershed between industrial society and what he called "the post-industrial society."

The same transition is often called the white-collar revolution. What it means is that most people work either at the management of industry or the provision of services. Agriculture, mining and manufacturing cease to be predominant. With this goes greater expenditure on services which may include such diverse activities as education and foreign travel. Food and consumer goods are less conspicuous in the family budget, in line with the old economic doctrines that there are limits to the amounts of basic commodities that people can consume.

The speed of the white-collar revolution in the United States has been quite remarkable. When people elsewhere have sought to emulate the United States, this change in the pattern of work has been as much an inducement as the economic growth which made the changes possible. Since 1900, the proportion of Latin workers in the United States' working population has decreased from 37 percent to less than 10 percent. Most of the slack has been taken up by an increase of the proportion of workers in the United States who work in commerce and administration. Although the statistics are a little misleading in that they span a period during which increasing numbers of women have gone out to work, usually at jobs classified as white-collar jobs, the change certainly reflects the ways in which people in the United States spend their personal income. Foreign travel may seem conspicuous in the American way of life, but education occupies a much larger fraction of the total wealth of the United States—5 percent of the GNP. Are these changes seriously to be deplored?

Leisure is another index of the change. In manufacturing industry in the mid-1960s, the average working week was forty-one hours, but if the pattern of the American economy remains the same as it has been—by no means a safe assumption—there will be a sharp decrease in the length of the working

The Doomsday Syndrome

week in manufacturing industry from the mid-1970s on. The problem, if it is a problem, arises because productivity in manufacturing industry in the United States is still growing so quickly that there will either have to be a sharp reduction of the labor force or some radically new outlet for manufactured goods. Will foreign aid be one way of diverting what promises to be the excessive productive capacity of the United States in the decade ahead?

To say that there will be more leisure is also to state a problem. In the 1950s, people like Dr. David Riesman were ready to welcome the prospect of more leisure because they despaired of the possibility of making work more meaningful. Now, it is almost as common for people to bemoan that nobody knows what to do with leisure. Nobody will pretend that the problem does not exist. In advanced societies, people may be as ill-prepared for the benefits of the post-industrial society as are the subsistence farmers of India and Pakistan to face the prospect of a mercantile society. But problems like these are challenges of a kind which it is impossible to shirk. The prospect of more time on people's hands is, of course, a challenge as well as a discouragement. The result could be enlightenment and not the opposite.

The post-industrial society is characteristically a society with egalitarian tendencies. So much has been apparent for more than a century. Almost exactly a century ago, Alfred Marshall said: "The question is not whether all men will ultimately be equal—that they certainly will not be—but whether progress may go on steadily, if slowly, till by occupation at least, every man is a gentleman." This is in part a declaration that some forms of work can cramp if not destroy the spirit, and in spite of all the talk of how the new technology is dehumanizing, who now afflicted by technology would willingly settle instead for the life of a Victorian laborer or a latter-day peasant farmer on the Bay of Bengal?

Marshall's comment was also an economic prediction—industrialization will bring a narrower spread of family income.

Prosperity Is Possible

One of the striking features of the recent economic history of all advanced nations, whatever their political positions, has been the tendency for the economic gap between the rich and poor to diminish. The mechanism, of course, is easy to understand. Industry depends on skill, and skilled people can make economic demands on their employers. Although the continuation of the process of social change which began with the Industrial Revolution is not certain to bring liberty, equality and happiness, there is at least a good chance that it will do so. Moreover, the chance is greater now than it used to be.

It goes without saying that the developing nations of the world are still a long way from what Dr. Daniel Bell calls the post-industrial society. Moreover, given the uncertainties about the usefulness of economic statistics such as the GNP for comparisons of the advanced and developing nations, and the inaccuracy of social statistics for many parts of the developing world, it is hard to form an accurate picture of how rapidly the processes of change can happen in the developing world. Plainly, much will depend on how quickly some measure of stability is found for the size of the population. Although the rapid pace of technical change in the industrial societies of the West has in recent years created the impression that the gap between advanced and developing nations is constantly being widened as a consequence of technical innovation, this is now perhaps a less serious cause for concern than it has been, not only because developed nations have now acknowledged, in principle at least, their obligations towards those still developing, but also because of the qualitative changes that have taken place in recent years among which the mercantilism following on the green revolution may in the long run be the most conspicuous.

But what is the value of technology if its unpleasant side effects outweigh the benefits? It is proper to acknowledge that even when technical innovations bring no unexpected side effects, their direct effects may entail unwelcome change. Even the

The Doomsday Syndrome

development of typewriters, uncomplicated innovations, would mean that legions of copperplate clerks were out of work. But is it true, as Dr. Jack D. Douglas says, that "the threats to our natural environment from the multifarious forms of pollution, all of which stem directly or indirectly from the advance of technology, have put an end to the bright dreams of technological utopias"?

Three simple truths about technological innovation help to put these questions in perspective. First, side effects have always accompanied industrial activity, as the metallurgical slag heaps of the Western world will testify. Many of the side effects accompanying Victorian innovation were much more damaging even than the carbon monoxide which motor cars produce. Second, technical innovations come about only if they offer some decisive advantage over techniques which already exist or if they promise some previously nonexistent benefit. In the circumstances, the positive benefits of some innovation are always sufficient to make it worthwhile to spend money on the avoidance of unpleasant consequences. The best way of dealing with carbon-monoxide pollution, in other words, is not to do away with motor cars but to ensure that combustion is more accurately controlled in internal-combustion engines. And third, there is no reason why communities should not decide whether to allow technical innovations to be introduced and, if necessary, to devise laws to regulate their use. It is in this spirit that society has so far refrained from using the technology of nuclear weapons for blasting harbors and canals, as the United States Atomic Energy Commission has been pleading for a decade to be allowed to do. The benefits are problematical, the risk of incidental damage is not negligible and all concerned (apart from some officials of the AEC) appear to have accepted that the game is not worth the candle.

The fear that computers will help to rob people of freedom has a special place in the literature of doomsday, but the shadow of Big Brother is as insubstantial as any other. In the rich literature

Prosperity Is Possible

of the struggle between the individual and the bureaucracy, the fear has frequently arisen that malevolent or even self-satisfied bureaucracies would seek to use machinery to keep their constituents on some straight and narrow path. And is not the Tower of London full of the instruments by means of which monarchs tried to make sure that their intentions, sometimes felt to be in the interests of their subjects, were properly respected? The modern equivalents are supposed to be the techniques of mass communications and the use of computers. What is the truth?

To the extent that science and technology are blamed for what seems to be a threat to individual liberty, it is relevant that much of contemporary science must have helped to undermine many individuals' sense of personal identity. Even such abstract developments in science as the recognition that living things first sprang from the more or less random synthesis of organic chemicals in the primitive atmosphere of the earth 3,000 million years ago raise problems for those brought up to believe that life began quite differently. The vast scale of the universe, the possibility that what seems from the earth to be the universe is merely some isolated backwater in a much larger and still problematical scheme of things and the growing conviction that other kinds of living things will one day be found elsewhere in the universe are disturbing ideas. The anxiety which has attached to molecular biology, and the fears often expressed about the supposed horrors of genetic engineering, are signs of how profoundly people's confidence in the autonomy of human beings has been undermined by discovery. And if it is possible to simulate by means of electronic computers the functioning of, say, a city so as to predict precisely how it will respond to some change or other, is that not also an affront to the common but mistaken view that human behavior is essentially unpredictable?

Machines which can think in some sense are a more direct assault on what is thought of as liberty. All kinds of schemes have been put forward to suggest how computers may be used

The Doomsday Syndrome

to rob people of their freedom. Some people fear that the large computer files now maintained by governments for storing information about people's income tax, for example, might be used also to keep detailed records of how they have been educated, how their careers have developed and how they might be coerced into some unwelcome course of action. Or computing machinery might be used to make sure that social benefits are distributed only to people with patterns of behavior prescribed by the central government—those who have voted for the government of the day might have first claim on the schools or hospital services, for example.

The flaw in these arguments is that even the vast computers which now exist could not easily be used for such ambitious tasks. No amount of electronic wizardry can do much to simplify the present problems of handling, even with computers, very large files of statistical information. Even to store on a computer the names and addresses of all the people in countries such as the Soviet Union and the United States would require that something like a hundred thousand million items of information should be stored. With existing machinery, it would take close on a day to search through this file of information to discover, for example, some particular person's address. But if more information is to be stored, and if more complicated searches are to be made, the time taken and the cost involved become extremely large. Even when computers are still faster than at present, the gulf between the magnitude of the mass of information about individuals which might be stored and the amounts of information which computers can sensibly be expected to handle would remain. In other words, however hard they try, governments will probably discover that the detailed control of individual destiny by means of a computer is either unrealistic or inordinately expensive.

The possibility that commercial computers may be used to interfere with individual privacy is more worrying. Already there have been complaints in the United States that organizations which set up in business to vouch for the credit of private

Prosperity Is Possible

citizens will, when computers are fully used for this kind of work, be more efficient than at present and therefore more able to damn a person's credit rating wrongly. Undoubtedly, there is plenty of scope for such applications of computers, as indeed for computers to store and later to recognize the names of people suspected of traffic violations (which has already made New York City notorious but not noticeably more effective in hunting down people with unpaid parking fines). And it remains something of a puzzle that immigration officials in the United States still have to refer to a loose-leaf book whenever a foreign visitor presents a passport and a request for entry. Why is the blacklist not already on a computer?

In all these possible applications, however, the technology of computers will serve only to make more efficient tasks which are already attempted. If the result is intolerable, the moral is not that computers are malevolent but that the tasks which they are used for, and which are already being undertaken, are themselves intolerable. In other words, if too rigorous an application of the rules by which the credit bureaus function may have the effect of perpetrating an injustice against some unsuspecting individual, then the credit bureaus should not be allowed to operate as they do even at present. Questions like this are, after all, entirely within the competence of governments.

Much the same can be said of the fear that the new electronic technology will help to make propaganda more efficient. It is no accident that the leaders of political coups always have radio stations high on their list of buildings to be occupied. The loudspeakers to be seen on many village lampposts in Eastern Europe are another manifestation. And 1984 in Orwell's sense is possible only with such efficient methods of observation and communication that no person is able without breaking the rules to enjoy privacy. Here again, however, it is not technology which should be blamed but the motives of those who seek to use it malevolently. No doubt Nazi Germany would have welcomed the television set, but the 1930s were also a telling

The Doomsday Syndrome

proof that in the mounting of an efficient propaganda campaign, the medium is less important than the message. Low-frequency radio receivers were quite good enough for Hitler and Goebbels.

That most complaints about the use of the mass media as instruments of propaganda should at present come from the United States—with its two television receivers for every five people—is another of the paradoxes with which the doomsday movement is suffused. To be sure, commercial advertising is presumably effective enough in the eyes of those who pay for it to justify the cost, which presumably implies that the opinions and choices of those who see broadcast commercial advertising have been influenced. It seems also to be clear, however, from the running battle between the American television networks and successive administrations, that the content of television broadcasting has been if anything unwelcome to the Administration. Television in the United States has probably helped to bring about a change of policy on Vietnam. For that matter, it has also been influential in spreading news of the supposed environmental crisis. Perhaps the most serious complaint against the new mass media is that they can exaggerate public issues. The question of whether they can be used malevolently by central governments is, however, the same as the question how are they to be regulated. This has always been the case, even when the only methods of broadcasting were town criers. Whether the new mass media become intolerable instruments of propaganda will be settled not by a better understanding of how they function, but by political decisions, of an entirely familiar kind, about how channels of communication should be controlled. Big Brother is a political animal, not a creation of technology.

Among the chief targets of the environmentalists is the modern city, which has often seemed to be the institution that combines all the evils of the modern world. Cities, after all, are notoriously the sources of pollution. The largest of them, New York

Prosperity Is Possible

and London, for example, are such prolific sources of heat that the temperature in the center, at least in the winter, will tend to be several degrees above that in the surrounding countryside. Cities are also crowded places where social problems are most conspicuous—where the welfare roll is most crowded and where the murder rate is highest. To what extent has the new technology contributed to these problems? To what extent might the new technology help to make them go away?

Most of the complaints now everywhere to be heard about the modern city seem to be uninformed by an appreciation of the role of the city in society, not merely now but for the past 3,000 years. Mr. Lewis Mumford—now, as it happens, one of the despondent—has most sensitively described the function of the city in his monumental book *The City in History*. Cities are not simply places for people who have nowhere else to be. From the beginning, the propinquity which city life provides has been a social and economic asset. The whole is greater than the sum of the parts. The other side of the coin is that cities must bear the brunt of the change brought about by the transformation of agriculture and industry. Since the nineteenth century, new industries have flocked to the cities as have workers displaced from the land. What happened a century ago in Manchester and Birmingham is now happening in Nairobi and—although this is a different case—Calcutta. Is it any wonder that cities should be the places at which social problems burst through the surface?

To hope that cities will one day be free from problems like these is to hope for such a degree of stability within society that industrial and social change will be at an end. The practical question is to know how best to strike a balance between the economic health of society at large and the social and environmental problems of the modern city. The first guiding principle is that it is not possible to cure the problems of the city by curing the symptoms. Mr. Charles Abrams has pointed eloquently to the folly (in New York) of seeking to put an end to slums by providing alternative housing at rents far beyond the

The Doomsday Syndrome

pockets of the slum dwellers. In the same way, welfare relief, necessary though it may be, is not a sufficient solution to the problem of unemployment and impoverishment. The problem of city transport will not be solved simply by legislating against the motor car.

The motor car, however, has undoubtedly helped to change the shapes of cities. Within the present century, the population of the largest cities has grown but (with a few exceptions) has also become more thinly spread. In Boston, for example, the population density at the center was 220 to the acre in 1900 and 69 to the acre in 1950. Between 1900 and 1940, the central density in Philadelphia fell from 180 to the acre to roughly 90 to the acre. The central density in London is now less than a fifth of what it was in 1801. The benefits for the suburban commuters are plain enough—the illusion of country life combined with the stimulation of working in the city. But may this be a case in which the public good is not the simple sum of the interests of individuals? The suburban sprawl is an offense against the countryside. The traffic congestion in the city streets is a consequence of the daily commuting journeys as of the intensive business and social life of the city.

The question is to know how to strike a better balance between the interests of individuals and of the community as a whole. This again is an economic question, and it is hard to see how the ideal pattern for any modern city can be discovered until some attempt is made to reflect the real costs of city life in the prices people pay for services and amenities. Should those who operate motor vehicles in crowded cities, for example, pay simply for the fuel they consume in doing so, or should they also pay their share of the cost of setting aside land for city streets, for building new access roads and even, on occasion, for taking steps to remove air pollution and the like? Nobody can be sure just precisely what would be the extra cost to the operators of motor vehicles of such measures, but there is a good chance that if real costs were charged, people would be less inclined to live in the suburbs, with the result that some at least of the most obvious problems would tend to disappear.

Prosperity Is Possible

People would begin moving back to the city centers, for example.

The undoubted defects of city life must thus be laid at the door of city administrations, not technologists—not even automobile engineers. Their failure, indeed, is one of the many ways in which technological innovations provide less than their potential benefit by being required to fly in the face of simple economic principles.

One of the most conspicuous features of the modern city is not the dominance of technology but its neglect. Even in what is often called the electronic age, opportunities for replacing messenger boys by communications circuits are outrageously neglected. City administrations and property developers conspire to erect huge office blocks without considering how those who work in them will make the journey. Arrangements for enabling people to move about within cities remain primitive. Most city administrations worry about such things as the location of offices, dwelling and amenities, but always on such a tiny scale that they are unable to do more than perpetuate the errors of their predecessors. Many environmentalists would suggest that the city as such is an abomination, but others will be more anxious to ensure that cities become as pleasurable as technology can make them.

The case of the modern city is yet another proof that technology is by no means the irrepressible autonomous agent which it is sometimes supposed to be, most conspicuously by Dr. Jacques Ellul. The record of the past few years, in Western Europe and in North America, shows quite clearly that communities are continually electing not to take up innovations of one kind or another. One striking illustration is the decision by the United States Congress in 1971 not to continue spending money on the development of a prototype supersonic civil aircraft. Ironically, by the time the decision to cancel had been taken, so much had been spent on the project that it was illogical not to have seen how the prototype would perform in flight.

Successive British governments elected not to introduce first

The Doomsday Syndrome

television and then color television as quickly as they might have done for fear of reducing the rate of personal saving. Most countries forbid really fast motor cars—or at least neglect to provide roads on which they can be driven. In many cities, techniques for building tall buildings are never used because planning authorities consider, perhaps rightly, that amenities will be irreparably damaged.

The running battle in the past few years between the residents of New York and the Consolidated Edison Company, which makes and sells electricity in the city, is a vivid proof of what communities can do to stem what they think of as the juggernaut of technology. By proposing, in 1962, that there should be a nuclear power station within the city limits, the generating company clearly posed the questions of how much New York was prepared to pay for its electricity and whether it would prefer power stations within the city or on the banks of the Hudson, still largely unspoiled. In the event, the community has gone on increasing its consumption of electricity and at the same time has set its face against the nuclear power station, has sanctioned a conventional power station (the Astoria plant) but has restricted the output of electricity from it and has set its face against a pumped storage system a few miles up the river. By the exertion of public pressures, New York has electricity shortages instead of power stations. The next step is to work out ways of running the city at a reduced voltage.

By now, there is ample evidence that the most interesting problem of modern technology is not that of coercion but that of choice. The mere existence of the environmental movement implies that radical changes in the pattern of technology are conceivable. But there can be no simple strategy for deciding the directions of technical innovation. To be sure, where most humdrum technology is concerned, the problem of choice can be left to the manufacturers. In the West, for example, it is for typewriter manufacturers to back their judgment of what kinds of innovations would be beneficial with the money which they

Prosperity Is Possible

have to lay out to support development. Elsewhere, other criteria may be used in deciding when some minor improvement should be introduced. Few governments are willing—let alone competent—to be arbiters in decisions like these, but the community does have a proper interest in providing a framework within which manufacturers may operate freely. It is proper but also traditional that governments should require that even minor improvements of technique should not be allowed to damage the interests of consumers and the environment. Electrical products, for example, must be designed so as not to electrocute those who use them. Food additives must be tested before they are used. Motor cars must be reasonably safe to drive.

Even in the regulation of conventional technology, however, mistakes are possible. The new safety regulations for motor cars in the United States may be a step backwards, for example—nobody can be sure at this stage whether the air bags which are supposed to inflate between the front seat passengers and the windshield whenever there is a collision will actually save lives. Here, as in the prescription of what is safe and what is unsafe in the use of drugs or synthetic chemicals, deciding where to strike a balance is never easy.

In the Western economy, private individuals have helped to shape the pattern of innovation by their decisions to spend money on new products, motor cars and food, for example. On the other hand, governments tend to have the decisive say in regulating the development of the electronic computer industry, telecommunications and ship development and it is no surprise that in these roles they have been far from perfect. Sometimes governments have chosen to fly in the face of the long-term interests of their citizens in keeping alive technologies which are unlikely to be of value to the society concerned. In the same spirit, the United States' journeys to the moon, successful within their own terms, can hardly be counted an economic or a social gain for the people of the United States, which is another way of saying that resources to the value of $20,000 million have

The Doomsday Syndrome

been wasted. A good part of the disillusion with technology springs from the irrationality of decisions like this. The Apollo program has probably also contributed to the sense that technology is a juggernaut which can be stopped or diverted from its goal only with the greatest difficulty.

Governments can have a decisive influence on the pattern of development of high technology, for the cost of opening up a new field may be far greater than private corporations can afford. To acknowledge that the system does not always function perfectly is not a proof that technology is out of control. In Britain, for example, governments since the Second World War have helped to support the development of new aircraft even though the chances now seem small that commercially viable aircraft would result. In the United States, the Apollo program is only one of many ill-thought-out decisions by the administration. Until very recently the same has been true of the technology of cancer therapy. Projects like these, however, are exceptional and, however large, they represent only a small part of a nation's spending on technical innovation. It follows that modern technology has made it necessary for governments to set up machinery for making decisions in the shifting sands where science, technology and the interests of society come together.

But why not dispense with technical innovation and thus avoid the problems it creates? After zero population growth might come zero innovation. The chief objection is that innovation is at some level inseparable from industry. Even if governments were to elect not to spend money on research and development or on the training of scientists and engineers, ways would be found, as in the nineteenth century, of continually improving the performance of the machines already in existence. And if it is hard to quantify the economic benefits of new expenditures on research and development, decisions not to spend money would be quickly reflected in loss of competitiveness in markets overseas. In short, as long as there is international trade, and as long as some nations are prepared to

Prosperity Is Possible

base their exports on technical innovations, technology is unavoidable.

International connections are likely to be increasingly important. In the past few years, it has become painfully apparent that there are urgent reasons why advanced societies should provide those which are economically impoverished with large amounts of foreign aid. In this sense, economic growth has naturally an important part to play. For even if the advanced communities should decide that they no longer wish to see an increase in personal affluence at home, only by an increase of the output of manufactured goods or agricultural products will it be possible to provide developing countries with tangible help. Although countries in receipt of foreign aid are increasingly anxious to be given money and not goods, it is possible to use pound notes or dollar bills only by exchanging them for goods or services which must ultimately be provided by the donors. Even if, in some communities, the prophets of doom were able to persuade a majority of the people in advanced societies to settle for their present levels of prosperity, it would be an international tragedy if the industrial economies of these countries were not encouraged to grow so as to provide the materials necessary for removing the disparity between nations.

Technology can make a direct contribution to the improvement of the lot of developing nations. Over the years, there has been a continuing argument about the extent to which developing countries should adopt the technology which has been the foundation of economic advancement in Western Europe and North America. Even quite recently, countries such as India, not by any means well endowed with resources, have spent large sums on the development of such things as nuclear power stations and even space rockets. What purpose have these served? Would it not have been better to spend the resources instead on other kinds of equipment, for irrigation perhaps? The short answer, indeed the only answer, is that a dash of high technology may be useful even in developing countries as a means of stimulating interest in developing the skills of bright

The Doomsday Syndrome

people who might otherwise emigrate or avoid technology altogether.

The developing nations also present a unique range of problems in technology. In Africa, for example, it remains a puzzle to know how best to develop tropical agriculture—the groundnuts scheme is still too fresh in people's minds for that to be forgotten. Elsewhere, the management of underground water resources may be an overwhelming problem. How to extract water from the Indus basin year in and year out without accumulating intolerable quantities of salt in the ground and without using up the reservoir? In the particular ways in which they occur in developing nations, these problems present a challenge which is altogether different from that with which conventional technology is familiar.

But in connections like these, science and technology are not so much to be regarded as straitjackets for society but as tools by mean of which practical social problems may be solved. Is it reasonable also to consider that this influence is malign?

What Can Be Done?

8

The hallmark of the doomsday movement is gloom. Among those who consider that the pace of growth of the world's population is a serious impediment to economic growth in the developing countries, for example, only some appear to share the Ehrlich view embodied in declarations such as "the battle to feed all of humanity is over." Among those who consider that environmental pollution is a nuisance, only some go on to echo Dr. Commoner's view that "the emergence of a full-blown crisis in the ecosystem can be regarded, as well, as the signal of an emerging crisis in the economic system." In doing so, as it happens, they dodge a great many practical questions which, if answered, could help immediately with the improvement of the environment—the development of effective legislation for the control of polluting discharges, for example. And when the doomsday men suppose that present directions in biological research embody serious threats to the integrity of the human race, they make a whole string of assumptions that medical men will in future behave malevolently, quite out of character with their traditions. The doomsday movement is dedicated, in other words, to the view that the worst will always happen.

Against this background, it is not surprising that prophecies of cataclysm abound in the doomsday literature. Dr. Commoner says that "the world is being carried to the brink of ecological disaster not by a singular fault, which some clever scheme can correct, but by the phalanx of powerful economic, political and social forces which constitute the march of history." This theme which informs what might be called the extreme doomsday movement, is that cataclysm is almost but not quite inescapable. The great issue, for the modern world as with the inhabitants of the biblical Sodom and Gomorrah, is whether it can mend its ways in time to escape disaster.

The Doomsday Syndrome

The results are usually naive. They are well illustrated by the comprehensive recipe for survival published by *The Ecologist* in January 1972 under the banner "A Blueprint for Survival." According to the editors of the journal, one of the horrors to be avoided is the "Collapse of Society" when "at times of great distress and social chaos, it is more than probable that governments will fall into the hands of reckless and unscrupulous elements who will not hestitate to threaten neighboring governments with attack, if they feel that they can wrest from them a larger share of the world's vanishing resources. Since a growing number of countries (an estimated 36 by 1980) will have nuclear power stations, and therefore sources of plutonium for nuclear warheads, the likelihood of a whole series of local (if not global) nuclear engagements is greatly increased."

And what is the solution? *The Ecologist* goes on to describe "a new social system" which is on the face of things as frankly utopian as anything Godwin wrote (see Chapter 2). The authors would "promote the social conditions in which public opinion and full public participation in decision making become as far as possible the means whereby communities are ordered." In particular, police forces would be dispensed with. From this it follows—so the argument goes—that society must be decentralized to small communities but, then, with small-scale industries made integral parts of small communities, "it is much more likely to encourage product innovation because people clearly want qualitative improvements in a given field rather than because expansion is necessary for that industry's survival or because there is otherwise insufficient work for its research and development section." But such communities are said to have other advantages—people will "enjoy the rewards of the small community, of knowing and being known, of an intensity of relationship with a few rather than urban man's variety of innumerable superficial relationships." And in the process of changing society, the editors of *The Ecologist* "emphasize that our goal should be to create community feeling and global awareness rather than the dangerous and sterile compromise

What Can Be Done?

which is nationalism." William Morris would hardly have put it differently.

This recipe, of no great distinction in itself, is nevertheless a vivid illustration of the extent to which the environmental crisis is regarded by its chroniclers as the kind of milestone in human affairs which can only change the course of history, possibly for the better but more probably by catastrophe. The most serious weakness of this position is that the facts do not usually support it. The growth of the world's population is not nearly as inexorable as the environmentalists say. The threat of famine is receding, not coming closer. Minerals are now more plentiful than ever, whatever the more distant prospects. Lake Erie is not dead, and genetic engineering is neither a threat nor even a practical possibility.

But nobody will pretend that there are no problems to be solved, many of them the unforeseen consequences of technical innovation, and the second important weakness in the extreme environmentalist position is that it pays too little attention to the ways in which existing techniques, chiefly legal and administrative, have been used to remedy public nuisances. And is there any reason why the continuing pollution of Lake Erie should not be controlled by the devices which have been used to keep other bodies of water clean—the prohibition of the discharge of untreated sewage or other chemical effluents, for example? Is there any reason why those who complain of air pollution in cities should not be enabled to breathe the cleaner air which they yearn for as a result of sensible traffic planning and regulation? Indeed, the environmentalists who shake their heads in sorrow over what they call the ecological catastrophe neglect not merely what might be done to restrict the public nuisances of which it is now easy to complain—they also ignore what has been done already. And is it not the case that protests about aircraft noise have so far prevented New York from finding a site for a fourth airport and have required the British government to place a site for a third airport on the estuary of the Thames, close on fifty miles away? Is it not the case that air

The Doomsday Syndrome

pollution has been decreasing for the past decade in British and American cities? That the pace of population growth in a great many developing countries has begun to decline as those populations have learned through prosperity and education to follow the ways by means of which the now advanced communities have learned to moderate the size of future generations?

The third weakness of the extreme positions which now compel public attention, at least in the English-speaking countries of the North Atlantic, is that it ignores what might be done. One of the most misleading and potentially damaging errors in the metaphor of spaceship earth is that it suggests that the environment of the earth is not merely delicately balanced—which is half true—but that its ingredients are for practical purposes predetermined. Although in the most literal sense of all, there is no serious prospect that human beings will ever be able to make new kinds of raw materials with which to work, the record of the past two million years shows plainly enough that the survival of the human race is not dependent merely on the availability or the shortage of particular raw materials or even on a favorable climate, but on the deliberate exercise of human ingenuity. To assume that the equipment of spaceship earth consists merely of the stock of elements—things like iron and silicon—with which it was endowed 4,500 million years ago is willfully to ignore the way in which people, even the most primitive people, have by ingenuity helped to ensure their survival or at least that of their children and grandchildren. Now, as throughout the past two million years, it remains a surprise that this species has kept alive against all the odds. No doubt the strangest irony of the extreme environmentalist position is that it has come into the open at a time when human beings are more than ever able to mold the environment in which they live, using it where possible, putting up with it where necessary.

The world is not in nearly as bad a state as the Commoners and Ehrlichs say it is. Moreover, the present discontents cannot be laid entirely at the door of technology, and it is a non-

What Can Be Done?

question to ask—as many people do—will the technology that has brought us to this pass be able to find a way out again? Indeed, the ways in which the machinery of society needs to be adjusted so as to diminish problems as diverse as those of pollution and the sense of alienation between science and society are familiar and ancient. How can a balance be struck between the interests of individuals and larger organizations, what constitutes the common good, in what ways must political machinery be strengthened so that communities can choose between novel kinds of opportunities? What can be learned from the past? What needs to be done to strengthen existing institutions?

In the past two years, in the United States in particular but in Western Europe as well, a great deal of constructive work has been done on these problems, especially the abatement of pollution. It remains a puzzle why so little use is made of existing law. In Britain, after all, a man who creates a nuisance for his neighbor can be sued. There are often legal definitions of what constitutes a nuisance—putting up a building in such a way that a neighbor is deprived of light can be prohibited. People may now be alarmed to see how far rivers have been polluted with effluent, but they should first of all reflect that much of what is now recognized as pollution is a monument to the complaisance of previous generations.

In the peculiar circumstances of the United States, where people are fond of saying that pollution knows no frontiers, the most serious impediments to improvement are the barriers which separate the jurisdiction of municipal, state and federal governments. To urge that the United States government should protect the environment is to ask that it should devise a system of interlocking carrots and sticks that will persuade governments at a lower level to act sensibly. In the past few years, it has been helped enormously by the willingness of several states—New York, California and Illinois, for example —to adopt legislation that reflects federal decisions. This explains how fitful has been federal intervention in environmental improvement.

The Doomsday Syndrome

In the circumstances, it is perhaps an unexpected triumph for good sense that so much has been done in recent decades to look after the improvement of the environment. The conservation movement in the United States has been supported generously by the federal government since the beginning of the century. President Lyndon B. Johnson in 1965 spelled out a program of financial assistance for conservation and the improvement of the environment. It was itself a landmark. At the beginning of 1970, President Richard M. Nixon introduced a measure that would spend some $4,000 million of federal money over three years as a federal contribution to approved municipal programs for the improvement of water quality. By the beginning of 1971, several new developments had taken place in the United States. The Administration first of all set up the Council on Environmental Quality, with responsibility for making policy on the environment. Later in the year, there followed the Environmental Protection Agency, charged with executing policy, but with responsibility to begin with largely for air and water pollution—the supervision of policy on pesticides, traditionally with the Department of Agriculture, was not transferred to the EPA. The Food and Drug Administration, with responsibility for contaminants in food, was similarly left alone.

By a mixture of cajolery and persuasion, the EPA seems to have been able to exert a noticeable influence on municipal care for air and water pollution. In 1970, the agency estimated that rather more than $2,000 million was spent on capital equipment for the treatment of water pollution, and that a further $17,000 million would have been invested in the following four years. At the beginning of the agency's existence, water pollution was the chief contender for public funds but it is clear that capital investment in equipment for cleaning the gases from industrial machinery and motor cars is going to cost an increasingly large proportion of the total as the years go by. Between 1970 and 1975, the EPA estimates that more than $60,000 million will have been spent on air and water cleaning.

What Can Be Done?

As in Britain so in the United States, the concern about air pollution which has influenced public policy throughout the 1960s has already brought some benefits. In Chicago, for example, air pollution seems to have reached its peak in 1965 and since then the concentration of both sulphur dioxide and carbon monoxide in the atmosphere has decreased, carbon monoxide most spectacularly. In Denver, Philadelphia, St. Louis and Washington, D.C., there has been a substantial improvement in the quality of city air since the mid-1960s. But monitoring, an expensive activity, is still far from thorough.

The precise reasons why city air appears to have become cleaner are not understood, although it may well be that the cities where the pollution is most severe have set out deliberately to enforce standards. This certainly explains why air pollution in New York has diminished since its peak in 1968. If this explanation is correct, the outlook is of course cheerful, for it implies first of all that regulations on the use of machinery can have important consequences. And although the total amount of smoke, carbon monoxide and sulphur dioxide released into the atmosphere in the United States continues to increase from one year to the next, it now appears that greater proportions of it must be discharged in rural atmospheres where natural dispersion is more efficient.

Nobody should be surprised that simple restrictions on the kinds of machinery in use and the ways in which they may be used should have such an effect. In London, after all, the Clean Air legislation of the 1950s, which has progressively required that different regions in the United Kingdom should burn no fuel which could emit smoke, has enormously improved the quality of the atmosphere. The most startling result has been the disappearance of polluted fog (called smog) from London. It must be acknowledged that confusion which arises in the United States because the federal government is able only to specify standards at which motor cars will be manufactured for example, but must let local authorities police the enforcement of these regulations, is a serious barrier not merely to

The Doomsday Syndrome

cleaner air and water but to a legal framework that will seem equitable to all who are affected by it.

There is no reason why straightforward legislation should not be used to regulate the forms of pollution which are chiefly a public nuisance within a nation's frontiers. Although at the beginning of their existence, both the Council on Environmental Quality and the Environmental Protection Agency in the United States were exposed to all kinds of temptations to adopt the environmental message as a banner, in the event they have turned out to be rather hard-headed organizations, as much concerned with the economics of pollution as with the crusade against it. The nearest equivalent agency in Britain is the Department of the Environment, an amalgam of government departments dealing with matters as different as transport and housing policy. The sharpest difference between British and American practice is that the Department of the Environment is its own critic on matters of the management of the environment.

The problem of enforcement is especially difficult in the United States because of the distribution of executive responsibility between the different levels of government, but there are also technical problems long since typified by the attempts in Britain to define smoke pollution by means of a crude visual standard which an inspector holds up before his eyes and the difficulty of knowing when a heavy lorry may be emitting more than a prescribed amount of invisible carbon monoxide. But, in controlling the pollution from internal-combustion engines, in the United States it has been necessary to lay down standards which apply to motor vehicles as manufactured. Although allowance has been made for a measure of deterioration, it will be hard to make sure that negligent servicing or improper operation will not break the rules.

This is why there is great interest in schemes for restricting some forms of pollution by the application of the price mechanism. There is, for example, a scheme in the United States to restrict the use of lead in gasoline (petrol) by putting a tax on

What Can Be Done?

lead-based additives, and in February 1971 the EPA was at work on a scheme for imposing charges on sulphur-dioxide emission. There has also been talk of using such devices for persuading manufacturers to restrict the amounts of pollution in the effluents which they discharge to the atmosphere and to rivers. The justification for these devices is that they help to smooth the transition from one state of affairs where some source of pollution is uncontrolled to another where it does not exist because it has been priced out of existence. The principle is that those whose activities pollute the atmosphere should be made to pay for the privilege of doing so. Plainly, similar arrangements can be used to regulate other forms of public nuisance—a tax on DDT, for example, might help to strike a balance between the interests of farmers to use as much DDT as may be necessary to kill unwanted insects and the interests of the community at large to see that the use of DDT is restricted, if only for the sake of wildlife. Taxes are by no means a panacea for public nuisances, but they are a powerful illustration of what can be done by administrative methods which already exist to moderate insults to the environment.

Understandably, the new machinery for the regulation of pollution is least well equipped to decide just where to draw the line between the tolerable and the intolerable. Quite apart from the difficulties of predicting what forms of pollution will spring from what kinds of activity, there are also few ways in which the balance between cost and benefit can be discussed in economic terms in circumstances in which the interested parties can put their case intelligently and can be questioned intelligently. Although the committees of Congress in the United States have welcomed the environment movement as a device for asking unfamiliar questions of unaccustomed witnesses, they have not been especially good at recognizing that the first step in sensible regulation is to strike a sensible balance.

To judge from its second report, published in 1971, the Council on Environmental Quality is evidently hoping for great things from a novel administrative device promulgated in April

The Doomsday Syndrome

1971. Since then all federal departments, agencies and establishments have been required to make an assessment of the consequences of any new proposal from the construction of a building or the operation of a new manufacturing establishment, which might "significantly affect the quality of the human environment." This has the practical effect of requiring the Atomic Energy Commission to file what are called "impact statements" which for better or worse ensures that the AEC is no longer both the source of proposals for using nuclear energy in the United States and the arbiter of when these uses are likely to be safe. What the council hopes is that it will be possible to extend this procedure to cover all activities which are supported wholly or in part by federal money—in other words, publicly sponsored research on a new type of aircraft would allow the Environmental Protection Agency to ask hard questions about the environmental effects of that aircraft. And because one striking feature of the new procedure is that the impact statements, as they are called, should be open to public comment from outside the federal government, it is plain that the new administrative device will serve sometimes to prevent foolish projects and sometimes as a lightning rod to disarm ill-informed opposition.

More to the point, the Environmental Protection Agency in its first two years did much to throw light on the economic aspects of pollution in the United States, partly with the help of committees of the U.S. National Academy of Sciences. In 1971, for example, the agency was able to record not merely the slow but steady decline of air pollution in sixty important cities in the United States, but also to understand the limitations of what Congress had done in its hasty setting of standards for motor-vehicle exhaust fumes. The regulations which Congress had promulgated would imply something like an extra $250 on the cost of each new automobile, but even so it remains to be seen whether it will be possible for manufacturers to comply with the regulations due to come into force in 1975. (A report from the National Academy of Sciences at the beginning of

What Can Be Done?

1972 suggested that there was still some way to go before suitable engines would be available.) If at some stage in the 1970s, suitable engines become available, the exhausts from American automobiles will be the cleanest in the world, at least if the regulation can be effectively enforced.

What will all this cost? The programs of air and water pollution control mounted in the United States were reckoned by the Council on Environmental Quality in 1971 to cost a total of $61,700 million between 1970 and 1975, and a further $43,500 million would be spent on programs for solid waste disposal. By 1975, the annual cost of these programs will be $16,500 million. By then the Council on Environmental Quality estimates, 1.5 percent of the GNP of the United States will be spent on pollution control. The direct economic penalty is clearly small, but some industries will be more seriously affected than others. The cost of water treatment at paper mills, for example, is likely to exceed 1.6 percent of the value of the paper manufactured in the United States and this will entail both an increase in the cost of paper and a deceleration of the pace at which American forests are cut down to feed the paper mills—an uncovenanted benefit for the conservationists. Other industries will be significantly affected by air pollution control. The Council for Environmental Quality has estimated, for example, that the capital cost of bringing iron and steel plants up to the new standards will consume something like 10 percent of the steel industry's capital expenditure.

The result will be that the prices of many manufactured products will be changed and, as a result, there will be small but significant changes in the pattern of consumption. The community, of course, will gain an improvement of air and water quality when the polluters are saddled with the costs of abating their pollution, but there is nothing in this prospect to bear out Dr. Commoner's declaration that pollution is so inseparable from industry, and that industry in a free-enterprise society can survive only if it grows, that there must be radical changes in the structure of the private enterprise system. And,

The Doomsday Syndrome

by extension, there is no reason why the prospect of comparatively painless air and water pollution control in the United States should not be applicable in the other industrialized communities where the same or similar standards are enforced.

But what use are these attempts to improve the environment if at any time new industries may establish themselves, bringing new kinds of pollution in their train? Since 1970, legislation in the United States has required that potentially polluting enterprises should bear responsibility for demonstrating that their activities do not offend against the environment and the law. The amendments to the Clean Air legislation of 1970, for example, require that factories should demonstrate that their emissions are not hazardous in whatever sense the Environmental Protection Agency may define, and similar regulations now apply both to the dumping of solid waste in the oceans and to the marketing of new chemicals. So long as the Environmental Protection Agency enjoys political support in Washington and the cooperation of state and municipal authorities, there is no reason why the United States should not in future enjoy as much clean air and water as it is prepared to pay for.

Substantial inconsistencies remain, however, within the apparatus of the federal government. It is still not clear, for example, whether pesticides are the responsibility of the Department of Agriculture (which has an interest to see that they are used as much as possible) or the Food and Drug Administration (which tends to take a more skeptical view but which is habitually so weak that it can hardly make itself heard). The Environmental Protection Agency has had, since 1971, responsibility for operating a registration procedure and for setting the standards for regulating the use of pesticides, but the effectiveness of these arrangements will not quickly be demonstrated. And what is to be done about the control of water pollution caused by the run-off from agricultural land, especially now that intensive animal farming means that large quantities of animal excreta find their way untreated into local rivers? Nodoby should be surprised if, by the end of the 1970s,

What Can Be Done?

stock farms are required to process their effluents with as much care as human sewage is dealt with.

The success with which the United States has tackled these serious insults to the environment can in principle be repeated elsewhere. In Britain, indeed, where Clean Air legislation goes back to the 1950s and where the control of water pollution has a still longer history, there is every prospect that seemly standards will be promulgated and enforced without imposing an intolerable burden on industry or on the national economy. One result, of course, will be that new industries are less free to exploit parts of the country not yet industrialized, but that too should be a benefit which the conservationists will acclaim.

It goes without saying, however, that these steps are only a beginning. So far, for example, too little attention has been given to the design of cities that will allow large numbers of people to live and work together without creating the sense of congestion of which everybody complains. Both in the United States and in Western Europe, too little has been done to develop methods of mangement for national parks and nature reserves that will allow access to the public without at the same time inviting destruction or despoliation of the regions themselves. If there should come a time when visits to such places are restricted or perhaps rationed, communities such as that in Britain will have a more real excuse than at present to say that the country is overcrowded—and they will also have a powerful incentive to increase the acreage of the national parks.

In short, there is no reason why well-ordered communities such as those of Western Europe and the United States should not be able, with the machinery which exists at present, to decide for themselves what amenities they will secure and then to pay the cost of them, either in taxes or in higher prices. To pretend otherwise is to make mountains out of molehills, and familiar molehills at that.

Environmental problems which cross national frontiers are a more serious affront to the effectiveness of the legislative ma

The Doomsday Syndrome

chinery which exists. The Rhine, long known as an international sewer (which nevertheless still supports more fish than the Thames) is polluted because sovereign nations will not restrict their pollution of the river for the sake of others. The Baltic Sea, potentially as vulnerable to pollution as Lake Erie, now takes large quantities of treated and untreated sewage and industrial effluent from the countries around its shores. Even the Mediterranean, a much larger mass of water, could some decades hence be damaged by a greater load of pollution than can be dealt with naturally. What can be done to dissuade the nations concerned from fecklessness?

The essence of the difficulty is what Dr. Garrett Hardin has described in the context of the United States as "the tragedy of the commons"—the tendency of independent groups so to overexploit common resources as to despoil them. The complaint applies not merely to the tendency to pollute the atmosphere or the oceans without consideration for other users but also to the temptation for nations to make excessive inroads on fish stocks, on resources of raw materials such as petroleum and even, by overbreeding, to create excessive demands on the capacity of the surface of the earth to grow food. The question is how sovereign nations are to be persuaded that their long-term interests require moderation.

Although there are a great many problems which need urgent attention, and although the International Whaling Commission has conspicuously failed to preserve stocks of whales in the South Atlantic in the face of the determination of countries such as Japan and the Soviet Union to kill more animals each year than the population can support, it would be wrong entirely to ignore the precedents which exist for international action in the common good.

The steps taken in 1971 by the Northwest Atlantic Fisheries Commission to conserve commercial stocks of cod and haddock (see Chapter 3) are a telling illustration of what can be done. In the long run, there is no reason why substantially similar arrangements should not be made to safeguard the stocks of

What Can Be Done?

other commercial fish, but it would be wrong to underestimate the difficulties. To begin with, too little is known about the reproductive habits of important fish such as the salmon of the North Atlantic, the anchovies in the Eastern Pacific and the tuna fish of the Pacific and the Atlantic. There is also a need for greater flexibility in the marketing of fish, for in northwestern Europe in particular, much of the tendency towards overfishing stems directly from the chauvinistic competitiveness of the fishing industry.

Where international pollution is concerned, as in the Baltic and the Rhine, there is no reason why similar international commissions should not be established to work out annual quotas of pollutants which member countries must not exceed. To be sure, present understanding of how international waters like these should be handled is incomplete, but modest programs of research could quickly lay the foundation for meaningful regulations. If the United Nations Conference on the Human Environment arranged for Stockholm in June 1972 had been planned in a more practical manner, it might have contributed significantly to the setting up of international instruments along these lines.

More serious international problems would arise if it could be shown that worldwide contamination by materials such as DDT or mercury is a hazard to human life. As things are (see Chapter 4), the nations which are injudicious in their use of these materials suffer directly from this practice. There is no substantial evidence that DDT used in the United States is carried in hazardous quantities elsewhere, for example. But if there were a serious source of strictly worldwide contamination, it would be necessary that legal instruments for regulating it should also be thoroughly international.

The difficulties are best illustrated by supposing that carbon dioxide in the atmosphere from the burning of a fossil fuel might at some stage in the future become a real and not a hypothetical threat to the climate on the surface of the earth. Then it would be necessary for nations to agree on quotas to

The Doomsday Syndrome

restrict the discharge of carbon dioxide. Plainly such a system of international control would be an infringement of what many nations consider to be their sovereign rights. It is also hard to guess at the principles on which national quotas would be established. Would industrialized nations be required to restrict their emission of carbon dioxide so as to allow those still growing to use more fuel? Evidently there would be awkward problems for the international lawyers to surmount, and suggestions that the atmosphere might be cleansed of carbon dioxide by changing the behavior of ocean currents are for the time being at least fanciful. In the circumstances, it is just as well that the threat of calamity by the greenhouse effect is at once uncertain and remote.

The more immediate need is for more efficient monitoring of the atmosphere and the seas. At present, for example, the only reliable measurements of the carbon-dioxide content of the atmosphere come from the single observing station maintained by the United States at Mauna Loa in Hawaii. Nobody can tell whether the apparently accelerated rate of carbon-dioxide accumulation in 1969 and 1970 is a worldwide or a regional phenomenon. The concentration at Mauna Loa increased by 2.6 percent in the two years, compared with the annual increase of 0.7 percent in the previous decade, but the extra carbon dioxide may have a natural source, possibly volcanic. Until there is a network of observing stations, all of them measuring the same quantity with roughly similar techniques, it will be hard to know what is happening to the concentration of carbon dioxide in the atmosphere.

There is a similar need for systematic monitoring of the other constituents of the atmosphere—dust particles, gas such as sulphur dioxide and even persistent pesticides (which seem to be distributed over great distances by the atmosphere and not the sea). And what about the mechanisms by which DDT or mercury are scattered? What are their concentrations in the water of the open seas? These and other questions need answering, not so much to avoid imminent calamity but because

What Can Be Done?

techniques for making the measurements are now available and because questions of worldwide pollution could at some stage be more threatening than at present. One issue to be faced is that the cost of thorough monitoring could be very large. Will those who now complain about pollution be willing to contribute towards the bill?

How will the work be done? Although the World Health Organization of the United Nations has done much in the past few years to lay down acceptable standards of contamination by pesticides and other potential sources of pollution, international responsibility for humdrum work such as the monitoring of atmospheric constituents is still very much at the mercy of chance. The World Meteorological Organization is well suited to the monitoring of air pollution. But should there be a United Nations organization for the environment? This is a red herring. Where monitoring is concerned, it is inevitable that nations with ambitions to know what they drink and breathe will go to some trouble to make measurements and keep statistics. What needs to be done internationally is to coordinate this work, making sure that the same standards are used in different places and that the information which nations need individually is also made available internationally.

The moderation of population growth in the world as a whole, held by many to be the most urgent task, is only indirectly an international problem. For once it is established (see Chapter 2) that the communities which suffer most from rapid population growth are those which inflict this penalty on themselves, enlightened self-interest is a sufficient motive for improvement. In spite of the gloomy prophecies of recent years, the governments of developing nations are well aware of the balance that must be struck between population growth on the one hand and economic and social advancement on the other.

The results are already apparent in Southeast Asia as a whole, in many of the countries of Latin America and elsewhere in the world. Fertility is declining. It is not merely pointlessly gloomy but misleading to pretend, as the doomsday men pre-

The Doomsday Syndrome

tend, that this process will not spread throughout the developing world. Is it not more reasonable to suppose that the trend towards declining fertility which has already begun will spread and even accelerate? And is it not seemly that the advanced nations of the world, which have themselves only recently emerged from the demographic transition, should attribute to less fortunate nations the capacity to be at least as capable of social adjustment as they have been themselves?

That said, it must be acknowledged that the population problem is indirectly international. To the extent that population growth prevents developing nations from being as prosperous as they might be, growth helps to prolong the period during which the economic gap between the rich and the poor countries of the world will persist. In the long run, this is a more serious threat to international well being than any real or imaginary threat to environmental stability. But the remedy for this state of affairs has been amply described in recent years. Foreign aid by advanced societies to those less fortunate could be a sufficient means of providing the incentives necessary to bring demographic stability to the developing nations in the years immediately ahead. It remains of course a scandal that advanced nations have so far been parsimonious in the amounts of foreign aid which they are willing to provide and foolishly discriminatory in the ways in which they have distributed it, but is there not the strongest reason why those who preach demographic disaster should direct their efforts where they would be most valuable, in persuading the governments of developed nations to spend more on foreign aid?

In the doomsday literature, it is common to deride the contributions which science and technology can make to the abatement of environmental problems. Dr. Rene Dubos, in *Reason Awake,* complains at the foolishness of relying on what he calls "technological fixes." In reality, however, to the extent that the environmental problems of which he and others write are realities, there is powerful evidence that research and development have

What Can Be Done?

an important contribution to make to the creation of a society which is at once humane and able to take charge of its own affairs. Nobody pretends that technology by itself could be a sufficient cure for present ills, for legal and administrative procedures, national and international, are indispensable.

The truth is, however, that in the modern world, science and technology have become essential components of the resourcefulness and ingenuity which the human race must exercise if it is to continue to survive. If the discovery of metal tools made possible the preservation of neolithic society, the development of the instruments of the new technology will help to ensure the survival of contemporary society. Until recently at least, so much has been taken for granted. One of the abiding flaws of the doomsday literature is that it ignores the contributions which science and technology are at present making to the solution of contemporary problems.

Medical research, which has admittedly made possible the abrupt reduction of death rates in developing countries since the Second World War, may yet contribute in important ways to the reduction of fertility. In the long run, reducing infant mortality in developing countries may be as important (see Chapter 2) as the provision of still more convenient techniques of contraception. Is that to be scorned? And can it sensibly be held that the impending success in the treatment of presently intractable forms of cancer, and the further decrease of mortality among the middle aged in advanced societies, will be unwelcome, even if one side effect may be an increase in the size of some populations? The children who are by these means helped not to be orphans might be asked for their opinions.

To the extent that many of the social problems of developing countries are consequences of poor communications and the incarceration of too many people in agricultural communities, there are even important benefits to be won in the immediate future from the development of telephones, television and other devices in telecommunications. In advanced societies, at least, the experience of the past few years has shown quite clearly

The Doomsday Syndrome

that these have important contributions to make to education and to social mobility, which in turn are among the more important prerequisites of stability, demographic and otherwise. Is it not mistaken to suppose that these developments, valued as they are in advanced societies, have no value elsewhere in the world? Is that not an assumption calculated still further to increase the sense of deprivation with which the less fortunate nations are saddled?

In the years ahead, as in the present and in antiquity, science and technology are indispensable instruments in the improvement of resources. The agricultural revolution in Europe in the eighteenth century, like the green revolution now under way in Asia, was made possible by a better understanding of the ways in which plants can be made to grow and yield good crops. In agriculturally advanced communities, in North America and Western Europe for example, these developments have brought unexpected side effects—it is necessary, for example, for the plant breeders to keep at least one step ahead of the plant diseases which are unavoidable in intensive agriculture. But to describe such a balance between practice and discovery as a technological fix is no more meaningful than to complain that the animal husbandry of the early neolithic societies was mistaken because it created a need for veterinary science. And at present the prospect is that scientific techniques of plant breeding and agriculture will make possible not merely still further increases of the yield of crops in Asia but the development of crops which provide a better diet and will prepare the foundations for productive fish farming in fresh-water ponds as well. In short, scientific research and the promise which it holds for the years ahead has made the threat of famine go away.

In exactly the same way, the contributions which science and technology have made in recent years to the improvement of natural resources have meant that nations no longer need to fear that their survival will be threatened by a lack of essential raw materials. The threat of a scarcity of energy, real enough in the 1950s, has already been dispelled. Is that a mere "techno-

What Can Be Done?

logical fix"? Research and development have also helped not merely to make it possible to exploit metal ores which would previously have been unworkable but have made possible the substitution of comparatively plentiful materials for those previously in short supply. But this is a continuing and accelerating process. Even if supplies of some materials, petroleum for example, are dramatically much smaller a century from now than they are at present, in gloomy forebodings about impending scarcity it is surely appropriate to give at least some weight to the way in which scientific research and development have provided the human race with more freedom and flexibility than in the past.

For advanced and developing communities alike, technology as it is at present and the innovations now in prospect also promise a continuing improvement in economic resources. Although Dr. Commoner complains that technology means industry and industry means pollution, the creation of egalitarian and socially progressive societies in the developing nations will be possible only if there are ways in which whole populations can be provided with food, housing, health care and education. The necessary pooling of common tasks is possible only if science and technology are used as ways of increasing the productive capacity of human hands and muscles. The machine, in other words, however it may be hated, is no less important now and in the decades immediately ahead than has been the wheel. And who will call that a technological fix?

But science and technology have done and will do more than lighten labor and avoid drudgery. The temper of modern society owes much to the temper of modern science and in particular to the precept that understanding is the most secure foundation for innovation. Ironically, of course, a good many of the hypothetical calamities to which the environmentalists draw attention have been recognized only because of the understanding which science has brought. Who would worry about DDT if it had not been for the invention of powerful techniques of chemical analysis, gas chromatography for example? Who would

The Doomsday Syndrome

worry about mercury pollution except when there is overt toxicity if it had not been for refinements of chemical analysis? Who would fear the effects of carbon dioxide in the atmosphere if it had not been for the still rudimentary understanding of the atmosphere which the past few decades have brought?

The other side of this coin is that the rational temper of modern science has also helped with the solution of serious social problems. Disease has not of course been eradicated, but it is no longer regarded as a visitation by evil or hostile spirits. City planning, and the amenities which might flow from decent city planning, are now amenable to objective discussion. And society itself can be rationally described. If, as was undoubtedly the case, the habitation of spaceship earth, as it is called, was in part secured in megalithic times by the understanding of the way in which the sun and the moon move across the sky, is it not now foolish to disregard the contributions which scientific understanding and technological development can make to survival and the humane life? One of the most serious errors in the extreme environmentalist position is that by supposing that science and technology have nothing but useless gimmicks to offer the modern world, an indispensable aid to continued survival may be overlooked.

It is too soon to know what permanent effect the more extreme branches of the environmental movement will have had, but they have helped to dramatize a set of problems that might otherwise have been neglected. Public affairs are constantly refreshed by the challenges of those who ask that caricatures of the real world should be taken at their face value and the environmentalists deserve some credit for having pinpricked public administrations into actions that would not otherwise have been natural to them.

The movement as a whole is of course a symptom of the times but especially of the present condition of the United States. Since the beginning of the 1960s, American society seems to have been tormented with self-doubt. Civil rights came first,

What Can Be Done?

then Vietnam, now the environment. Outsiders, anxious to please, or at least not to give offense, are bound to ask, while trying to share the sense of doom, whether the fad will last, and for how long. And how much of it stems from an affluence which others cannot yet pretend? What will be the effect of draconian measures against pollution in the United States on imports of less hygienic machinery from elsewhere? Why is it that the people in Washington are so zealous in their public declarations on the environment and so apparently incompetent to persuade municipal authorities to put principle into practice?

One disturbing interpretation is that anxiety about the environment is a convenient lightning rod for diverting anxiety from other topics. And it would be true of course that if everybody was to die tomorrow of mercury in tuna fish, there would be no need to worry now about the problems of next week— foreign aid, relations with mainland China, the social not the technical problems of the urban conurbations and the problem of the young. Although an ardent concern for the environment often seems like social prudence, the fact that the environmental movement has managed to unite the extreme left and the extreme right and to bring together some of the very old and the very young (not to mention Mr. Ralph Nader) may sometimes be held to be suspicious. Is it just possible that the environmental movement is a way of expressing anxiety in public, in good and varied company and without the risk of being accused of making mischief?

The way in which the movement's message has been greeted outside the United States, with a mixture of curiosity, politeness and alarm, is less of a feather in anybody's cap. It is true that some governments, that of Sweden for example, have welcomed news of yet another crusade to fight. Governments like the British, more occupied with such goals as economic growth, have made a dutiful acknowledgment of the environmental problem by renaming a government department, appointing a standing Royal Commission and making a number of public speeches. A part of the trouble, unfortunately, is that one of the

The Doomsday Syndrome

compromises not far beneath the conscious level in most British minds is how much of a rather well-nurtured environment should now be exchanged for how much economic growth. May it not be a little embarrassing to have to be putting out flags for the environment and still hoping that industry will not merely prosper but expand?

Elsewhere, there has been frank disbelief about the motives for the movement's sudden growth. People in India are as tired of being told by Americans that they should be sterilized so as to damp down the population explosion as were Kenyans tired of being told by the British in the 1950s to stay on their farms so as not to lengthen the unemployment queues in Nairobi. In the past twenty-five years, the governments of the nuclear powers and would-be nuclear powers have become extremely skilled at managing to avoid the threat of war, and indeed they seem somehow to have organized a framework within which nuclear war is less believable than at any time since the Second World War. But the same nations have become much less sensitive in their dealings with the developing countries, or the UDCs as they tend to be called in the literature of the environment. Yet countries such as India and Brazil are sovereign nations: there is no requirement in international law nor precedent in the practice of more prosperous nations to suggest why they should regulate their own affairs in such a way as to conform with standards set by other people.

The political consequences of this tactlessness by people from industrialized societies are serious. For more than a decade it has been clear that the most urgent task in the relationship between advanced societies and the rest is to bridge the economic gulf that separates them. Then there will be a chance to stabilize the world's population. Then there will be time to regulate pollution internationally. So is it not good politics first of all to work for enough foreign aid to put international relations on a basis on which the threat could effectively be dealt with?

The offense which the doomsday men (but not all environ-

What Can Be Done?

mentalists by a long chalk) have given to intellectual life is much more serious. When people say, as Dr. Ehrlich has done, that he will be glad if his somber prediction turns out to be false (see Chapter 1) because then, at least, people will have survived, they are playing a mean trick. The common justification is to say that it is necessary to exaggerate to get people stirred, to get things done. But people are easily anesthetized by repetition and there is a danger that, in spite of its achievements so far, the environmental movement could still find itself falling flat on its face when it is most needed, simply because it has pitched its tale too strongly. The cases of phosphate detergents and cyclamates were close calls.

This is one reason why the environmental movement would be strengthened if it had a wider perspective. It is forever saying that society must learn to balance cost and benefit and then negelecting to point out that economists and others have already done a good deal to show how calculations like these should be performed. The movement's lack of a sense of history is also maiming. Not merely are there lessons to be learned from the past, but some of the conflicts which have been provoked by the movement's attack on the establishment are explicable only historically. Just as it gives offense to tell developing nations not to build blast furnaces that pollute the air, so it gives offense to suggest to relatively poor sections of the community that the time has come for the search for material prosperity to cease. May this explain why black people are conspicuous by their absence among the environmentalists in the United States? In reality, of course, even countries such as the United States, rich as they are, still need a good deal more economic growth to be able to afford to pay the teachers who will be needed to teach the disadvantaged children. If there is to be an accommodation between prosperity and pollution, it will have to be worked out in the familiar political arena. Social security, welfare and educational policies will be as prominent as decisions on acceptable standards of air pollution.

Luckily, there is nothing in the record of the past few years

The Doomsday Syndrome

that points to an impending cessation of the progressive liberalization and enrichment of society which it was permissible, in Alfred Marshall's time, to call progress (see Chapter 7). If anything, the process is accelerating. People shake their heads over the way in which the population of the world might be doubling once every thirty-five years, but the population of the universities in Western Europe and North America has for some time been doubling in less than twenty years and the population of secondary schools elsewhere in the world is growing still more quickly. Further, there is no doubt that programs for research and development already begun contain the seeds not merely of further economic growth, much of it free from pollution, but also opportunities for ordinary people to enjoy benefits which have previously been beyond reach.

The environmentalists are fond of using the eloquent metaphor of spaceship earth but this is not the most important point to make about the way in which living things have managed to survive for 3,000 million years and, so far, to evolve. Although everybody seems prepared now to accept that other planets elsewhere in the galaxy are likely to have living things on them, nobody makes light of the evolutionary barriers which the human race has had to surmount. After two million years of near extinction, is it any wonder that instinct should lead to temporary overfecundity? The truth is that the technology of survival has been more successful than could have been imagined in any previous century. It will be of immense importance to discover, in due course, the next important threat to survival, but the short list of doomsday talked of in the past few years contains nothing but paper tigers. Yet in the metaphor of spaceship earth, mere housekeeping needs courage. The most serious worry about the doomsday syndrome is that it will undermine our spirit.

Postscript

Since the British edition of this book was published, there has been an event of some importance. An organization known as the Club of Rome has published an account of a study carried out at Massachusetts Institute of Technology by Dr. Dennis L. Meadows and his colleagues which, under the title *The Limits to Growth* (Universe Books, New York), purports to show that many of the more gloomy prophecies of the environmentalists can be upheld by mathematical calculations carried out by electronic computers. But, as will be seen, this study suffers from many of the faults of the qualitative arguments of the environmentalists not equipped with large electronic computers and qualifies for Dr. Gunnar Myrdal's description of the study as "pretentious nonsense" (in a Dutch television program broadcast in May 1972).

The Limits to Growth is based on a computer simulation of the world. The idea is that the computer is programed to store information about such quantities as the population of the world (for this purpose broken down separately into the population of children between zero and fifteen, the population of adults of reproductive age between sixteen and thirty-five and the population of those whose reproductive life is over). The same computer stores a number indicating the amount of money invested in industrial capital, a number indicating the amount of arable land, another which is supposed to stand for the stock of unrenewable resources and one which is meant to be a measure of pollution. The object of the exercise is to calculate how these and several other variable quantities will change in the course of time. The stock of nonrenewable resources, for example, will decrease in the course of time as resources are used up, and this rate of consumption will be determined in part by the size of the world's population and by the quantity of resources consumed

The Doomsday Syndrome

each year by a single individual, which is in turn dependent on the amount of industrial output per head and ultimately, in part at least, on the rate of investment in new factories of various kinds. Dr. Meadows and his colleagues argue quite properly that with a model like this, it is possible to calculate the changes which are likely to come about in the course of time in the various quantities with which their computer is equipped to deal. They go on to calculate that if there is "no major change in the physical, economic or social relationships that have historically governed the development of the world system," there will come a point in the next century when the diminishing stock of natural resources brings about a decrease of industrial growth, a consequent decrease in the amount of food available per head of population and then, in due course, a return to the bad old days of the eighteenth and nineteenth centuries, when the death rate increases rapidly because of starvation and when even a rapidly increasing birth rate is unable to prevent a decline of population.

The first thing to be said is that there can be no reasonable objection to the use of computer models in an attempt more fully to understand the relationships between the quantities which describe the condition of the world at any time. Dr. Meadows is also right to claim that his computer model of the world is more sophisticated than any other so far devised. Unhappily for him, it does not follow that the modeling process is free from error. In the past few years, there have been several attempts to construct computer models of small parts of what Dr. Meadows calls the world system—national economies, for example. These computer models have rarely been of practical use in helping to forecast the behavior of the British or the American economy, for example, although they have been instructive in helping to throw light on unexpected relationships between varying quantities such as industrial output and employment. For the truth is that even the best possible computer model is no better than the asssumptions about the real world with which it is provided. And even very large computer models,

Postscript

such as that which Dr. Meadows has used, are never large enough to take account of all the possible relationships between one thing and another. It is no wonder that the Club of Rome study has been forced to make drastic simplifications which even extreme environmentalists usually manage to avoid.

The first and most serious complaint against the Club of Rome study is that its authors have been forced to describe the world in oversimple terms. Their error is what the economists call aggregation. On population, for example, they have been compelled by the limitations of their equipment to describe the total population of the world by three numbers, with the result that their calculations are unable to take account of the way in which the pattern of population growth differs markedly between developing countries and advanced countries. On pollution, represented by a single number in the computer calculation, they are compelled to assume that this is at any time determined by the scale of industrial and agricultural output and are thus unable to make allowance for the way in which pollution of various forms might be drastically reduced, either by devoting industrial resources to the abatement of pollution or by changes in the pattern of industrial output and in particular the replacement of polluting industries by others.

These simplifications, apparently built into the Club of Rome's computer model, make nonsense of the study. So far as can be told from *The Limits to Growth*, for example, the world's stock of nonrenewable resources—metal ores especially—has been represented by a single number. In one particular calculation, it was assumed that the amounts of nonrenewable resources in the earth's crust in 1970 were the equivalent of 250 years' supply at the then rate of consumption. On the face of things, this was a generous assumption by Dr. Meadows and his colleagues, for the known reserves of a great many common materials such as lead and mercury are unlikely to last for nearly as long as that. But the history of the past few decades has shown clearly enough that relatively scarce materials are constantly being replaced by more common ones—copper, for

The Doomsday Syndrome

example, is being steadily replaced by aluminum in many parts of the electrical industry. By representing the total stock of nonrenewable resources by a single number in the computer calculation, Dr. Meadows and his colleagues have implicitly rejected the contribution which this process of substitution can make to the amelioration of resource scarcity. Moreover, by assuming that the present stock of raw materials is to be represented by a single number, they have ruled out the process by means of increasing scarcity and the increased prices which it brings stimulate exploration for new materials and also make it economic to exploit ores of lower quality. In other words, in constructing their computer model, Dr. Meadows and his colleagues have built in artificial restraints on the development of their world system. In the circumstances, it will be no surprise to those who know computer models that the computer calculations suggest that at some stage in the future, catastrophic instabilities may arise.

This is merely one example of the way in which the MIT computer model, for all its complexity, does not correspond to the real world. Another assumption which Dr. Meadows and his colleagues have made is that there is a simple relationship between life expectancy and the average level of nutrition. The raw materials for this assumption are the figures for life expectancy which the demographers compile for countries of various types, some rich and some poor, and the available statistics for the amount of food (in terms of calories) which the populations concerned consume. It is no surprise in countries in which at present the daily consumption of food is the equivalent of 2,000 calories a day or less, that life expectancy is much lower than in the well-fed countries of the West. But it is of course absurd to jump from this simple observation to the assumption that Dr. Meadows and his colleagues make in carrying out their computer calculations that at some stage in the future, the life expectancy of the world's population as a whole will be determined by the amount of food available per head and by the relationship between nutrition and life expectancy thrown

Postscript

up by present statistics. For the truth is that in the developing countries where nutrition is poor and life expectancy is low, starvation is by no means predominant among the causes of early death. The poor nutrition and the low life expectancy of the impoverished countries are no doubt both consequences of the underlying poverty which prevents these countries from investing in public health services as well as agricultural development. But it is a kind of nonsense to assume that the relationship between nutrition and life expectancy which Dr. Meadows and his colleagues have discerned in current statistics implies a cause-and-effect relationship that will, moreover, endure for decades to come. One of the difficulties with *The Limits to Growth* is that a detailed assessment of these weaknesses cannot be attempted on the basis of what has so far been published. A detailed statement of the assumptions on which the model has been constructed will be available only towards the end of 1972, and only then will its relationship with the real world be determined. The first publication suggests that the Club of Rome has given a great many hostages to fortune. And it is hard at this stage to know what to make of the claim, running through the Club of Rome report, that the study is meant only as an admonitory projection into the future, not a prediction. This, of course, is a familiar academic escape from responsibility. Yet *The Limits to Growth* does at one point assert that: "We can thus say with some confidence that, under the assumption of no major change in the present system, population and industrial growth will certainly stop within the next century, at the latest." It is true that this sentence includes the familiar reservation of the extreme environmentalists, "under the assumption of no major change in the present system," but in the circumstances the Club of Rome should not be surprised that *The Limits to Growth* has been publicly regarded as a prophecy.

References

CHAPTER 1: IS CATASTROPHE COMING?

Paul R. Ehrlich, *The Population Bomb*, Ballantine Books, 1968.

Paul R. and Anne H. Ehrlich, *Population, Resources, Environment*, W. H. Freeman, 1970.

Barry Commoner, *The Closing Circle*, Alfred A. Knopf, 1971.

Rene Dubos, *Reason Awake*, Columbia University Press, 1970.

Eugene Rabinowitch and G. Hecht, *Explaining the Atom*, Gollancz, 1955.

P. M. S. Blackett, *The Political and Economic Consequences of Nuclear Energy*, Harrap, 1948.

Herman Kahn, *On Thermonuclear War*, Oxford and Princeton, 1960.

Rachel Carson, *Silent Spring*, Alfred A. Knopf, 1962.

Barry Commoner, *Science and Survival*, Viking Press, 1967.

C. S. Wallia (ed.), *Towards Century 21*, Basic Books, 1970.

Jack D. Douglas (ed.), *The Technological Threat*, Artemis Press, 1971.

Jacques Ellul, *The Technological Society*, Alfred A. Knopf, 1964.

Adlai Stevenson, United Nations, October 1964.

Environmental Quality, Second Annual Report of the Council on Environmental Quality, 1971.

CHAPTER 2: THE NUMBERS GAME

Paul R. Ehrlich, *The Population Bomb*.

David Brower, *The Environmental Handbook*.

William and Paul Paddock, *Famine—1975!*, Little, Brown, 1967.

Thomas Malthus, *Essay on Population*, for example, ed. Michael P. Fogerty, Everyman Library, 1958.

Godwin, W. *Enquiry Concerning Political Justice, and Its Influence on Morals and Happiness*, 3rd ed. London, 1798.

Condorcet, Marquis De, *Sketch for a Historical Picture of the Progress of the Human Mind*, trans. J. Barraclough, New York, 1955.

Gertrude Himmelfarb, *Victorian Minds*, Weidenfeld & Nicolson, 1968.

William Petersen, *The Politics of Population*, Gollancz, 1964

Paul R. and Anne H. Ehrlich, *Population, Resources, Environment*.

Donald J. Bogue, "The End of the Population Explosion," in *The Public Interest*, 1967.

Rapid Population Growth—Consequences and Policy Implications, Johns Hopkins, 1971.

Colin Clark, *Population Growth and Land Use*, Macmillan, 1967.

United Nations Demographic Yearbook, 1969, United Nations, 1970.

The Doomsday Syndrome

D. Friedlander in *Demography*, Vol. 6, 1969, p. 359.

Census 1971, England and Wales, Preliminary Report, HM Stationery Office, London, 1971.

World Population Prospects, 1965–2000 as Assessed in 1968, Working Paper No. 37, Population Division, United Nations Department of Economic & Social Affairs, December 1970.

United States Bureau of the Census, 1967.

Rene Dubos, *So Human an Animal*, Charles Scribner's Sons, 1968.

CHAPTER 3: THE END OF THE LODE

Barry Commoner, *The Closing Circle*.

David Ricardo, *Principles of Political Economy and Taxation*, Everyman, 1926.

John Stuart Mill, *Principles of Political Economy*.

Vance Packard, *The Waste Makers*, David McKay, Inc., 1960.

Resources for Freedom, Report of the President's Materials Policy Commission (the Paley Commission), 1952.

Hans H. Landsberg, Leonard L. Fischman and Joseph L. Fisher, *Resources in America's Future—Patterns of Requirements and Availabilities 1960–2000*. Johns Hopkins for Resources for the Future, Inc.

Stephen H. Spurr, "Developing a Natural Resource Management Policy," in *No Deposit—No Return*, ed., Huey D. Johnson, Addison-Wesley, 1970.

Paul R. Ehrlich, *The Population Bomb*.

Dirck Van Sickle, *The Ecological Citizen*, Harper & Row, 1971.

Third World Food Survey, FAO, 1963.

The State of Food and Agriculture 1970, FAO, 1970.

The World Food Problem, Vols I & II, Report of the President's Science Advisory Committee, The White House, 1967.

Economic Survey of Asia and the Far East 1969, UN, 1970.

World Energy Supplies 1965–1968, Statistical Papers Series J. No. 13, UN, 1970.

Statistical Yearbook 1970, UN, 1971.

M. King Hubbert, "Energy Resources," in *Resources and Man*, published for National Academy of Sciences by W. H. Freeman, 1969.

Gerald Manners, *The Changing World Market for Iron Ore 1950–1980*, Johns Hopkins Press for Resources for the Future, Inc., 1971.

Harold J. Barnett and Chandler Morse, *Scarcity and Growth—The Economics of Natural Resource Availability*, Johns Hopkins Press for Resources for the Future, Inc.

CHAPTER 4: THE POLLUTION PANIC

John W. Gofman and Arthur R. Tamplin, *Poisoned Power*, Rodale Press, 1971.

Rachel Carson, *Silent Spring*.

Barry Commoner, *The Closing Circle*.

References

The Biological Impact of Pesticides in the Environment, Environmental Health Sciences Center, Oregon State University, 1970.

Thomas H. Jukes, "DDT and Tumours in Experimental Animals," in *The International Journal of Environmental Studies,* October 1970.

Chlorinated Hydrocarbons in the Marine Environment, National Academy of Sciences, 1971.

Joint Survey of Pesticide Residues in Foodstuffs Sold in England and Wales, 1 August 1967—31 July 1968, County Councils Association and others, 1971.

Report of the Secretary's Commission on Pesticides and Their Relationship to Environmental Health, Parts I and II, U.S. Department of Health, Education, and Welfare, 1969.

Report of the DDT Advisory Committee, Environmental Protection Agency, 1971.

Annual Report 1970, WHO International Agency for Research on Cancer, 1971.

A. J. Wilson, Jr., J. Forester and J. Knight, *Chemical Assays,* U.S. Department of the Interior Circular 335, August 1970 (Gulf Breeze Lab., Florida, Progress Report FV 1969).

Man's Impact on the Global Environment, SCEP Report, MIT Press, 1970.

Harold Johnston, "Reduction of Stratospheric Ozone by Nitrogen Oxide Catalysts from Supersonic Transport Exhaust," *Science,* August 6, 1971.

Mercury in the Environment, U.S. Geological Survey, 1970.

Mercury in the Environment—The Human Element, Oak Ridge National Laboratory, 1971.

Survey of Mercury in Food, Report of Working Party on the Monitoring of Foodstuffs for Mercury and Other Heavy Metals, Ministry of Agriculture, Fisheries and Food, 1971.

Report of the Advisory Committee on 2, 4, 5-T, Environmental Protection Agency, 1971.

Toxicological and Environmental Implications on the Use of Nitrilotriacetic Acid as a Detergent Builder, U.S. Senate Committee on Public Works, 1970.

Lake Erie Report—A Plan for Water Pollution Control, U.S. Department of the Interior, 1968.

Environmental Quality, Second Annual Report of the Council on Environmental Quality, 1971.

The Economics of Clean Air, Report of the Administrator of the Environmental Protection Agency to Congress, 1971.

Allen V. Kneese, "Background for the Economic Analysis of Environmental Pollution," in *Swedish Journal of Economics,* March 1971.

Allen V. Kneese, Robert U. Ayres and Ralph d'Arge, *Economics and the Environment—A Materials Balance Approach,* Resources for the Future, Inc., 1970.

J. C. Headley and J. N. Lewis, *The Pesticide Problem: An Economic Approach to Public Policy,* Resources for the Future, Inc., 1967.

CHAPTER 5: ECOLOGY IS A STATE OF MIND

Paul R. and Anne H. Ehrlich, *Population, Resources, Environment.*
Leo Marx in *Science*, 170, 945; 1970.
Report No. 92-H 11 of Subcommittee on Air and Water Pollution of U.S. Senate Committee on Public Works, 1971.
Barry Commoner, *The Closing Circle.*
Garrett Hardin, "Not Peace, But Ecology," in *Diversity and Stability in Ecological Systems*, Brookhaven National Laboratory, 1969.
The Nation's Estuaries: San Francisco Bay and Delta, California, Subcommittee of the U.S. House of Representatives Committee on Government Operations, 1970.
Max Nicholson, *The Environmental Revolution*, Hodder & Stoughton, Ltd., 1970.
Guy-Harold Smith (ed.), *Conservation of Natural Resources*, John Wiley & Sons, Inc., 1950.

CHAPTER 6: MAN-MADE MEN

Jean Rostand, *Can Man Be Modified?*, Librairie Gallimard, 1956.
H. J. Muller, "What Genetic Course Will Man Steer?," in *Proceedings of the 3rd International Congress on Human Genetics*, Johns Hopkins Press, 1967.
Sir Macfarlane Burnet, *Genes, Dreams and Realities*, Medical and Technical Publishing Co., Ltd., 1971.
J. R. S. Fincham, *Microbial and Molecular Genetics*, English University Press, 1965.
Carl R. Merril, Mark R. Geier and John C. Petricciani, "Bacterial Virus Gene Expression in Human Cells," *Nature*, October 8, 1971.
See, for example, Victor Chapman and Ralph Riley, "Homoeologous Meiotic Chromosome Pairing in Triticum aestivum in which Chromosome 5B is Replaced by an Alien Homoeologue," *Nature*, April 25, 1970.
R. G. Edwards, "Problems of Artificial Fertilisation," *Nature*, September 3, 1971.
Landrum B. Shettles, "Human Blastocyst Grown in Vitro in Ovulation Cervical Mucus," *Nature*, January 29, 1971.
D. G. Wittingham, "Survival of Mouse Embryos After Freezing and Thawing," *Nature*, September 10, 1971.
L. E. A. Rowson, "Egg Transfer in Domestic Animals," *Nature*, October 8, 1971.
F. C. Steward, *Growth and Organisation in Plants*, Addison-Wesley, 1968.

CHAPTER 7: PROSPERITY IS POSSIBLE

Barry Commoner, *Science and Survival.*
Rene Dubos, *Reason Awake.*
Barry Commoner, *The Closing Circle.*

References

Kenneth E. Boulding, "Fun and Games with the Gross National Product —The Role of Misleading Indicators in Social Policy," in *The Environmental Crisis*, ed., Harold W. Helfrich, Jr., Yale University Press.

Paul R. and Anne H. Ehrlich, *Population, Resources, Environment*.

J. K. Galbraith, *The New Industrial State*, Hamish Hamilton, 1967.

Jacques Ellul, *The Technological Society*.

Lewis Mumford, *The City in History*, Weidenfeld & Nicolson, 1958.

Daniel Bell, "Notes on The Post-Industrial Society," in *The Public Interest*, Vol. 1, No. 2, April 1967.

United Nations Statistical Yearbook, 1970.

Jean Gottman, *Megalopolis*, MIT Press, 1961.

David Riesman, "Leisure and Work in Post-Industrial Society," in *Mass Leisure*, ed., Eric Larrabee and Rolf Meyersohn, The Free Press, 1958.

Jack D. Douglas (ed.), *The Technological Threat*.

CHAPTER 8: WHAT CAN BE DONE?

Barry Commoner, *The Closing Circle*.

The Ecologist, Vol. 2, No. 1, January 1972.

Environmental Quality, Second Annual Report of the Council on Environmental Quality, 1971.

Catalog

If you are interested in a list of fine Paperback
books, covering a wide range of subjects
and interests, send your name and address,
requesting your free catalog, to:

McGraw-Hill Paperbacks
1221 Avenue of Americas
New York, N.Y. 10020